KINGDOMS AND
STRONGHOLDS OF
THE CRUSADERS

KINGDOMS AND STRONGHOLDS OF THE CRUSADERS

T. S. R. Boase

171 illustrations, 17 in colour

THAMES AND HUDSON · LONDON

Printed and bound in Great Britain by Jarrold and Sons Ltd, Norwich

ISBN 0 500 25029 4

Contents

Preface

The history of the crusades has been admirably told and discussed in many
works. This short study is primarily concerned with the lives led by the
settlers, the motives that inspired them, and their own complex personal
relationships. In a work of this scale much must be generalized, and facts,
particularly dates, stated with an unargued certainty that they cannot
claim. Scholars familiar with the subject will recognize the views that
I accept, and also my great indebtedness to many writers, to whom in the
absence of footnotes no full acknowledgment can be made. I have tried in
the Bibliographical Note (p. 254) to indicate my gratitude to them. The
many friends, old and new, with whom over a period of some fifty years
I have discussed crusading matters, know I am sure how much I have
valued our interchange of views. I must, however, in particular express
my thanks to Père Coüasnon of the École Biblique in Jerusalem for the
time he has spent in showing and discussing with me the work of restoration, which he has so admirably supervised, in the Church of the Holy
Sepulchre.

T.S.R.B.

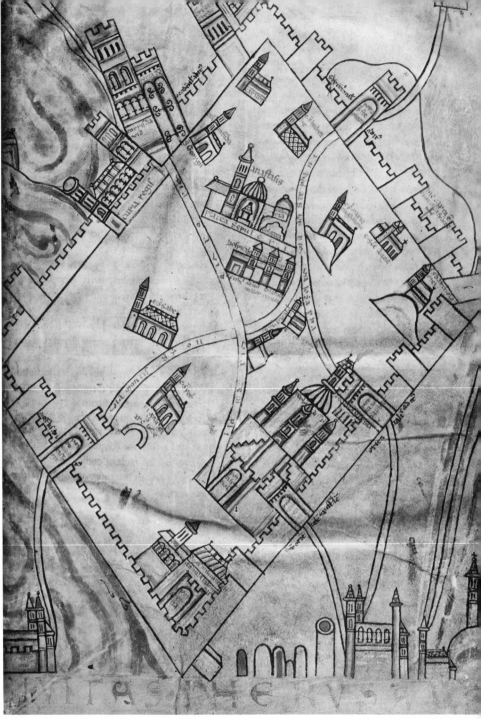

2 Plan of Jerusalem. The 'Cambrai Plan' dates from the closing years of the crusaders' occupation of the city, after the bell-tower of the Church of the Holy Sepulchre had been built (*c.* 1170). It shows both the tomb and the Mount of Golgotha within the Church.

The settlement of the Kingdom   1

The year 1071 was a disastrous one for Byzantium. In April, after a three years' siege, Robert Guiscard, the Norman leader who had so strongly established himself in southern Italy, occupied Bari, and ended the imperial hold over that area, which, disturbed and frequently nominal as it had been, dated back to the days of Justinian. On 26 August, at the other end of the Empire, north of Lake Van near the town of Manzikert, the Selchukid sultan Alp Arslan defeated a large Byzantine force, led in person by the emperor, Romanus Diogenes, who remained a prisoner in the hands of the victor, the first emperor to be a Moslem captive. By December the Normans, with their ships that had defeated the Byzantine fleet in the port of Bari, were blockading Palermo, and on 10 January 1072 they entered the city, completing their conquest of Sicily and ending its two centuries of Saracen domination. The central Mediterranean was now controlled by a Christian power, rapidly developing its naval resources and looking for new fields of conquest. A short way south of Bari lay the old Roman port of Egnazia, from which the Via Egnatia, the highway from Durazzo to Thessalonica and Constantinople, took its name. Bari had replaced it as the main port, but the eastern links remained, and soon Guiscard and his son, Bohemond, were to cross the Adriatic to campaign in Macedonia and Thessaly. To Byzantium, weakly held by short-lived emperors, it was as urgent a threat as that of the Selchukid advance in Asia Minor.

In the shifting pressures of central Asia, bands of Turkomans, nomadic tribes, had been moving westward, becoming converts to Islam as they made contact with the Arab world. Two grandsons of Selchuk, the leader whose name became that of the dynasty, Tughrul-Beg and Chagri-Beg, adopted, almost inevitably, a policy of territorial settlement. In 1055

9

Tughrul-Beg entered Baghdad, and received from the caliph wide administrative powers with the title of sultan. His sphere of influence was Mesopotamia up to the borders of Byzantium, while his brother was established in Khurasan and Persia, territories eventually united with Mesopotamia under his son, Alp Arslan, sultan from 1063 to 1072, the victor of Manzikert.

These events did much to change the balance between the two great religious divisions of Islam, the Sunnites and the Shiites, that went back to the disputes over the succession to the prophet Mohammed. The Selchukids were Sunnites, attracted by the clear-cut rules of Moslem orthodoxy, untroubled by the more mystical speculations of Shiism. On entering Baghdad, they had freed the Sunnite Abbasid caliphate from a century of domination by the Shiite Buwaihids, a family that originated from the Persian town of Shiraz. This left the Fatimid empire of Egypt, at the height of its power under the long reign (1036–94) of the eighth caliph, al-Mustansir, as the great representative of Shiism, and therefore the suspicious foe of these changes in Baghdad. Under al-Mustansir and his vizier, the Moslem Armenian Badr al-Jamali, Cairo received its great circuit of walls and its magnificent gateways, landmarks in city architecture. But for the moment Egypt bided its time.

3 One of the gateways of Cairo designed in 1087 by Armenian architects. The bevelled voussoirs (gadroons) on the side arches were a form of Eastern decoration much copied by the crusaders.

10

4 Alexius Comnenus in his imperial robes presents Christ with the volume of dogmatic extracts from the Fathers, an arsenal of orthodoxy against schismatics, that he had ordered to be composed.

The accession in 1081 of Alexius Comnenus to the imperial throne brought a new and vigorous personality to cope with Byzantine distress. From the striking narrative of the *Alexiad*, written by his daughter Anna with much style, learning, insight and partiality, we know more about him than about most of his contemporaries. His abilities deserved such informed repute. By 1091 the Normans had been driven out of Durazzo, Robert Guiscard was dead and his son Bohemond engaged in civil disputes in Italy; mutual distrust of the Normans in the Adriatic had led Alexius to make a treaty with Venice in 1092, opening to them the ports of the empire on very favourable terms, an all-important step in the growth of Venetian trade. The Pechenegs, a people of Turkish extraction settled on the northern banks of the Danube and the most dangerous of Byzantium's Balkan neighbours, had been practically wiped out in a decisive victory followed by a grim massacre. In Asia Minor little headway had been made against the Turks, but on the death of sultan Malik Shah in 1902 the Selchukid power disintegrated into struggles among rival claimants. Alexius was able to form an alliance with Kilij Arslan, who held Nicaea and Iconium (Konya), against the emir of Smyrna, whose ambitions threatened Constantinople and Iconium alike. There was a period of hard-won peace, much needed by the depleted finances of Byzantium.

In his wars, Alexius had been compelled to hire many mercenaries. The Scandinavian Varangian guard had been an established force for almost a century; the upheavals of Europe sent other contingents, Anglo-Saxons, Germans, the ever-restless Normans. Robert I, count of Flanders, returning from a pilgrimage to Jerusalem in 1087, had for two years aided Alexius, and promised to send him a contingent of 500 mounted Flemings. Memories of this negotiation persisted, and a spurious or at least much re-edited appeal from the emperor to Flanders was to be used as later crusading propaganda. Alexius was seeking also papal help in recruitment. Already under Gregory VII (pope 1073–85), papacy and empire had found some common ground in suspicions of Norman power in southern Italy, though on the papal side there were many fluctuations of policy. Now, with the accession of Urban II in 1088, Alexius was prepared to discuss again old controversies of recognition and seek agreements with the papacy which would facilitate Western mercenary aid. In 1095, when Urban held a council at Piacenza, a Byzantine embassy was present with sad accounts of the overthrow of the Christian churches of Asia Minor, those historic churches of Paul's missionary journeys, whose names if not their exact locations were so familiar to Western churchmen. From Piacenza, Urban moved north to visit Cluny, where he himself had once been prior.

No century had as yet been so well informed about Islam and its teachings. As the *reconquista* advanced in Spain, Cluniac monks followed in its path: along the great pilgrim route to Compostella they had their hospices, and the *Livre de Saint-Jacques* was probably a Cluniac product. This learned centre could not fail to have some knowledge of the civilization of Toledo and Cordova; in the twelfth century it was a Cluniac abbot who had the Koran translated into Latin. To Western Christendom, the Saracens represented the main body of unbelievers. The Jews held a special, in some ways intermediate, position; the eastern boundaries of Germany were wild lands of heathen tribes; but the Saracens stood for a consolidated body of heathen thought, and one about which, in France and Italy, there was some reasonable knowledge. In Spain and Sicily there were Arabic-speaking Christians, who were aware of the higher culture of the Arab world. Born in Bukhara and dying in 1037 in Isfahan, Avicenna, whose writings are the great touchstone of medieval Arab learning, had resources of both Western and Eastern writers such as no Latin could draw on. But the popular picture was comparatively little affected by these localized contacts. Bede's definition of the Moslems as sons of Ishmael still gave them their place in Biblical cosmology, and disputes as to the origin of their name, Saracens, when they were descendants of Hagar not of Sara, proved more attractive to medieval inquirers than any attempt to appreciate their theology. As the wars in Spain were intensified, propaganda took on a simpler, blacker picture, readily adapted to crusading requirements. Guibert of Nogent in his *Gesta dei per Francos*, in the first decade of the twelfth century, could write of Mohammed, or Mathomus as he calls him, that 'it is safe to speak evil of one whose malignity exceeds whatever ill can be spoken'.

At Cluny more informed appreciations could be expected, but it was knowledge of Moslem Spain, not of the doings in Asia Minor and Syria. And in 1095 the affairs of Spain were critical enough. A new wave of invaders from Africa, the Murabits, had inflicted a crushing defeat on Alfonso VI of Castile at Zallaca in 1086. Urgent appeals for help were sent to France, and among those who replied to them was Raymond of St Gilles, who was later to inherit the county of Toulouse and marry as his third wife the daughter of Alfonso of Castile. But the situation remained a perilous one, despite the brilliant and unscrupulous warfare carried on in Valencia by Rodrigo Diaz, who, as the Cid Campeador, was to become a very potent legend in Spanish history. In 1089 Urban had proclaimed that those who assisted in the rebuilding and defence of Tarragona would share in the same aids to salvation as those who made the pilgrimage to Jerusalem. When Urban came to Cluny there must have been much talk of Islam and of Spain, and at some point on his journey Urban met or exchanged messages with Raymond of St Gilles, a man who had close interests in the Spanish wars. Here in south-west France it was Spain that was the holy war, and Urban's wider schemes must have come primarily from his own meditations on events. From Cluny he went to Clermont, where on 18 November 1095 he opened a council whose main business appeared to be enforcement of ecclesiastical reforms, the Truce of God, and the adultery of the king of France with Bertrada of Montfort, countess of Anjou. It was only when the business was completed that Urban, outside the city, preached the crusade to a vast assemblage.

Of this sermon we have four accounts by men who heard it, those of Baldric of Dol, Robert the Monk, Guibert of Nogent, and Fulcher of Chartres. All wrote some time after the event, and naturally enough,

5 Urban II in 1095 visited Cluny on his journey to the Council at Clermont and consecrated the great new church there, where he himself had formerly been a monk.

without benefit of shorthand notes, differ considerably in their reporting of it. It is clear, however, from their words and from letters sent out by Urban, that great stress was laid on the devastation of the Eastern churches and in particular 'of the holy city of Christ, made illustrious by His passion and resurrection'. 'Altars are overturned and defiled with filth: . . . need it is indeed to hasten to your eastern brothers conversant as they are with blows.' The statements were emotional and very general, and owed much to pilgrims' reports. The overland route no longer lay through Byzantine territory; Antioch, 'the church of St Peter', and Jerusalem were in Selchukid occupation; and though there does not seem to have been, at least by 1095, any marked oppression of the local Christian communities, there had been some pillage when the towns changed

The pope is on the left, the abbot, St Hugh, opposite him. Though painting almost a hundred years later the artist is clearly familiar with the ritual.

hands. The Church of the Holy Sepulchre had been destroyed in 1008 under the fanaticism of the Fatimid caliph al-Hakim, but in the mid-century it had been largely rebuilt with financial aid from Byzantium, and was a splendid new building rather than a devastated ruin. Nor were the local Christians anxious for intervention, always prejudicial to their status if not to their lives, and there is no recorded appeal from them. It was indeed a favourable moment with the break-up of Malik Shah's empire and the civil turmoil consequent upon it, but of this neither Urban nor the crusading leaders showed any real awareness. Intelligence of such far-off events was very random, and collection and analysis of it entirely unorganized. It was with a singularly blind trust in God that the crusade moved on its way.

15

More realistic was the pope's hope of peace in Europe, of the end of fratricidal strife between Christians. The Truce of God, the suspension of all warfare for fixed periods, figures prominently among the acts of the Council. 'Fight now against the unbelievers, you who are wont to wage private wars against the faithful . . . now there will be the enemies of God on one side, His friends on the other.' And to further this, any who set out 'not moved by desire of earthly gain, but only for his soul's salvation and the deliverance of the Church, will thereby do penance for all his sins, having made true and full confession of them'. This is how Urban defines it in one of his letters; and in the documents where crusaders assigned their lands in their absence to the care of some monastery or other authority, the phrases 'for the remission of our sins', 'for the salvation of our souls', constantly recur. The concepts of pilgrimage were now transferred to a Holy War, with an explicitness that had been accorded to no earlier venture. Popular imagination gave its own vividness of interpretation. Those who died on the crusade – or rather on the 'journey', for 'crusade' is a later term – were martyrs assured of instant entrance to paradise. As an early crusading song has it:

Who thither fare
And find death there
Heaven's joys will gain
And with the saints remain.

More directly practical concerns were not neglected. The crusaders themselves were placed under the protection of the Truce of God, and the papacy guaranteed the safety of their families and lands during their absence. In return they were contractually bound by their oath of participation. Not the least of Urban's innovations were the sign of the cross distributed to those who volunteered, and the firm pledge exacted that they would complete the undertaking. It was needful to give permanence to enthusiasm. It was also necessary to raise funds. The crusades were to give rise to many financial expedients. These were still in the future, and in the days after Clermont the only clear steps taken were the raising of loans on the lands of departing crusaders. In the vast enterprise that he had launched, without in all likelihood foreseeing the magnitude of the response, there were innumerable details to be considered. Urban was a man of remarkable grasp and administrative ability; that was proved beyond doubt; but no one could control this upheaval of Western Europe without some chaotic accompaniments to it.

It was an age of popular preaching, with an audience that was ignorant, inflammable, and desperate. The year 1095 had been one of severe famine

16

6 Peter the Hermit preaching the crusade. By the thirteenth century, when this illustration was made, Peter's prime part in the crusade was generally, though inaccurately, accepted.

throughout north-west Europe. Sigebert of Gembloux described it as 'a calamitous year, with famine everywhere and the poor harassing the rich with theft and fire'. The land was unable to maintain its inhabitants, and the peasant population could not be held on its barren fields. This at least seems the explanation of the crowds following itinerant preachers, some of whom (such as Robert of Arbrissel or Bernard of Tiron) were, with the help of more educated supporters, to found communities. One of these preachers was known as Peter the Hermit, and crusading propaganda became his chief and fatal theme. Numbers are unascertainable with any precision, but the prelude to the main crusade was the passage of large undisciplined hordes from France and Germany, plundering their way through Europe, horrifying Byzantium with their uncouthness, and ending miserably in a massacre by the Turks on the southern shore of the Bosphorus. They were followed by the organized forces of the crusading leaders. Their numbers too must remain a matter of speculation, but the arrival in the winter of 1096–97 of these various contingents, and their handling by the Byzantine authorities, certainly required some administrative skill on both sides. This was far from the recruitment that Alexius had looked for, but he was prepared to put it to his purposes, and in particular to secure from the leaders an oath to restore any Byzantine territories that they conquered. The presence of his former opponent, Bohemond, was a disturbing factor, but the Norman proved more amenable than had been expected.

17

7, 8 Now little remains of the great walls of Antioch, built by Justinian after an earthquake in 528, and even the citadel (left) is a shattered ruin. But until the mid-nineteenth century much of them still stood (right). Since then, earthquakes have shaken them down and builders have carried off the stone.

THE FOUNDING OF THE KINGDOM

The situation, though the crusaders probably knew little of it, had changed considerably. The main Turkoman bands had been withdrawn from Syria by Tutush, brother of Malik Shah, in a bid for power in Mesopotamia, and for the time being, even after Tutush was killed in battle in 1095, they remained there. Two sons of Tutush, Ridvan at Aleppo and Dukak at Damascus, disputed the Syrian succession, with insufficient forces to prevent independent emirates being established at Antioch, Shaizar and Tripoli. In Egypt the caliph al-Mustansir had died in 1094, his vizier Badr al-Jamali in 1089. The latter was replaced by his son, al-Afdal, but the succession to the caliphate was disputed. The heir was Nizar, the eldest son; al-Afdal, seeking a more biddable master, secured the appointment of a younger brother, al-Mustali. Nizar was soon killed, but the dispute split the Shiite world, where theories of direct succession had religious force. In particular the Ismailian sect, whose headquarters were at Alamut in the Elburz mountains but who had considerable influence in Aleppo, finally broke away from any Fatimid allegiance. Egypt, however, still held the Syrian coastline as far north as Tyre, and in August 1098, encouraged by news of the crusading victory at Antioch, al-Afdal reoccupied Jerusalem, driving out the Turkoman Artukids who held it.

18

The latter moved northwards, establishing themselves at Mardin in Mesopotamia, and are a family of whom much was to be heard in crusading history. In Asia Minor the first success of the crusaders in taking Nicaea had forced Kilij Arslan of Roum into alliance with his usual rivals, the Danishmendids of Sebastia (Siwas), another of these Turkoman settlements, but his defeat by the Franks at Dorylaeum drove him eastwards, not only allowing passage to the crusading army, but enabling Alexius to reoccupy the western coast as far as the gulf of Antalya. Pergamon, Ephesus, Laodicea, the ancient Christian names, were once more under Christian control. For a time Antioch checked the crusading advance, but when the crusaders' capture of it was followed by their victory, against considerable odds, over a relieving force from Mosul, the way into a divided Syria lay open to them. On 15 July 1099, when they entered Jerusalem, they had added a victory over Egypt to their almost unbroken triumphs.

Whereas the siege of Antioch, with its immense Byzantine walls surrounding its precipitous hillside, had halted the crusade for the best part of a year, that of Jerusalem was accomplished in little more than a month. The city was strongly garrisoned, but it was only a year since the Fatimid mangonels had battered down the walls. The defences had been repaired, but the bundles of hay and mattresses hung on them by the besieged to deaden the shock of missiles showed that there were still doubts about their strength. The strongest point was the citadel, the so-called Tower of David, commanding the gateway to the Jaffa road. The splendid Herodian masonry was still largely in place, and it was not stormed but was surrendered to Raymond of Toulouse, in return for a safe-conduct for its garrison – a sensible bargain all the more striking compared with the horrible slaughter that took place throughout the rest of the town. With the citadel in his hands, Raymond, the acknowledged leader of the march south from Antioch, might well expect to have the governance of the city.

Some days later, the leaders met to discuss their problems. There were immediate tasks, such as the burial of the victims of the massacre, for the city was full of dead bodies and 'fearful stench', and the disposal of the

9 The Tower of David. The Herodian Tower of Phasael was thought by the crusaders to have been built by king David, and was therefore the suitable dwelling

booty; but the prime need was for some organized government. Nothing indicates that any thought had been given to future policies once Jerusalem was taken. The feudal West was used to frequent shiftings of tenures and estates without disruption of the basic agricultural system. The Franks had no understanding of the particular problems of Syria, and, with the possible exception of Bohemond's nephew Tancred, little experience of settlements involving mixed races and religions. The immediate requirement was a ruler, preferably with royal status, to establish some chain of responsibility. The ecclesiastics made a bid for priority in the election of a patriarch, but since the death of Adhémar of Le Puy, the much-respected papal legate, in the camp at Antioch, there was no clerical candidate who could command rapid assent. The lay leaders, in a gathering that presumably included their tenants-in-chief, went ahead with their business. The most prominent figures were

for their kings. Round it they built their castle, much rebuilt since then and recently considerably restored.

Raymond, count of Toulouse; Godfrey of Bouillon, duke of Lower Lorraine, and his elder brother, Eustace, count of Boulogne; Robert, count of Flanders; Robert Curthose, duke of Normandy; and Tancred, nephew of Bohemond and representative of the Italo-Norman interests.

They formed in themselves a striking cross-section of crusading motives. Raymond had a certain seniority in age and status. He had succeeded to his county in 1088, and had almost certainly had experience of warfare in Spain against the Moors. His second wife had been a daughter of Roger of Sicily, his third of Alfonso of Castile. He had been the first great noble to adhere to the crusade and had possibly had prior discussion with Urban about the great design. Godfrey had held his duchy as long as Raymond his county and was now in his early forties. He had inherited Lorraine from his maternal uncle, Godfrey the Hunchback, the husband of the celebrated Matilda, and their political and matrimonial disputes had involved Godfrey in the struggle between empire and papacy. If papal policy regarded the crusades as a means of removing some of the turbulence of Europe, Godfrey was well placed to appreciate the need for it. For one who had warred against the papacy, the crusade might indeed have a particular expiatory value, and behind Godfrey was his mother, the saintly Ida, a lady of strong character and much devotion. His brother Eustace had come on the crusade with Stephen of Blois. He, like

10 Robert Curthose died in 1134 in the castle of Cardiff, having been a prisoner for twenty-eight years of his brother, Henry I. Even before his death this unhappy crusader had become something of a legend, and the thirteenth-century oaken figure on his tomb is a romantic tribute to his memory.

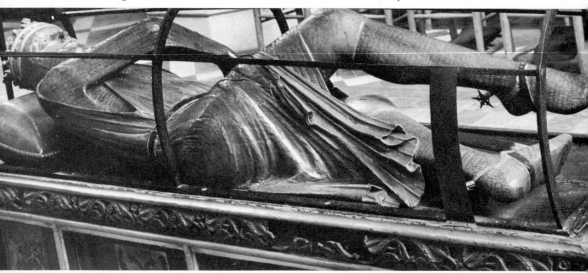

Raymond and Godfrey, had held his title for some twelve years, but he had achieved little prominence in the crusade and, as did Robert of Flanders and Robert of Normandy, intended to return to the West once Jerusalem was taken. Godfrey's third brother, Baldwin, had left the main crusading force, to seize lands for himself at Edessa. Robert of Flanders had, through his father's pilgrimage and dealings with Alexius, some knowledge of the East. He seems also to have had real zeal 'to check the wickedness of the pagans'. Robert Curthose had a very different background. Displaced by his younger brother, William Rufus, in the kingdom of England, he was being hard put to it to retain control of his duchy. Papal intervention secured peace between the brothers, and Robert pledged his duchy to William, in return for a loan of 10,000 silver marks to finance his expedition. It was a complete example of the papal appeal to cease from fratricidal strife, and to take 'the way of Jerusalem' against enemies from without. For Robert himself it was a chance to distinguish himself in a new field and to shake off the cares of state. There is little sign in Normandy of much religious enthusiasm; a comparatively small number of landholders, some fifty in all, are recorded as mortgaging their lands to proceed to Jerusalem; and one or two of Robert's contingent, such as his uncle, Odo, bishop of Bayeux, were men who had good reasons for a temporary absence. Tancred had taken the cross along with his uncle, Bohemond. He was barely twenty, with no landed prospects of his own, bred in the south Italian tradition of conquest and raids against Byzantium, and with some knowledge of the Moors and their customs. Among his followers, as we know from an account written by one of them, the *Gesta Francorum*, there was much simple enthusiasm on which Bohemond had played when at Amalfi he tore his rich cloak into strips to make crosses for his recruits; but the careers of both uncle and nephew show hard-headed practicality rather than emotionalism, and Bohemond had, disregarding his oath to Alexius, stayed to organize Antioch and had not as yet completed the pilgrimage to Jerusalem.

Raymond of Aguilers, chaplain to the count of Toulouse, tells us that the crown was offered to his master, who refused 'to take the royal name in that city', but would give his assent if another took it. William of Tyre, writing after the event, adds the gloss that Raymond's followers hoped that if he did not obtain the kingdom he would return home, and so raised difficulties. There are hints here of intrigues and negotiations, but the elderly count, blind in one eye since his wars in Spain, seems to have lacked convincing appeal to the mixed crusading following, and it was Godfrey to whom the kingdom was given, though, with pious humility, he took as a title only that of Advocate of the Holy Sepulchre.

11 Godfrey of Bouillon
setting out on a crusade.
This rendering, from a
French version of William of
Tyre's *History*, is more than
a century after the events
depicted, but the painter
catches the spirit of his
theme. The eagle, so prominently displayed, is unlikely
to have figured on Godfrey's
banner (above).

12 Crusaders attacking a
Saracen town.

14 Baldwin receiving the
surrender of Edessa in 1099.
The artist, almost certainly
working in Acre in the late
thirteenth century, has made
a real attempt to differentiate
the crusaders and the Armenians. Turbaned Turks look
on in the background.

24

13 The death of Godfrey of Bouillon, from a late fifteenth-century French version of William of Tyre's *History*.

Cairo was not long in reacting to the loss of Jerusalem. Al-Afdal had hoped at first for an alliance with the crusaders and had sent an embassy to Antioch; negotiations were discussed and Frankish envoys returned with the Egyptians to Cairo, where they remained for almost a year. They rejoined the crusaders' southern march with proposals from the vizier, who was also treating with Alexius Comnenus, for an agreement as to unarmed pilgrimages to Jerusalem. They were proposals that the crusaders could not consider. Al-Afdal was thinking in terms of the eleventh-century Byzantine conquest that had been limited to northern Syria; the Franks on their side could not forgo the liberation of Christ's homeland, 'that city in which He himself suffered for us'. Since Western status was so closely based on landholding, this territorial mysticism had a peculiar significance, and the tolerant, civilized Fatimids were as much infidels, *pagani*, as the ruder marauding Selchukid emirs. The massacre that took place when the crusaders captured Jerusalem – a vengeance, as it seemed to the perpetrators, on the enemies of Christ – finally decided al-Afdal that an alliance was hopeless, and within three weeks of the taking of the city, he in person led a large Egyptian force to Ascalon, where his

15 The ruins of Ascalon, the city that so long defied the crusaders, as drawn by the nineteenth-century traveller Comte de Forbin.

16 The long-disputed ground of the fertile coastal plain as seen from the walls of Ascalon.

fleet could join him. Godfrey moved with great speed, leaving Jerusalem practically denuded of troops. On 12 August he surprised the Egyptian forces, unprepared for battle, and completely routed them. It was a victory that certainly was won against great numerical odds. A rich booty was taken in the enemy's camp, and Ascalon offered to surrender. The offer, however, was made to Raymond, not to Godfrey. The garrison that the former had allowed to depart from the Tower of David, the only survivors of the massacre of Jerusalem, were in the town and mindful of his good faith. Godfrey, however, could not brook so immediate a disregard of his authority. A dispute broke out among the leaders, and the chance of taking Ascalon was lost. It was one of the most fateful errors of the whole crusade. For another fifty years Ascalon was to be a port of call for Egyptian navies that the crusaders could not challenge, and a base from which the southern coastal plain, the fertile lands of the Kingdom, could be constantly raided. Godfrey's intransigence cost his successors dear.

The failure at Ascalon made the securing of other ports an urgent matter. Godfrey concentrated on the fortification of Jaffa, taken by the Genoese while the crusaders were besieging Jerusalem, and on an

17 Jaffa, where so many pilgrims landed, still retains its medieval appearance in this drawing (1834) by William Bartlett.

unsuccessful siege of Arsuf. Robert of Flanders and Robert of Normandy, their vows accomplished, marched northwards and homewards. Raymond went with them for part of the journey, eventually going on to Constantinople, where Alexius found him the most congenial and reliable of the Latin lords. Tancred, who combined strategic sense with self-interest, was occupying southern Galilee as a principality for himself and a barrier against the Selchukids in Damascus. Godfrey was left with very meagre forces, insufficient for any major enterprise: William of Tyre estimated them at 500 knights and 2000 infantrymen. Some reinforcements came when Bohemond of Antioch and Baldwin of Edessa marched south, tardily fulfilling their pilgrimage to Jerusalem, and, on their return, left some of their knights behind them. It was a sufficient demonstration of Frankish power for several of the coast towns, Arsuf, Acre, Caesarea and even Ascalon, to offer annual tributes to preserve their trade. Conquest began to pass into settlement.

In the thirteenth century, when the *Assizes of Jerusalem* were compiled, Godfrey was thought of as a lawgiver; the codification of law contained in the *Lettres du Sepulchre*, deposited in the Church of the Holy Sepulchre

28

and lost when Saladin took Jerusalem, was believed to be of his making. Some beginning of regulations there must have been, but the system of government seems to have been of gradual growth. Godfrey had been elected by a somewhat random assembly of the leaders of the crusade, many of whom had shortly returned home. To the thirteenth-century legalists he had been elected by the barons of the Kingdom, the High Court. In fact the first fiefs were distributed by Godfrey personally, inasmuch as any sanction was sought for their occupation, and it was only gradually that the concept of a court of the local baronage was established. Tancred's principality of Galilee was his own conquest. Gerard of Avesnes was given the fief of St Abraham of Hebron by Godfrey. When he had been captured at Arsuf, the Moslems hung him in chains on the walls, a favourite practice; despite their close friendship, Godfrey had not stayed his archers and the unhappy Gerard was drawn up covered with arrows. But he had survived and might well claim some compensation. Godfrey had little time for further action; in July 1100 he sickened of a fever and died. He remains a shadowy figure, but he left behind him the repute of 'a true Confessor of Christ'; legend made him into the crusading ideal. 'He had', wrote Matthew of Edessa, 'the sword of Vespasian, that sword that had taken Jerusalem.' Albert of Aix already knew of Godfrey's legendary ancestry (the story of Godfrey's grandfather, Helias, closely parallels the legend of Lohengrin), but William of Tyre 'purposely omitted' the story as it seemed to him 'to be without foundation', though in other respects he gives Godfrey higher praise than any known facts seem to justify.

This unexpected decease raised the question of succession to the leadership of the Kingdom. It was complicated by the recent arrival of the patriarch Daimbert, archbishop of Pisa, who, backed by Bohemond and Tancred, and his own Pisan fleet, had secured the deposition of the recently nominated Arnulf of Choques, the adroit and perhaps unscrupulous chaplain of Robert of Normandy. Arnulf had, after many inquiries, discovered the True Cross and the slab on which Christ's body had lain in the tomb. These were hidden before the siege of Jerusalem by the Greek patriarch Symeon, who then took refuge in Cyprus, where he had recently died. Daimbert was aiming at a theocracy under patriarchal control, and Bohemond and Godfrey both recognized his suzerainty. For Bohemond this gave a Latin confirmation to his principality of Antioch, steadily challenged by Alexius Comnenus; to Godfrey it was a weakening of his already insecure position. On his death his followers, in consultation with the dispossessed Arnulf, seized the Tower of David and sent urgent messages to Godfrey's brother, Baldwin of Edessa. By a rapid march,

18 The crowning of Baldwin I as king of Jerusalem. The coronation is shown according to the French rite, not as described in the *Assizes de Jérusalem*. From a thirteenth-century copy of William of Tyre's *History* illustrated in France.

19 The interior of the Church of the Nativity at Bethlehem where Baldwin I was crowned. The pillars are those of the sixth-century church, but the original vista through to the apse is now closed by the eighteenth-century screen.

forcing his way through Moslem opposition at the Dog River, north of Beirut, he reached Jerusalem, and on Christmas Day Daimbert, accepting defeat, crowned him king in the Church of the Nativity at Bethlehem. The ambiguous title of Advocate was abandoned, and as king Baldwin I became the real founder of Outremer, the Latin settlements beyond the sea.

He was a very different man from his brother. Third in his family, he was a landless man, and it had long been clear that for him the crusade was an opportunity for territorial gain. His expedition to Edessa could be considered a sound strategic move, cutting across the Euphrates, barring one of the routes between Asia Minor and Baghdad, and separating Aleppo from Mosul. It also gave control of a landing-stage on the Euphrates for goods going to the Syrian ports. But it is unlikely that the knowledge was available to make such judgments. The crusaders were working without maps, and most of their topographical information must have been acquired on the spot. Baldwin had Armenian contacts through a certain Bagrat or Pancrace, who had been with the crusading troops since Nicaea, and could supply him with local information. He had also already diverged from the main body into an Armenian sphere of influence at Tarsus, where he found Tancred on a similar errand, and the first civil bloodshed of the crusade occurred. The dismemberment of Greater Armenia and the dispersion of its people before Selchukid pressure had begun in 1021, and in 1042 Kakig II of Ani was given territory in the neighbourhood of Caesarea; but he was treacherously assassinated by the Greeks, a murder that became a dark legend in Armenian history. With the extinction of his dynasty, various Armenian leaders, among them Roupen and Oschin, occupied castles in the Taurus and began to advance into the coastal plain. At Melitene, an Armenian, Gabriel, who had adopted Greek Orthodoxy, held the town for Byzantium, but was hard-pressed by the Danishmendid emirs. Edessa was governed for Byzantium by an Armenian, Toros, and had a large Armenian population. In constant danger from the Turks, they welcomed Baldwin's capture of Turbessel, west of the Euphrates, and then his advance across the river to Edessa, even though his party of eighty knights was no substantial reinforcement. Adopted as heir by Toros, Baldwin soon encouraged a rising in which Toros was killed. Bagrat next incurred Baldwin's suspicions and was put to torture, escaping afterwards to the safety of the mountains. To the Latins, the Armenians were territorial rivals and also schismatics. Armenian disillusionment was not long in coming. Matthew of Edessa, who lived through the period, could write of how 'they came to break the Christian's chains, to free the Holy City of Jerusalem from the yoke of the infidel, and to seize from Moslem hands the venerated tomb that received a God', but soon they seemed to him 'madmen, who practised cruelties of every kind'. Baldwin's career had hardly been an edifying one. Very tall, well-made, dignified and circumspect, he had, however, the manner and ability suited to kingship; and a strong man was sorely needed, for his reign opened with a disaster for which he had no responsibility.

The news of the capture of Jerusalem had roused immense enthusiasm throughout the Christian world. Returning warriors were eagerly listened to, and no doubt stressed the needs and opportunities of these new Christian lands. From Lombardy, Germany and France, large contingents took the road eastward, among them Stephen of Blois (son-in-law of

William the Conqueror) who had deserted the crusading host at Antioch when events there were at their lowest ebb, and now sought (induced, it was said, by his wife's reproaches) to make amends for his pusillanimity. Numbers are uncertain as ever, but to contemporaries the movement seemed equal in size to the original crusading armies. All are agreed that there were too many women and non-combatants; this was a migration almost more than a military expedition. As such it would have been invaluable to the Latin states, but there was little hope that it could safely traverse the perils of Asia Minor. The folly and obstinacy of the Lombards destroyed for the first and largest detachment what little hope there was. Bohemond in the previous autumn, answering an appeal for help from Gabriel, the Armenian ruler of Melitene, was captured by the Danishmendids and carried off by them to remote Neocaesarea in north-eastern Asia Minor. The Lombards insisted that a diversion should be made in order to release him, and instead of striking south by the direct route, now largely under Byzantine control, they turned eastward. It was a threat that once more induced the Selchukids of Roum and the Danishmendids to abandon their normal hostility and to unite against the Franks. A terrible slaughter followed, from which only some of the mounted men escaped. With morale restored and high, the Turks turned on two other detachments, one under William of Nevers and one under William IX, the poet duke of Aquitaine, and destroyed both of them. Only a few of the leaders and some more cautious men, such as the chronicler Ekkehard, abbot of Aura in Bavaria, who took ship from Constantinople, reached the Kingdom. Among them was Stephen of Blois, who at last, having endured so much, found the requisite martyr's death in a battle at Ramla, where his sensible plea for greater caution had been disregarded. To Western crusading enterprise, these disasters were as discouraging as they were stimulating to the Moslems. The Byzantine hold on Asia Minor, regained after the victories of the first crusade, was once more shaken; and Outremer was left unreinforced and unpopulated.

COMMERCE

Fulcher of Chartres, his well-informed chaplain, tells us that Baldwin brought from Edessa 200 knights and 700 foot, his *exercitulus* he calls it, his little army, and that in his early days in Jerusalem the king had only 300 knights to garrison Jerusalem, Jaffa, Ramla and Haifa. It was only after hard fighting at the narrow pass of the Dog River that he had been able to force his way through to Jerusalem. Fulcher engagingly admits, in telling of the battle, that he would much rather have been at Chartres or Orleans. It seemed a miracle indeed that with such exiguous forces they could defeat

20 The taking of Jerusalem in 1099, as depicted by an early fourteenth-century French artist. The costumes are of his time, but the details of the attack are carefully followed.

and take captive the surrounding enemy or force them to pay tribute. In such a situation, now that the land route had proved so disastrous, control of the coast as the link with the West became all-important, and as long as the main ports remained in Moslem hands they were harbours for the Egyptian fleet, from which it could attack crusading communications. By 1104, with the help of the Genoese, Arsuf, Caesarea and Acre were in Baldwin's hands. In 1110, still aided by the Genoese, he captured Beirut and in the same year Sidon was taken for him by a band of Norse crusaders, who, under their king, Sigurd, had been at sea for three years and had already fought the Moors in Spain; but these seasoned men were seafarers not settlers. Despite their experience, they were hard-pressed by Fatimid ships from Tyre, and it was only the intervention of a Venetian squadron that turned the day. These successes had been furthered by the fact that, to the north, Tortosa and Tripoli were now in Christian hands, the former captured with the aid of the battered remnant of the carnage in Asia Minor, the latter surrendered in 1109 to Baldwin backed by Genoese and Provençal ships, and handed over to Bertrand, natural son of Raymond of Toulouse, as count of Tripoli. Raymond himself had died in 1105. He had been in Constantinople in 1101 when the crusading bands passed through, had joined them there, and shared in their defeats and desperate escapes. Of the first crusaders he was the most persistent and most frustrated; when many of his Provençal followers returned homewards he had stayed resolutely in the Holy Land, both a devotee and a colonist. Shrewd enough to appreciate that the Byzantine alliance was both a check on his rival, Bohemond, and essential for the policies of Christendom, he had some diplomatic ability but lacked decision and luck in bringing his designs to effective conclusion.

The all-important naval aid of the Italian cities was far from disinterested. The Genoese had been first in the field. In November 1097 a fleet of twelve galleys had come to St Simeon, the port of Antioch, at a critical moment of the crusading siege. Again it was a Genoese fleet, under William Embriaco, of a family that was to play a great part in Outremer, that came to Jaffa while the crusaders were besieging Jerusalem. Their ships, it is true, were destroyed by a raid of the Alexandrian fleet from their base at Ascalon, but, forced to take to land, they played an effective role in the siege-works at Jerusalem. The Pisan fleet that came in the summer of 1099 under the archbishop Daimbert was the largest as yet to reach Syria, and established Pisan claims to quarters in Jaffa and Jerusalem; but under Baldwin, whose accession they supported, the Genoese dominated the scene. Baldwin conceded to them, in each of the towns conquered with their assistance, a third of the town, and equivalent territory outside the walls to ensure their

21 Christ ruling the world, with Jerusalem at its centre. The Omphalos, the central point, was marked in the Church of the Sepulchre. From a thirteenth-century English psalter.

supplies. These grants were inscribed on a golden plaque placed behind the high altar in the Church of the Holy Sepulchre. Not only were they allotted quarters in the towns but they were also given many exemptions from customs duties, and a certain judicial independence under their own *vicontes*. Gibelet, the ancient Byblos, was ceded by Bertrand of Tripoli to the Genoese, who installed Hugh Embriaco there. The great keep that still stands, built out of Phoenician ruins but Western in design, must have been erected by them in the first half of the century and is one of the most impressive remaining works of the early times of the settlement.

22 The castle of Gibelet, one of the earliest crusading castles, with a central keep as in Western models. It was largely built out of the ruins of ancient Byblos.

In the winter of 1111, from November to the following April, Baldwin laid siege to Tyre. It was, always with the exception of Ascalon in the south, the one port still in Moslem hands; but Baldwin was depending on Byzantine naval aid, and the Greeks were not prepared to challenge Fatimid naval power, unless Baldwin guaranteed support for their claims on Antioch. Tyre, impregnable from the land behind its strongly guarded isthmus, the town that had so long resisted Alexander the Great, remained untaken, and it was not till 1124 that the second Baldwin captured it and completed the coastal line of ports.

This taking of Tyre marks the first large-scale intervention of Venice in crusading affairs. Genoa and Pisa were at war with one another, and their galleys were busied in home waters. Baldwin II entered into negotiations with Venice. The moment was propitious, for relations were temporarily strained between Venice and her earlier ally, Byzantium, but the Republic struck a hard bargain. Its merchants were to have a quarter, free of all customs duties, in every town of the Kingdom; a third of the city of Tyre when taken, and the same in Ascalon if they aided in its capture; they were to have an annual payment from the royal revenue of 300 bezants, and they even demanded, though this was refused, a controlling voice in the rate of customs-dues chargeable on other nationals. These were terms never fully realized, and Venice can never have intended to have a *fondaco* (a warehouse, from the Arabic *fonduk*) in every town, but they gave a great reserve of powers, a bargaining point for future negotiations. The Venetians' seamanship was, moreover, brilliantly demonstrated when, in a battle off Acre, they outmanœuvred and almost completely destroyed the Egyptian fleet. Tyre was blockaded, and starved into surrender.

Life in these Italian settlements was highly cosmopolitan. The market-hands, the dockers and porters were drawn from the local inhabitants or from slaves, given as a share of the spoils after some victory or bought on Eastern markets. Visiting merchants made their stay, and commerce was, except in periods of active warfare, not limited by religious scruple. Moslems could come and go on the trade routes, and the decline of piracy in the eastern Mediterranean benefited both religions. The developments in shipbuilding in the Italian arsenals led to a steady increase in tonnage; in the twelfth century the average was about 500 tons, in the thirteenth increasing to 600. The Genoese favoured the *bucca*, a large sailing-ship; the Venetians preferred the smaller, more easily manipulated galley. Normally these ships were two-deckers, but in the thirteenth century a third deck was sometimes built. Venice built for St Louis in the thirteenth century a ship with an over-all length of 110 feet and a maximum beam of 41 feet, carrying 1000 men and 100 horses. The bills of a Genoese sailing show that 1100 pilgrims were being carried in addition to 75 mariners. Spices, for which the Western world had an endless demand, bulked large in the commodities, but silks and muslins, cotton, woven textiles, glass-ware, Damascene steel, alum, precious stones, and metals including gold and silver, were other articles of Eastern export. From the West came velvet, linen, and woollen goods. The normal sailings, 'passages' as they were called, were in spring and autumn.

This expanding trade was based on a monetary system of random complexity. The basic and most respected coinage was that of Byzantium, the gold bezant or hyperperon. Closely rivalling it in general confidence was the golden dinar or marobotin of the Arab empire. Both were assayed at a minimum of 3·5 grammes of gold, though there were variations in the gold content, and coins could be quoted with specific reference to their date or their design. In the West, calculations were still made on the Carolingian formula of libra, solidi and denarii, but the denarius, the silver penny, was the only current coin, and much trading was still conducted by barter. Gold supplies in the West had been steadily declining. Barbarian burials, Viking pillage, the dedication of plate and exhaustion of mines had all taken their toll since Carolingian times. Gold-dust was still collected from some of the rivers, the Rhinegold for one, but this was a slow and minimal form of production. It was not until the thirteenth century that new mines in the eastern Alps and Silesia were worked. The quest for gold is an underlying motive in these journeys to the East. It was only in 1140 that Roger of Sicily coined his gold ducat, and more than a hundred years later that Florence, to compete with Eastern standards, took over the coin; it was stamped with the city's own lily, and gradually became known as the *fiorino d'oro* or florin. In practice, however, calculations in golden coinage were met by payments in smaller silver denominations, often the product of local mints held by some seigneurial right. The *cambiatores* (money-changers) were very important in these transactions, and in Jerusalem the Latin and Syrian changers were assigned specific areas in the replanning of the town carried out by queen Melisend.

These Latin changers were members of a burgess class represented in the Kingdom by many other trades. The shops of the goldsmiths and drapers are mentioned in documents, and there were presumably Latin merchants independent of the Italian states. Zeal for the crusade was not limited to the knightly class, and trading and industrial openings were more tempting than those the West generally offered. There were non-combatants on the great expeditions, or at least men unattached to particular levies, and there were many more who came on pilgrimages and stayed to prosper.

38

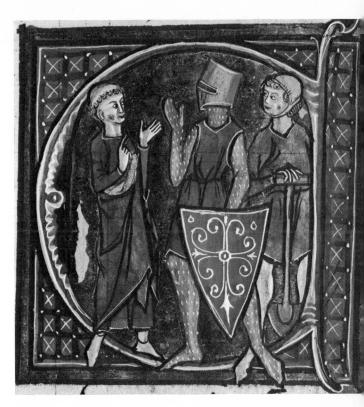

23 The three important orders in medieval life: the cleric, the knight and the labourer (the church, chivalry and the soil). The developing class of merchants did not fit easily into a stratification of society based essentially on the agrarian economy of northern Europe.

Certainly there were some master-builders and stonemasons, supervising local labour in the great building programmes of the Kingdom. Names, when they occur in charters, often give places of origin: Sancho the Gascon, Peter the Catalan, Gerard the Fleming. There was in Jerusalem a babel of tongues and dialects, controlled in official documents by the use of Latin and dominated by a French-speaking court and aristocracy. The *jongleurs'* poems, as they have come down to us, use the same language, but there must have been many problems of communication in this very diverse society.

The courts of burgesses provided rules and authority for these men of the middle class. In the thirteenth century, thirty-seven of these courts are listed, held in the main towns, some of which were rather settlements round a castle such as Kerak, Monréal and Darun, than actual townships. The courts were under a *viconte*, but gave their decisions through a jury of twelve, and dealt with cases, including capital crimes, in which burgesses or a burgess and an indigene were involved. Cases between a burgess and a knight might be withdrawn to the High Court. Though employed in their various civil tasks, the burgesses in this frontier world could not be exempted

39

from military service, or for that matter risk being unarmed. As with the Italian *fondachi*, the first duty was defence of their own locality, but contingents could also be summoned for wider campaigns, 500 from Jerusalem and Acre, 300 from Nablus, 150 from Ascalon, 100 from Tyre and Jaffa, 50 from Caesarea and Arsuf, a list that, though certainly incomplete, suggests the scale of population in the main centres.

Far more numerous than the Latin burgesses were the local inhabitants, ranging in occupation from well-to-do merchants, no doubt with their eastern skills often outwitting the immigrant Latins, to peasants labouring on the land, exposed to all the incidents of plundering raids. The Syrians, the common term for the local Christian communities, preserved, for their own disputes, their ancient courts under a *rais*; some *rais* were men of wealth and standing.

RELIGIOUS QUESTIONS

The Latin Church, faced with Greeks, Jacobites, Nestorians, Georgians and Armenians, exercised on the whole a sensible tolerance. Matthew of Edessa, it is true, writes that at Easter 1101 the sacred fire failed to light in the Sepulchre because the Franks were occupying the monasteries of the local churches and, 'most detestable sin of all', were placing women (presumably nuns) in them. This proof of divine displeasure at once brought a change of heart. It is likely enough that under inexperienced Frankish management the ceremony of the Holy Fire miscarried, and it may well have been a warning of the need for tact in local ecclesiastical affairs. The long history of Christian dispute had left many variants of belief among these churches. Jacobites, Georgians and Armenians all rejected the doctrines of the Council of Chalcedon (451) as to the double nature of Christ, but their monophytism varied, the Jacobites following the teaching of Eutyches, while the Armenians had remained less sharply separated from the teaching of the Orthodox Church, and in fact more cordial towards Rome than towards their ancient enemies though none the less critical of it. The Nestorians, probably never a large group in Jerusalem, had a great tradition of theological writing in their Mesopotamian monasteries, and the subtleties of their speculations must have been singularly incomprehensible to Western clerics. For those who had come to Jerusalem in simple faith, the niceties of definition over which the East had so long laboured must have seemed curiously remote. Relations, however, were reasonably cordial. Visiting pilgrims of these sects made no complaints about their treatment and some churches remained in their hands or were shortly restored to them. Among the great building activities of the twelfth century, the Armenian cathedral of St James has a

40

distinguished place; the Syrian church of St Mark is clearly twelfth-century work; and the Georgian church of the Holy Cross is known to have been restored. Many others, such as the often mentioned Jacobite church of St Mary Magdalen or the Hospice of St Saba, must have undergone similar rebuildings or restoration.

When the crusaders found themselves in possession of Jerusalem it was an almost empty city. Since the oppression under al-Hakim in the early eleventh century the Christian community had enjoyed reasonable tolerance. In the words attributed to Urban at Clermont, the sufferings of the Eastern Christians was one of the exhortations to the crusade, but it was the coming of the crusaders and the capture of Antioch that provoked the Moslems to persecution. Many Christians were killed or driven out of the city. The Jews were allowed to remain, but it was ill for them to be thus laid open to suspicions of complicity, and they perished almost completely when the crusaders burned their synagogue, or so at least an Arab source tells us. The Christian sources, retailing without compunction the massacre of the Moslems, do not mention this atrocity; it might have seemed equally praiseworthy to many of them, but the Church had condemned the earlier crusading pogroms, and little was said of this latest revolting episode.

The Moslem victims in a massacre that spared neither age nor sex were another matter. Here the violence of a harsh, cruel society was intensified by a sense of religious justification. This was vengeance on the children of the devil who had defiled the sacred sites with their filthiness and slain and tortured the faithful. Raymond of Aguilers describes how, as the crusaders came down the coast through areas with Christian churches, they found the images, even those of God Himself, defaced by the Turks, and the eyes obliterated, as can often still be seen today. Against such blasphemers the more bloodthirsty passages of the Old Testament were freely quoted, and slaughter, sadistically satisfactory to these wearied troops, was carried out in the conviction that it was pleasing to God. 'The righteous shall rejoice when he seeth the vengeance, he shall wash his feet in the blood of the wicked.' Baldric of Dol, alone of the chroniclers, feels some need to apologize by stressing the presumption of the pagans in taking shelter in the Temple of the Lord. Not surprisingly the massacre resulted in the flight of many Moslems from the surrounding country. Equally predictably it induced the emirs of neighbouring towns, such as Caesarea and Arsuf, particularly after the crusading victory before Ascalon, to negotiate and offer tribute. Within two years of the taking of Jerusalem, Godfrey was entering into treaties with the Moslems. Colonization was a very different matter from crusading.

41

Moslems, however, were not allowed to return to Jerusalem. In its sparsely occupied state, such permission would have been too great a danger. Christian inhabitants had to be encouraged and a decree was passed granting possession of a house to a man who resided in it for a year and a day. Baldwin I took further steps in the last years of his reign, 'seeing', William of Tyre puts it, 'that the people of our country were so few in number and so needy that they scarcely filled one street'. A ceaseless traveller, with small bands of 200 knights, Baldwin had been to the Red Sea at Ailah and his final journey was to take him to 'wonder at the waters of the Nile'. He learned of the many Christian villages in the territories adjacent to the Kingdom, and offered liberal terms to any who came and settled in his capital. They came, William tells us, 'with their wives and children, flocks and herds, and all their households'. It was a genuine migration and it seems to have been the basis of a new prosperity for Jerusalem. It remained, however, a town of problems. Off the merchant routes, it did not share in the prosperity of the coastal towns, which steadily attracted the more enterprising immigrants. The Italian cities never opened *fondachi* there. On its stony hilltop, food supplies had to be carefully watched. Water, as until very recent times, was in short supply.

It was, however, the glorious and sacred city of Christendom's longing, the greatest goal of pilgrimage. Then as now, tourism was its most profitable industry, and presiding over its sacred associations was a body of ecclesiastics, certainly disproportionate to the numbers of the population. The patriarch Daimbert had been deposed in 1102 by a council in Jerusalem; none too soon, for he had been accumulating the lands and treasures of the local churches with little regard for the policies of the Kingdom, and had returned to fight his cause at Rome. In 1112, after two brief and ineffective patriarchates, Arnulf of Choques once more achieved the office from which Daimbert had evicted him. As archdeacon of the Church of the Holy Sepulchre he had been holding a central position, supporting Baldwin in his permission to the Greeks to continue to celebrate there. As patriarch he now regulated the chapter by installing Augustinian canons, and commenced the building of the new choir, the cloister and canons' quarters and the patriarchal palace. Given conditions in Jerusalem, this considerable building task must have been a prolonged business. Baldwin I had been crowned in Bethlehem, where the church had survived undamaged the iconoclastic fury of al-Hakim, but it was on Christmas Day, which might well have given the Church of the Nativity a peculiar appropriateness. The date at which this work was completed is uncertain. We know that at his death in 1118 Baldwin was buried beside his brother Godfrey in the Church of the Holy Sepulchre, but this was in the part that had been built in the mid-eleventh century and implies nothing as to the rebuilding of the choir. It is not until 1143 that the chapel of Calvary is more closely described as 'by the gate as one enters from the right'. By then the building must have been well advanced. As early as 1105 the Genoese had asked for their plaque to be placed in the circuit behind the high altar, so that it is possible the walls were begun even.then.

THE CHURCH OF THE HOLY SEPULCHRE ▶

24 Reconstruction of the Church of the Holy Sepulchre as restored in the eleventh century. The crusaders removed the eastern apse, and opened a way from the tomb to their new choir.

25 Interior of the rotunda showing the tomb edicule: drawn by Corneille le Bruyn in 1681.

26 Showing it as adapted for the Greek Orthodox rite: the crusading choir drawn by Corneille le Bruyn in 1681.

27 Domes and bell-tower. The scaffolding, put up after the earthquake of 1927, has at last (1970) been removed.

28 Upper windows of south façade, showing the elaborate carving and also the sad state of repair before recent restorations.

The church of Constantine had been partially destroyed by the Persians in 614, and rebuilt in 620. Destroyed again by the fanatical caliph al-Hakim in 1008, it had been rebuilt in the mid-eleventh century with a grant from the emperor Constantine Monomachus. This was the church that the crusaders found. The lower courses of the walls of the Rotunda, enclosing the Sepulchre itself, and the substructure of the whole platform on which it stands, bridging the small depression between Calvary and the hillside of the tomb, were Constantinian. The eastern end of the Rotunda had, in the eleventh-century rebuilding, been closed by a wall with three openings in its lower storey, of which the central one led to an apse. Beyond was a large two-storeyed cloister, with the chapel of Calvary at its south-east corner, and rising beyond it, close to the steps leading down to the cave of St Helena, another domed chapel. There were also chapels included in the northern cloister wing. The Martyrium, the basilican church of Constantine on the cloister space, had not been rebuilt, though the remains of the great eastern doorway leading to it were and still are visible. The crusading plan involved removing the eastern apse of the Rotunda, opening a central arch leading into a domed crossing with transepts, beyond which was a choir with a curved ambulatory and three apsidal chapels. The chapel of Calvary was revaulted and an outside stair-case and porch added to it. The whole design recalls the pilgrimage churches of southern France, but the tribunes are wider and higher, and, with the local use of a flat roof, have an even height throughout. The arches are slightly pointed, and the vaults are ribbed. As a building completed in the 1140s, it is architecturally advanced, and recalls in some of its details the work at Saint-Denis outside Paris. It was a vast enterprise to be undertaken in the conditions of the time, when defence works constantly called for masons, but it was the climax to the cult of the Sepulchre, so constantly reiterated in crusading statements.

Its inception must be credited to Arnulf, that ambiguous adroit charac-ter of whom William of Tyre so deeply disapproved. It was Arnulf too who had rediscovered the True Cross and the tomb slab. The demand for relics quickly became a major issue in Jerusalem. The tomb itself was enclosed in marble to prevent pilgrims from detaching fragments of the rock; when the Russian abbot, Daniel, wrote of it in 1107, this work had been carried out and the Franks had placed on the tomb edicule a figure of Christ in silver, more than life-size. But if the tomb was protected, there was certainly a brisk trade in relics, and the demand was a constant induce-ment to the supply. A pious nun, Hedwig, from Schaffhausen, came to Jerusalem, where she made friends with the Jacobite patriarch Samuel, 'a man of great age and full of sanctity', and an anchoress called Emihilta.

Samuel, she knew, had been involved in the hiding of the Cross and the slab in the days of the siege, and when they were handed over to the Latins he had retained some pieces for himself. Hedwig persuaded him to give her a stone 'by no means small' from the Sepulchre and a splinter of the Cross set in a crucifix. The latter was duly tested by immersion in water and was found to be genuine. Thus laden, Hedwig returned through many dangers to Germany. Engagingly she admitted on her return that, on one day's journey, she had proceeded some way before she realized that she had left her precious packages behind at the last stopping-place.

Arnulf was succeeded as patriarch by Gormond of Picquigny (1118–28), and after all the disputes and recriminations there was at last in the patriarchal chair a man who commanded universal respect and confidence; 'a straightforward, God-fearing man' was the repute he left behind him for William of Tyre to record. The patriarchate can have been no light task, for under its charge was the establishment of a Latin episcopate throughout the Kingdom, and this involved demarcation disputes with the patriarchate of Antioch, a more ancient and established diocese than that of Jerusalem. Behind the decisions to be made lay a confusing history of former bishoprics which since the Arab conquest had been mere names, held if at all *in partibus*. An added difficulty was the constant variation in nomenclature, so that it was often hard to know what place was intended. Anyone who has wrestled with the gazetteer of crusading Syria will have full sympathy with these clerical confusions. The solution gradually reached, in consultation with Rome and frequent visiting legates, was on the whole a sensible one, answering to existing facts, though early fluctuations of policy, such as the transference of an archbishopric from Tabor to Nazareth, inevitably provoked some discords. Under the patriarchate the three archbishoprics were Caesarea, Nazareth and Tyre, the last uneasily debated with Antioch. The suffragan sees of Jerusalem were Bethlehem, Gaza, Hebron, Petra and the combined see of Lydda–Ramla. Bethlehem already had its church, to which cloisters and additional monastic buildings were added. Hebron had a Byzantine church built in a Herodian enclosure, and here it was adaptation rather than a new building. At Lydda, Ramla and Gaza new churches were built, though re-using Byzantine material. Of these the best preserved is Ramla, an aisled church ending in three apses set in a rectangular chevet, the common pattern of the smaller crusading churches. The vaulting and capitals suggest a date in the third quarter of the twelfth century, when at last the capture of Ascalon had brought a new peace and prosperity to the coastal plain. Little is known of the southern diocese based on Petra, and there is no record of any cathedral being erected there.

29, 30 The church at Ramla, now a mosque: a typical small crusading church of the twelfth century.

The various ecclesiastical authorities, bishoprics and abbeys were considerable landholders, particularly the Church of the Holy Sepulchre,
whose estates lay largely within the royal demesne round Jerusalem, and
were a complicating factor in assessing the revenues due to the Crown.
The demesne itself extended from the Jordan valley to the borders of the
maritime plain and from Nablus in the north to the boundaries, never
perhaps very clearly defined, of the lordship of Hebron. The Crown also
retained in its direct control the towns of Acre and Tyre. The main
baronies, as they took shape during the twelfth century, were the principality of Galilee, the county of Jaffa and Ascalon, the lordship of Sidon,
and the lordship of St Abraham (Hebron) including Kerak and Monréal.
Of these the principality of Galilee was the largest in extent, and controlled
the important Damascus frontier. Tancred had overrun this area immediately after the capture of Jerusalem, and it looked for a time as though
he planned an independent dominion, with Tiberias as the capital and
Haifa as the port. His summons in March 1101 to Antioch to act as regent
for the captive Bohemond was a fortunate chance for Baldwin I; Tancred
retained a lien on Galilee but never returned to claim it. Baldwin gave it to
Hugh Falkenberg of St Omer, whose family held it, with some intervals,
till all was lost, in 1187, at the battle of Hattin.

The lords of Sidon represented another durable dynasty. Sidon was
given to Eustace Garnier, a Flemish knight first mentioned at the battle of
Ramla in 1105 and therefore probably not one of the original crusaders.
He already held Caesarea and later obtained an estate at Jericho from the
lands of the Holy Sepulchre as the dowry of his wife Emma, niece of the
patriarch Arnulf. It is permissible to think that 'niece' may have been a
cover for a closer relationship, and it would be of interest to know more of
this lady who was to be one of the early feminine factors in the affairs of
Jerusalem. Garnier was clearly a shrewd practitioner, and when Baldwin II
was captured in 1123, he was unanimously elected regent and as such
successfully repelled an Egyptian attack from Ascalon. He died, however,
three weeks after his victory, and was succeeded in Sidon by his son,
another Eustace, while Caesarea passed to a younger brother. The
Garniers intermarried with the Ibelins and the Courtenays, passing into
this network of interrelationships among the very limited landed aristocracy of the Kingdom, where, with male mortality in battle high, the
women frequently remarried, carrying their estates with them in their
own right as guardians for younger sons. The two ports, Sidon and
Caesarea, were a sound basis for the family, and at the latter Herod's

49

artificially created harbour, though already silting up, could be partially reopened. There were considerable remains of this Roman capital of Judaea, with the great theatre in which Herod Agrippa had been suddenly stricken to death. The crusaders did not attempt to occupy the whole of the ancient circuit, but the walls of the cathedral built by them still stand to some height.

The Le Puiset family in Jaffa were to have a less continuous rule and were to be involved in one of the great scandals of the time. The fluctuating relationships of the lordship of Hebron with that of the Terre d'Outre Jourdain were to see constant changes before they passed into the disastrous holding of Reginald of Châtillon.

Such tenants-in-chief were always to be a limited number. Further grants of fiefs with seigneurial rights were made later by Baldwin II, but many of their holders had but short-lived tenures. This transitoriness is emphasized by some of the assizes that must date from comparatively early times, though the thirteenth-century version in which they have survived makes exact dating difficult. Fiefs could pass, it was laid down, through a daughter, if there was no son, and could pass, failing any direct issue, to a collateral line: but if two fiefs were combined in one hand, as for instance had been the case of Caesarea and Sidon, one fief must pass to a younger son or other heir. A royal right, jealously watched by the nobles, was that of the remarrying of widows. These were questions that could be raised in the High Court, open to all tenants-in-chief but dominated more and more by a few families. Eventually it was to be opened, at least in theory, to sub-tenants, but this famous assize must await discussion at a later stage. Military service was, needless to say, a constant duty of all tenants. Around 1170 the royal demesne carried the service of 257 knights, the seigneurial lands 402, and ecclesiastical lands 16. Of these knights many were without lands and owed their services for an annual payment, a 'bezant fief', which seems normally to have been at the rate of 400 to 500 bezants a year. Land was scarce, and much of it needed constant protection from raids, though it is possible to overestimate the continuity of fighting. There were periods of comparative peace, particularly in the coastal zones, but garrison duties had to be maintained, and plundering raids undertaken as a source of revenue; the value of the latter was frequently offset by the need to ransom prisoners.

The Latins were largely centred in the towns or villages grouped round a castle. The *casali*, the hamlets where agriculture was carried out, were mainly inhabited by indigenes. These lands were divided into *carrucates*, a day's ploughing for a pair of oxen. The main sowing was in autumn, but it is likely, to judge by traditional practices, that land left

50

31 Crusader: from a psalter made for Westminster. He wears the chain armour and long surcoat, adapted in the East as protection against the sun, of the early thirteenth century.

fallow for the winter was sown in spring for a summer crop. Fruit trees, vines and olives were cultivated, and in some parts sugar-cane, a valuable export. There is nothing in our scattered knowledge of this subject to suggest that the Franks brought any new methods or organization into this village life. Some buildings that seem the work of crusaders suggest small manor-houses and mills and may imply a movement into the country in the mid-years of the century; and where the village was grouped round a monastery or a castle there could be some Latin supervision. But the normal pattern seems to have been small groups of houses, rather than consolidated settlements. Some of the chroniclers draw a cheerful picture of the country's prosperity. Fulcher of Chartres, writing after 1124, has a celebrated passage in which he praises the speed with which the settlers adapted themselves to their surroundings: 'For we who were Western have now become Eastern. Who was Roman or Frank has in this land become Galilaean or Palestinian. Already we have forgotten our native land. . . . Who there was poor, here God makes wealthy. Who had a few pence, here possesses innumerable bezants.' It does not altogether square with his own account of the course of events, but it must not be dismissed as mere propaganda, as a brochure to encourage further settlers. The Franks were amazed not only at the capture of Jerusalem but at the opportunities it opened up. A Moslem observer had grudgingly to admit that even the Moslem cultivators round Acre, once the days of massacre were over, were faring better than they had in the past. Some of the drive and initiative that brought these men over the long dangers to Palestine continued and animated their colonial efforts

Not only the enemy, but the climate also, could bring hardship. A lack of rain meant famine; there were plagues of locusts and other pests, and the twelfth century was a period when the seismic area of Syria was very active. Earthquakes are constantly reported by the chroniclers. There was one in Jerusalem on Christmas Eve 1105, 'at which', wrote Fulcher 'we were all greatly terrified'. In 1115, on the eve of St Andrew's Day, in the night, 'when', as Walter the Chancellor puts it, 'frail humanity is accustomed to apt and sweet repose', Antioch was severely shaken and many buildings fell in ruins. In 1157 a great earthquake, known as that of Hamah, overthrew castles and villages in the Orontes valley. Again in Antioch, in 1170, the cathedral church of St Peter crashed in ruins in a terrible upheaval. The wrath of God, as moralizing writers were ready to note, was ever calling his people to repentance. Plague too was constant, and the epidemics, though ill-defined, were certainly new threats to the settlers, exposed to diseases against which their homeland gave them no resistant immunity.

32 Massacre of the Witnesses: from an English thirteenth-century Apocalypse. Such scenes of horror were all too common in crusading history.

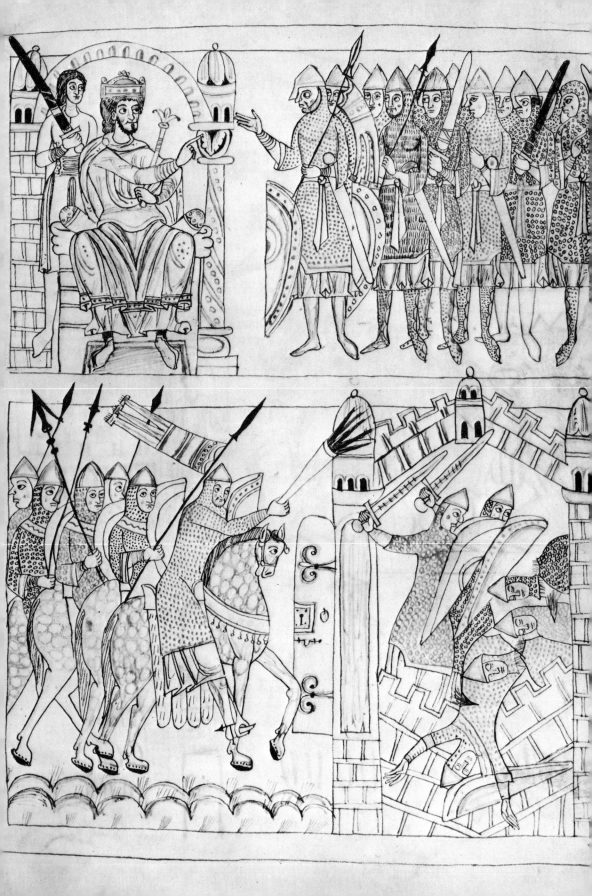

33 Nebuchadnezzar and his
warriors from this mid-twelfth-
century manuscript are wearing
the armour of the time, such as
was used by crusading forces.

34 The figure of Courage as
carved on the façade of Notre-
Dame at Paris in the early thirteenth century, is an ideal figure
of knightly virtues.

35 Combat of Roland and Ferragut, an episode from the *Chanson
de Roland*, dealing with the wars
against the Moors in Spain:
second half of twelfth century
from the Palace of the dukes of
Granada, Estella (Navarra).

Relations with the counties of Tripoli and Edessa and the principality of Antioch lacked any clear definition. Always in the background was the question of Byzantine rights, frequently denied, but never abandoned by the emperors. Raymond of St Gilles had professed himself an imperial vassal in opposition to the defiance of the Normans in Antioch, but on his death, with Tripoli still untaken, Baldwin had to intervene between the claimants, Raymond's cousin, William Jordan, count of Cerdagne, and his son, Bertrand of St Gilles, who arrived from France with an army of 4000 men carried by a Genoese fleet. William Jordan appealed for help to Tancred, already engaged in a fierce dispute with Baldwin of Le Bourg, count of Edessa in succession to his cousin, Baldwin I.

Of all the leaders of the first crusade, Tancred had the most remarkable and successful career. He had the advantage of youth, immense energy, complete lack of scruple, and single-minded concentration on his own interests. Bohemond's release from captivity in the summer of 1103 threatened his hopes, and Bohemond, aware that Tancred had done little to end his captivity and made no contribution to his ransom, relegated him to two small townships. But it was a very temporary setback. In January of 1104 a Moslem force from Mosul and Mardin advanced on Edessa. Bohemond and Tancred went to the assistance of Baldwin of Le Bourg and his chief vassal, Joscelin of Courtenay, lord of Turbessel, one of the survivors of the crusade of 1101 and the founder of a line that was to make its mark on the history of Outremer. In a disastrous defeat at Harran, south of Edessa, Baldwin and Joscelin were both captured, and Bohemond and Tancred escaped with difficulty. Tancred hastened to organize the defence of Edessa, but Bohemond, faced with the grave insecurities of these two northern states, decided to return to Europe and resume the old south Italian policy of an attack on Byzantium from the Adriatic ports. It was a venture that completely failed; Bohemond died in 1111, a disappointed man. Tancred was left in charge of both Edessa and Antioch. He was in no haste to secure Baldwin of Le Bourg's release, and it was only the constant dispute among the Moslem emirs that resulted, after four years' captivity, in Baldwin's return to Edessa in alliance with his former captor, Chavli of Mosul. Alarmed at Baldwin's reappearance, Tancred allied himself with Ridvan of Aleppo, and a civil war broke out between the two alliances. It was the negation of all crusading principles: Frank against Frank, each with infidel support. It brought Baldwin I north to Tripoli where he summoned Tancred and Baldwin of Le Bourg to meet him. Tripoli was now in the hands of Bertrand of St Gilles. Thanks to his French troops, the most notable reinforcement the Franks

36, 37 The tomb of Bohemond of Antioch at Canosa in his native Apulia, showing Moorish influence on the decorative details; the bronze doors were made by Ruggiero of Amalfi.

38 Marriages (so important in medieval diplomacy) and, as here, negotiations for marriage figure prominently as subjects in the illustrations of a magnificent fifteenth-century manuscript of the *History* of William of Tyre made in Flanders for an English king (?Edward IV). Baldwin I is negotiating with Sicily.

had yet received, the town had at length been taken. Bertrand did homage for it to Baldwin, while agreeing to cede Tortosa and Arqah to William Jordan to be held from Tancred. It was a short-lived compromise, for William was almost immediately after 'struck by a chance arrow' in a minor brawl, and on his death his lands reverted to Bertrand. Tancred did no homage for Antioch, but recognized himself as Baldwin's vassal for the vague rights he still held over the principality of Galilee, his insurance against the possible return of Bohemond. Peace was made between Antioch and Edessa, and Baldwin of Le Bourg's rights were fully recognized. In that year, 1109, the kingship of Jerusalem vindicated its power as a unifying element against the Frankish states.

Tancred died at the end of 1112, surviving by only a year the threat of his uncle's return. He had been an able warrior, tireless in battle and not unskilful in playing off the suspicions and jealousies of the Moslem emirates around him. In Aleppo in particular he had often found support from Ridvan, a strange character, deeply suspect to the other Moslem leaders, particularly to Maudud of Mosul, a strict, pious man who attempted to unite the Moslem states in a holy war, a Jihad, against the Franks. For to Islam the repulse of the infidel and the recapture of Jerusalem, sacred to

58

them as to Christendom, had full sanctions of piety. 'No tears are enough for Jerusalem', wrote Ibn al-Athir, 'for such a city they should fall in floods.' Maudud was an orthodox Sunnite, Ridvan had leanings towards the Shiites and in particular the Ismailian sect recently settled in the Ansaryah mountains. It was an Ismailian who struck down Maudud in front of the Great Mosque when he was visiting Damascus. Ridvan died the year following the death of Tancred. The two most striking personalities of northern Syria were removed. But Ridvan had retained Aleppo in Moslem hands, and without Aleppo, across the path from Antioch, Edessa remained dangerously exposed.

Antioch, in population and tradition, was a very different place from Jerusalem. A great Hellenistic city, famed for its luxuries and buildings, it had been reoccupied by the Byzantines in 969 and remained in their hands till occupied by the Selchukids in 1081. 'I thought', wrote the Syrian monk Michael, recalling the terrors of the Turkish capture, 'of the joys and dissipations of the Antiochenes, their excess of pleasures and amusements, their splendid robes.' It was still the old Antioch of its Hellenistic past. And the Turks had in fact been lenient victors: there had been no general massacre, such as there was when the crusaders took it seventeen years later and many native Christians perished in the general slaughter. Greek-speaking, Orthodox, with a long cultural tradition, the Christian population could teach the Franks many of the refinements of life. The Armenians, more recent citizens, had ties with their fellow countrymen in Cilicia, where the crusaders sometimes lent support, sometimes rivalry. The Franks adapted themselves all too quickly to this new life, with its palaces, its gardens and waterfalls at Daphne, its damaged but still notable splendours. Walter the Chancellor paints, with Puritan fervour, a picture of the licentious, gluttonous life of the city, where the women decked themselves with jewels to emphasize, not hide, their shameful parts, and called to passers in the street to come and lie with them. Tancred appears on his coins in the flowing robes of an Eastern potentate.

After the crusaders' capture of Antioch, the Greek patriarch, John, who had suffered much during the siege and been hung by the Turks in chains from the walls, was continued in office, but the refusal of Bohemond to recognize any Byzantine claims, and the creation of Latin bishoprics at Albara, Arta, Tarsus and Misis, required Latin patriarchal supervision. John, without in any way abdicating, withdrew to Constantinople, and the Latins, considering only his absence not his status, appointed a Latin patriarch, Bernard of Valence, who had been chaplain to Adhémar of Le Puy and recently created bishop of Arta. It was a fortunate choice. In his long patriarchate, 1100 to 1135, Bernard proved himself a worthy disciple of Adhémar. In emergencies, frequent enough, he steadied the morale of the city, and in disputes he was a conciliatory influence. He was succeeded by a very different character, Raoul of Domfront, a handsome man with a gift of pleasing and a ceaseless intriguer, who found much scope in the internal disputes of the principality. His career, however, ended with his deposition in 1139, when he was succeeded by Aimery of Limoges, whose patriarchate of fifty-four years was to make him one of the outstanding figures of the second half of the century.

Beside the long span of these patriarchs, the princes of Antioch were short-lived and the succession often a matter of dispute. When Tancred died, he had had no issue by his wife, Cecilia, a natural daughter of Philip I of France; the heir with the best legal claim was Bohemond's young son, but he was a child. The succession passed to Tancred's nephew, Roger. In 1115, he won a great victory at Danith over Bursuk ibn-Bursuk, who succeeded the murdered Maudud as representative of the Jihad and caliphate of Baghdad. It was a critical moment for the crusading states, and Roger's victory was aided by local emirs who feared this Mesopotamian intervention. The booty taken was estimated at a value of 300,000 bezants. Baghdad did not attempt a further invasion, and Roger enjoyed a prestige that was not to come again to his principality. But once the threat from Baghdad was removed, his former allies turned against him. In a campaign against Il-Ghazi of Mardin, in June 1119, the Antiochene forces were surprised by a forced march of the Turkomans through the hills, and were almost completely cut to pieces. Roger fell on the field. Il-Ghazi was a man who found pleasure in cruelty; the prisoners were tortured to death with all the refinements of Oriental ingenuity. The horror of it lives in the pages of Walter, Roger's chancellor, himself one of the captives, who, however, was held for ransom and lived to write his account, though, as he confesses, something worn by all that he had been through. Antioch was left almost defenceless, and Baldwin II of Jerusalem had to hasten northwards to its aid. The Field of Blood (ager sanguinis), as it was called by the Franks, ended this brief heyday of Antiochene prosperity.

The previous year the first Baldwin, sickening on a raid into Egypt, had been carried back to die in Jerusalem. He had been a great king and a skilful administrator: not a likeable man, but with a quick understanding of other men's motives. In his dealings with the northern principalities he showed a vision of a united crusading front, which if achieved might, against all odds, have given permanence to Outremer. It is sad that his greatest blunder came at the end of his career and very personally. He had no surviving heir: his first wife, Godvere, had died at Marash after the terrible crossing of the Anti-Taurus mountains in the autumn rains of 1097, and her young children seem to have survived her only briefly. By his Armenian wife, Arda, whom he soon neglected when her father failed to pay the full dowry, he had no family. She was placed in a convent and then allowed to depart to Constantinople. The marriage was never annulled, but Baldwin seems to have considered that it could be forgotten. These marriages with local women may well have been treated lightly at this stage, as they have been in other periods of colonial expansion. The king boldly proposed himself to the dowager countess of Sicily, Adelaide of Salona, whose son Roger had just come of age. The lady arrived with a rich dowry and received a splendid welcome at Acre, the first of the great displays which punctuate the disasters of crusading history. It was agreed that were there no children (Adelaide must have been nearing forty) the Kingdom should pass to her son, Roger of Sicily. But the dowry was soon spent by the needy Baldwin, and Adelaide discovered that his Armenian wife was still living. Baldwin, when struck down by sickness, was persuaded by the clergy of the sinfulness of his state, and Adelaide returned home, 'sad and sorrowing over the insult offered her as well as over the futile waste of her wealth'. William of Tyre continues: 'Her son was angered beyond measure . . . and conceived a mortal hatred against the kingdom and its people.' Thus was the Christian hold on the eastern Mediterranean divided. Norman control of Sicily and the subjugation of the Saracens there had opened a new epoch, and Roger was to extend his empire to include posts on the North African seaboard. A close alliance might have greatly changed the course of history, but instead there was this deep and never forgotten grievance.

39 The cope of Roger of Sicily made in Palermo (1133/34) and showing Eastern patterns, characteristic of Norman-Saracenic art.

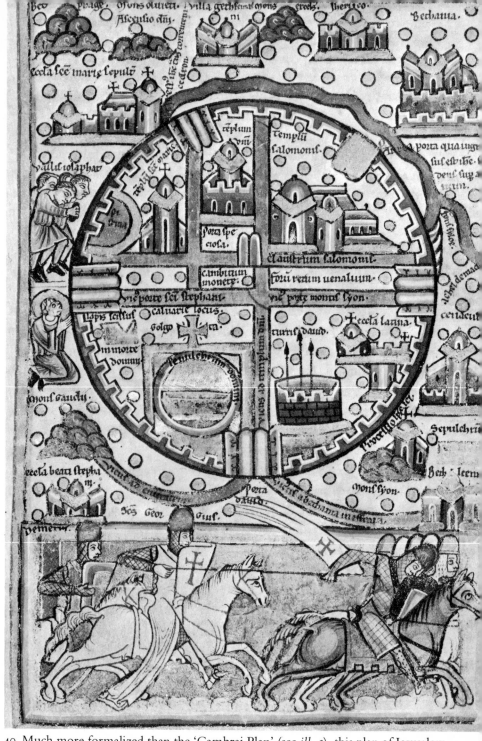

40 Much more formalized than the 'Cambrai Plan' (see *ill. 2*), this plan of Jerusalem, *c.* 1170, with its fighting warriors below, is propaganda rather than topography.

The defence of the Kingdom   2

BALDWIN II

Baldwin of Le Bourg, count of Edessa, was chosen by the patriarch and baronage in Jerusalem to succeed his cousin. His grandmother had been a sister of Eustace II of Boulogne, Godfrey's father. His mother, Melisend (from whom his more famous daughter was named), had two sisters, Alice and Isabella. The former married Everard of Le Puiset, and her three sons were already playing their part in the Holy Land; the latter married Joscelin of Courtenay, and it was their son Joscelin to whom Baldwin had given the fief of Turbessel. His own sister, Cecilia, had married Roger of Antioch. These close-knit family ties are characteristic of feudal Europe, and pre-eminently so of the crusading states. In the early days young relatives found a ready welcome there, and later the disparity in numbers of women to men, and the short expectation of life in these constant wars, led to much remarrying and consequent cross-kinships, not made any the less confusing by the recurrence of the same names throughout a family. The elective principle was retained in the kingship, but it was to a particular family that the electors looked. There was in fact some talk of approaching Eustace, Godfrey's third brother, but he had shown no inclination to return to Palestine, and must by then have been well advanced in age.

Baldwin of Le Bourg was an experienced leader, thoroughly familiar with Eastern problems and methods. Joscelin of Turbessel, despite the fact that there had been a quarrel between them that had led to his withdrawal to Jerusalem, led the voices in his favour, with seeming magnanimity but more probably with a strong hope or secret understanding that he would receive the county of Edessa. This was duly given to him, and he at once established his prowess in blows delivered against the infidel. It was as well that this fierce warrior was there in the dangerous years that followed Roger's death, and the enemy were at the gates of Antioch. Baldwin II went north and was given control of the principality. For four years he moved ceaselessly up and down Syria, confronting now Damascus, now Ascalon, now Aleppo, and maintaining his position against all of them. But, in 1122, Joscelin was surprised and taken prisoner, and the following year, marching to rescue him, Baldwin himself was defeated and captured by Belek, Il-Ghazi's nephew and ruler in Aleppo. They were imprisoned in Kharput, north-east of Melitene, where Belek had been increasing his dominions at Danishmendid expense, and it was from there that Joscelin made a dramatic escape. There seemed, however, little hope of securing the king's release, until a chance arrow ended Belek's career. His cousin, Timurtash, was ready to bargain. The sum, William of Tyre states, was 100,000 bezants and there were other clauses involving surrender of certain fortresses near Aleppo, and alliances against the Bedouin in the Jezireh. Baldwin's youngest daughter, Yvette, and Joscelin's son were among the hostages handed over. Ransom, however, was only for the highest placed and most essential. None was forthcoming for Galeran of Le Puiset, lord of Bira, cousin and fellow captive of Baldwin, who was soon after executed in captivity. Baldwin's failure either to hand over the fortresses or to join in fighting in the Jezireh may well have hastened Galeran's death.

Following his release Baldwin reached Antioch at the end of August 1124, cheered by the news of the capture of Tyre. The following year, by one of those rapid changes in fortune that makes these frontier wars so bewildering, he inflicted a crushing defeat on a Moslem force from Mosul and Aleppo, paying from the booty the full amount of his ransom and obtaining the release of the hostages. Each of the knights contributed a portion of his share for the release of the king's daughter, a child six years old.

41 A stretch of the Roman road that still exists between Antioch and Aleppo.

The second Baldwin was happier in his Armenian marriage than the first had been. His wife, Morfia, was the daughter of Gabriel of Melitene, whose wealth and backing had done much to establish Baldwin's early career in Edessa, but in 1103 Gabriel had been defeated and executed by Danishmend, the founder of the Turkoman line based on Sebastia, whose growing power was indicative of the new Moslem confidence in Asia Minor, after the crusading débâcle of 1101. The loss of Melitene blocked Latin hopes of a northern expansion based on their holdings of Marash and Mamistra, and it is hard to explain why Baldwin from Edessa had made no move to aid his father-in-law. Gabriel was disliked by the Armenians for his Greek Orthodoxy, and suspect as a former employee of Byzantium. There seems to have been a general opinion that his end was not ill-deserved. However, despite the failure to aid her father, Morfia seems to have been a loyal supporter of her husband, and in 1124 we hear of her busying herself over Baldwin's ransom. The accounts left by two native chroniclers, Michael the Syrian and Matthew of Edessa, reflect the liking of the Armenians for this second king who had come from Edessa, 'the most illustrious of the Franks, exemplary in the purity of his morals, an enemy of sin and full of kindness and modesty, even though tarnished by a greedy ingenuity for securing the goods of others'. It is a generous statement, for much of this greedy ingenuity had been at Armenian expense. In 1117, while still count of Edessa, Baldwin had overrun the territory of Bira on the Euphrates, south-west of Edessa, a region of strategic importance for it lay half-way between Edessa and his principal fief, Turbessel, but one that an Armenian chief had wrested from the Turks. It was to the ill-fated Galeran that this new fief was assigned. The same Matthew writes of Baldwin, while he chronicles this raid, 'he had more hatred against the Christians than against the Turks'. At this same time he imprisoned the Armenian Constantine of Gargar at Samosata; when the prison fell in an earthquake Constantine's body was found, thrown from the ruined tower, still chained to a column. He had been one of the chief supporters of the first Baldwin in his *coup* at Edessa; it was a tale that must have been much told along the Armenian network.

Once again the Kingdom of Jerusalem was without a son to succeed the father. Baldwin had four daughters, all of whom were to play roles of some moment in the history of the Latin states. The second daughter, Alice, was married in 1126 or early 1127 to Bohemond II of Antioch, who had arrived, a young and handsome man, to claim his father's inheritance. For Melisend, the eldest, it was clearly necessary to find a husband of some standing. An embassy was sent to Louis VI of France to ask his help, and a reply was received that testifies to the immense repute of the crusading

42 Enamel grave plate of Geoffrey of Anjou, son of Fulk of Jerusalem, husband of Matilda of England and father of Henry II: *c.* 1150, Le Mans cathedral.

Kingdom. Fulk V, count of Anjou, had already been on pilgrimage to Jerusalem and was known to Baldwin. A widower in his late thirties, he had decided to hand over his lands to his son Geoffrey, who had recently married Matilda, dowager empress and only child of Henry I of England. His mother was the celebrated Bertrada of Montfort, who had scandalized Europe by deserting his father to live adulterously with Philip I of France. Their daughter, Cecilia, Fulk's half-sister, was the widow of Tancred now married to Pons, count of Tripoli. Of Fulk's own family, one daughter, Matilda, had been betrothed to William of England, the ill-fated boy who perished in the wreck of the White Ship; another, Sibylla, was married to Thierry of Alsace, who had recently and unexpectedly succeeded to the county of Flanders. A man thus connected, one of the greatest noblemen of France, commended by the pope, could not be challenged by any of the crusading settlers. In 1129 Fulk reached Jerusalem, and the marriage with Melisend was duly celebrated.

Baldwin II died on 21 August 1131. Few of the first crusaders remained to survive him. Some two or three years previously, round the ripe age of seventy, another man had died to whom we and Baldwin are much indebted. Fulcher, canon of Chartres, had left for the first crusade with the forces of Stephen of Blois. He had almost certainly been at the Council of Clermont, and his account of Urban's speech, though no complete report, has the imprint of a deep impression received from the pope's words. He wrote, as he himself apologetically puts it, 'in a rustic style', but of 'things which I have seen'. In 1097, he became chaplain to Baldwin of Boulogne and went with him to Edessa and then to Jerusalem. His *Historia Hieroso-lymitana* was twice revised by him and ends in 1127. It is in the last recension that we find his famous passage on the new race of settlers, the orientalized Franks of whom, no doubt, it gives an exaggerated picture; but there were grounds of hope in those closing years of Baldwin's reign, where so much had been achieved, and where the royal court itself was now a family of mixed blood. The *Historia* was written to recount the deeds 'of so many martyrs, and who is so stony-hearted that hearing of these feats of God he will not break out in praises to him?' Fulcher had no doubts as to the divine sanction of the crusades, and no scruples about massacring the infidel. After the defeat of Kerbogha he states that the Moslem women in the camp were put to the sword, and follows it immediately with praise to God for deliverance from such dangers. He rarely comments or criticizes, and his unadorned tale inspires confidence. He was an honest man, with the faults and virtues of his time. Other writers, including William of Tyre, made much use of him, and he had no immediate successor. For some twenty years we lack a first-hand account of the Kingdom, and the want of it dulls the vividness of its doings.

THE POULAINS AND THE ARAB WORLD

The world to which Fulk came was a strange and complex one. There were interchanges of views as well as hostilities; and there was already a population of mixed blood, familiar with ways very different from those of the West. 'Those', wrote abbot Suger in his life of Louis VII, 'who are born of a French father and Syrian mother, or of a French mother and Syrian father are called *polini*.' James of Vitry, in the following century, writes the word 'pullani' and is not sure whether it meant that compared to the Syrians the crusading settlers were chickens, or that in the early days, since there were 'but few women, as compared with men in the army of the Western princes', the settlers fetched brides from the nearest Latin lands of Apulia. The normal use, however derived, was that of Suger. It is not surprising to find his comment in an account of the second crusade, the first occasion a full-scale Western expedition, led by two Western monarchs, found itself in contact with the way of life of the *poulains*, orientalized in their dress and habits, familiar with Moslem policies and ready for Moslem alliances.

These men had moved a long way from the views of pagandom in which the crusades had been launched. Even at the first contact, at Dorylaeum in 1097, the knight in Bohemond's army who wrote the *Gesta Francorum* said of the Turks that if only they stood firm in the faith of Christ no stronger or braver or more skilful soldiers could be found, and the *Gesta* was a widely read narrative. By the mid-century Otto of Freising could write: 'It is known that the whole body of Saracens worship one God and receive the Old Testament law and the rite of circumcision. Nor do they attack Christ and the Apostles. In this one thing alone they are far from salvation, in denying that Jesus Christ is God and the Son of God and in venerating the seducer Mohammed as a great prophet of the supreme God.'

The Arabs, on their side, were learning new appreciation of their invaders. Of this we have a remarkable picture in the autobiography of Usamah Ibn-Munqidh, a work more intimate and observant than anything in Western sources. Usamah was born at Shaizar in July 1095, three months before the crusade was launched at Clermont, and he died in Damascus in November 1188, a year after Saladin had taken Jerusalem. In his long life he covers the whole period of the Frankish hold of the Holy City, and in his closing years he wrote or dictated his memoirs. An old man, with his powers waning, he was in his own words 'chagrined at the feebleness of my foot and the trembling of my hand; while I write, my writing looks crooked . . . and my hand is too feeble to carry a pen'. But if the script faltered, the mind was still alert and the memories vivid.

He had been well placed to study the crusading invaders. The Munqidhite emirs retained a small area of independent rule round their castle of Shaizar, built on a rocky slope above the Orontes, where the river bends northward to take its course towards Antioch. Some twenty miles away, along a route which leaves the many windings of the river-bed, was the township of Apamea or Qalat al-Mudiq. Occupied by Tancred in 1106, it was for a time the crusading base for disputing control of the Orontes valley. To the north-east was the castle of Kafartab, another fiercely contested strongpoint. Till 1137 Usamah lived at Shaizar, but on his uncle's death he left for Damascus and from there went to Egypt, where he spent ten years involved, perhaps not always to his credit, in the intrigues and assassinations of the Fatimid court. Thence in 1154 he made his way to the service of Nur-ad-Din, and his long old age was spent under the protection of Saladin. On leaving Cairo he embarked his goods and family with a safe-conduct from Jerusalem on a Frankish ship, for the main sea communications were in Christian hands. It was, however, wrecked off Acre, and as a wreck the royal officers claimed the right of

68

43 Jerusalem and the pilgrim route from Jaffa: from Burchard of Mount Sion's *Description of the Holy Land*, made for Philip of Burgundy in 1455. The two towns in the foreground probably represent Ramla and Lydda.

plundering it. His family and retainers were left enough money to continue their journey, but all the goods were seized including his library of 4000 volumes. 'Their loss has left a heartsore that will stay with me to the last day of my life.' A learned, literary man, a poet, a brave warrior, something of a diplomatist, a great hunter who noted the habits of the birds and beasts he chased, and withal a compassionate man, aware of the suffering of the common people, particularly the old bereaved women, around him, he recounts many tales of battles against the Franks. In his first encounter with them, shortly after the Field of Blood in which Roger of Antioch had been killed, he charged a Frank on a black horse, ran him through and was sure he had killed him. But shortly after the fight a Frankish knight came to Shaizar, for between skirmishes visits were not infrequent, and asked 'to see the horseman who had struck Philip, for verily the Franks have all been astounded on account of that blow which pierced two layers of links in his coat of mail and yet did not kill him'. His admiration for the courage of these opponents constantly comes through his writing. Courage he thought their main virtue but he admits, while deprecating their judicial ordeals, that once in time of truce these same knights in the High Court gave a judgment in his favour. For the freedom allowed to their women he had nothing but wonder and contempt, and some of their medical practices inspired him with little faith though he was, rather surprisingly, prepared to learn and use some of their cures.

Arab Spain had been the great centre of medical studies, and the West had already learnt from these sources; but in the twelfth century the

44 Thirteenth-century siege warfare: an archer shoots from the walls, a besieger slings stones against them. From a French Bible of c. 1240, presented in the sixteenth century by cardinal Maciegowske of Poland to shah Abbas of Isfahan, who had the miniatures captioned in Persian.

45 A king presents a sword to a fully-armed knight; the gesture is symbolic of divine assistance. Initial from a late fourteenth-century Bible.

46 Arab doctors giving treatment: an illustration to a fourteenth-century copy of the treatise on surgery translated by Gerard of Cremona at Toledo in Spain in the twelfth century.

primacy in medical studies passed to the great hospital founded by Nur-ad-Din in Damascus. There botany and the use of herbs were much studied, and also there was a concentrated specialization on eye diseases, that most constant bane of the Middle East. Even operations for cataract seem to have been attempted. The crusaders, in particular the Hospitallers, were not unresponsive to these movements. As early as 1127 Stephen of Antioch was translating Arabic medical treatises into Latin. Theodore, also of Antioch, presumably a Greek by origin, was teaching at Jerusalem in 1184 and his pupil, a Syrian Christian, Jacob ben Saklan, was to become the leading figure in Damascene medical circles. It was said of him that he could give the page number for all his quotations from Galen, some of whose works he translated from Greek into Arabic. In Cairo under Saladin the learned Jew Maimonides was writing his treatises on hygiene. Spain and Sicily, with their easier accessibility, stimulated other branches of study. It was from visits to both places that Adelard of Bath (c. 1090– c. 1150) brought the use of Arabic numerals to the West. In astronomy (the astrolabe was an Arab invention), in optics, in an elementary form of physics, the Arab world was far in advance of Paris or Bologna. Few, probably, of the Frankish settlers in the Kingdom were able to grasp and appreciate these discoveries, but the contacts of the crusades must have hastened and intensified the reception of these new concepts.

Fulk knew Usamah well and talked often with him, and this Angevin count learnt quickly to understand the problems around him. The chief of these was the rise to power, based on Mosul and Aleppo, of Imad-ad-Din Zengi. The death in 1126 of Bursuk, of Mosul and Aleppo, struck down by an Ismailian, opened up three years of near-anarchy in Aleppo, an opportunity that was lost by the crusaders through the jealous disputes of the young Bohemond of Antioch and the ageing Joscelin of Edessa. In 1127 Zengi, whose father had governed Aleppo in the time of Malik Shah, was appointed atabeg of Mosul and the following year entered Aleppo. Bohemond and Joscelin both agreed to a truce with him, leaving him free to establish his control. The expulsion of the Franks was to be Zengi's final aim, but immediately he was determined to end the anarchy that had allowed the crusaders' success. He occupied Homs and Hamah and it was clear that Damascus was his next objective. The Frankish settlement could await a later fate.

It was a menace that was not clearly perceived. In Cilicia the Armenian Toros I, who for twenty-nine years, largely in alliance with Antioch, had maintained and expanded his power in the Taurus mountains, died in 1129 and a dispute broke out over his succession. Bohemond II could not resist intervening. Unfortunately for him, a Danishmendid force, with

47 View of Tripoli in the nineteenth century from John Carne's *Syria*, 1837. In the foreground is the much-rebuilt crusading castle.

similar aims, entered Armenian territory from the north. Near Mamistra the two forces met; the Antiochenes were cut to pieces, and Bohemond slain. His brief period of married life left only an infant daughter, Constance, as heir. His wife, Alice, a passionate, ambitious woman, claimed the regency, and when the king, Baldwin II, hastily came to Antioch, she closed the city gates against him. One of her messengers fell into the king's hands carrying a letter with an appeal for help to Zengi. The Antiochenes, not brooking a woman's rule, opened the gates to Baldwin, who banished his daughter to Latakia and entrusted the regency to Joscelin of Edessa. He, however, hardly survived the king with whom he had so long, sometimes in friendship, sometimes in enmity, shared the responsibilities and defence of Outremer. Laying siege to a Moslem fort, he was struck by a falling wall. It was clear that his wounds were mortal, but when news came of a Turkish inroad on the north of the county, the dying man had himself carried in a litter to do battle. His name and his coming turned back the raiders. 'Good my Lord God', said the aged warrior, 'I give you such thanks as I can that at my end you have been pleased that before me, half-dead and helpless, the enemy have fled and have not

73

48 An early tradition, accepted in the Middle Ages, told of the martyrdom of the prophet Isaiah by being sawn asunder. It was a fate that was said to have befallen some captured crusaders.

waited my coming. Good my Lord, I know that all this comes from your goodness and courtesy.' His son, Joscelin II, was of different stuff. Of mixed blood, being Armenian on his mother's side, he was small, dark, pleasure-loving and ingenious rather than courageous.

The death of Joscelin I and renewed plots by Alice, who now sought Byzantine aid, suggesting a marriage between Constance and the emperor's son, Manuel, brought Fulk north to Antioch. Alice's policy, whatever its motives, was sound. A close alliance with Byzantium was the only answer to the growing power of Zengi, though at the time he was busied with civil troubles in Mesopotamia. Unfortunately it was not a policy that the crusading baronage of Antioch would tolerate. Fulk had his own troubles. Pons of Tripoli refused allegiance to him; in Jerusalem there was a revolt led by Hugh of Jaffa. But the new king handled his affairs firmly. Hodierna, the third of Baldwin's daughters, was married to Raymond of Tripoli, who succeeded his father in 1137, when Pons was captured and killed trying to repel a raid from Damascus. In Antioch, Fulk arranged the marriage of Constance to Raymond of Poitou, a younger son of William IX of Aquitaine; he had much of his father's light-hearted dash and lack of scruple, and the good looks of his family. Raymond's niece, Eleanor, the reigning duchess, was queen of France, so that he, like Fulk, had no lack of good connections. Alice, still in her early thirties, would have liked him for herself, and in fact the patriarch, Raoul, persuaded her that this was the intention. Her disillusionment was not likely to make for contented family life, and the dowager princess once more retired to Latakia.

74

The story of Hugh of Le Puiset, count of Jaffa, is so full of incidents portraying the life of Jerusalem that it deserves recounting at length. The family of Le Puiset used, as so many feudal families, the same Christian name with distressing frequency. While one, Hugh, 'a villain, rich only in his own tyranny and that of his ancestors' abbot Suger calls him, was being subjugated by Louis VI in the French royal demesne, his uncle, another Hugh, joined in Bohemond's disastrous campaign against Byzantium. After its failure he went on to Palestine. Baldwin of Le Bourg was, through their mothers, his first cousin, and on his accession gave Hugh of Le Puiset the county of Jaffa. Another brother was that Galeran, lord of Bira, who shared Baldwin's captivity in 1123, but was left unransomed to his execution; according to one account this took the form of being sawn in two, a barbarous practice that even Saladin at times authorized.

The Le Puiset family may well have been somewhat on Baldwin's conscience. If so, there was a means of easing any remorse. Galeran's brother Gilduin, a Cluniac monk, had come to Palestine in 1120 and been appointed abbot of the Monastery of St Mary of Jehoshaphat in the valley of Kidron, in charge of the Tomb of the Virgin. The king made grants of land to the abbey, and it was under Gilduin that its great position and considerable wealth were established. Hugh I of Jaffa died shortly after the grant of his fief, and it was his young son, about thirteen years old, again called Hugh, who came to Palestine in 1120 to claim his inheritance, having hitherto been brought up in Apulia by his mother's relatives, she being a granddaughter of Robert Guiscard. He came in fact of good free-booting stock, with appropriately involved family connections. He was, William of Tyre reports, said to have been very handsome. By 1123 he had taken a wife, Emma, the niece of the patriarch Arnulf and widow of Eustace Garnier of Caesarea and Sidon, a lady much his senior for by her first husband she had two grown sons, Eustace Garnier of Sidon and Walter of Caesarea. It was the latter who, in the early years of Fulk's reign, accused his stepfather Hugh of plotting against the king, relying (William suggests) on the fact that the king was already jealous of the queen's liking for her attractive cousin. It was decreed that the accusation should be decided by single combat, 'according to the custom of the Franks', but Hugh of Jaffa failed to appear on the appointed day, and fled to the Egyptians at Ascalon. A combat between stepson and stepfather, with the queen's honour involved, might well have justified evasive action, but to seek help from the infidel, bringing them raiding into the coastal plain, was the deepest treachery. The patriarch William, who had succeeded in 1130, 'a sincere man, though but slightly versed in letters', intervened to make peace, and Hugh was pardoned but banished for

49 Cecilia of Tripoli appeals to her half-brother, Fulk, to rescue her husband (above); attack on Hugh of Le Puiset while playing chess in Jerusalem (below). From a mid-thirteenth-century copy of William of Tyre's *History*.

three years. While 'lingering in Jerusalem for his passage', he was playing dice, sitting before 'a shop in the street called the Street of the Furriers', when he was assaulted and seriously wounded by a Breton knight. Rumour at once began to name the king as the instigator, but under torture the assailant refused to implicate anyone but himself. He was slowly hacked to pieces in one of the few public executions recorded in the Kingdom. Hugh recovered from his wounds, and withdrew to his relatives in Apulia, where he was well received but died soon after. William of Tyre, our sole authority for this tale, rounds it off with an echo of Ovid's complaint over his exile. The queen, William adds, found it hard to forgive those who had attacked the count and besmirched her name, particularly a certain Rohard the Elder of Nablus. Years later we find this same Rohard among the queen's supporters against her son, Baldwin III. The old story had been forgotten and apparently forgiven.

In 1137, John Comnenus, angered by the marriage of Constance to Raymond, after Alice's approach for a Byzantine husband, appeared before the walls of Antioch. It was a critical moment in the affairs of the city. Fulk had come north to aid Raymond of Tripoli against a threat from Zengi, who had a large force in the neighbourhood of Homs. The Latins had been defeated, Raymond captured and Fulk, having taken refuge in the castle of Montferrand (Barin), had surrendered it in return for a free retreat for himself and his men, and the release of count Raymond and the other leading knights captured in the battle. Zengi entertained Fulk with full honours in his camp, a strange confrontation between the two leaders, but characteristic of the new freedom of intercourse.

Montferrand, Ibn al-Athir tells us, was of all the Frankish castles the one most damaging to the cause of Islam, so strongly placed that 'the birds had tired wings who tried to reach it'. It was a sad loss and with it went any hope of holding Rafaniyah, the fortified town guarding the foothills and the approaches to Homs. Neither of these places was again held by the crusaders, whose boundary here was driven back and control lost of the entry to the Orontes valley. The castle itself seems to have been completely destroyed in the great earthquake of 1170. Raymond of Antioch had come to the relief of Montferrand but had arrived too late. Then the emperor and the Byzantine forces appeared before Antioch. Fulk's counsel prevailed. He urged on Raymond the pledges taken by the leaders of the first crusade, and insisted that they should be honoured. Raymond, in the imperial camp, took an oath of allegiance to John. Fulk spoke of 'the treaties made by our ancestors'. Byzantine claims unfortunately had another basis, the oath taken by Bohemond I after his defeat in 1108, when from Italy, with complete heedlessness of crusading needs, he had invaded Byzantium and been forced to surrender outside Durazzo. These involved larger rights, and there were uneasy negotiations before a conclusion was reached. The following year John carried out a joint campaign with Raymond, the chief aim of which was the capture of Shaizar, the fortress of the Munqidhites on the Orontes. Zengi brought up relieving forces, but did not dare to risk battle with this combined force. He knew too that dissensions between the Christians were only thinly covered. Shaizar on its cliff above the river held out, despite the breaches in the walls made by the Byzantine mangonels, of which Usamah, though he was not himself present at the siege, heard many stories. Eventually, with little accomplished, the Franco-Byzantine force withdrew to Antioch.

Fulk meanwhile had made a treaty with Damascus, hard-pressed by Zengi. Tughtigin of Damascus, the wiliest of the Moslem opponents of

the first crusade, who had skilfully played off the Franks against Aleppo
and Mosul, died in 1128. His son, Bori, fell a victim to the Assassins four
years later, and power passed into the hands of Muin-ad-Din Unur, the
leading Damascene general. He had all his predecessor's astuteness, and it
was he who now came to terms with the Kingdom. It was for Fulk a
notable diplomatic *coup*, bringing to the Franks the control of Banyas, the
frontier citadel on the Damascus route, and definitely checking the
expansion of Zengi's power. Fulk could turn to castle-building in the
south of the Kingdom, where Ascalon still remained a constant menace.
These castles and the fiefs centred round them mark an important develop-
ment in the Kingdom. The site of Ibelin (Yabna) was on a hill rising above
the coastal plain between Lydda and the old Philistine town of Ashdod.
Its aim, William of Tyre tells us, was to check 'the insolent ravages of the
people of Ascalon'. Old masonry was used, and also the ancient wells. The
castle, of which today there are scant remains, had four towers, presumably at the corners of a quadrilateral, with an entrance in one of the walls
and no central keep, the typical Byzantine model that the crusaders copied.
William wrongly thought it the site of the ancient Gath. Ibelin was
assigned to Balian the Elder, 'a nobleman of great wisdom' and the
founder of the family of Ibelin which was long to play a distinguished part

50 The castle of Shaizar, the home of Usamah Ibn Munqidh, on the Orontes. This
Arab castle was never taken by the crusaders.

in the affairs of the Kingdom. He had been a vassal of Hugh II of Jaffa, but he had stood by the king at the time of Hugh's revolt. His origins are uncertain but he was probably a Norman of southern Italy. He married Helvis of Ramla, thereby consolidating a considerable estate.

The castle of Beth–Gibelin, again wrongly identified as Beersheba, controlled the route from Ascalon to Hebron. So successful were these two castles in curbing raids, and as a base for attacks against the city, that a third was built, at Tall as–Safiya, even nearer to Ascalon and known to the crusaders as Blanchegarde. As with all crusading castles, these new buildings provided protection for an agricultural area and attracted new settlers. At the same period, east of the southern end of the Dead Sea, Payan the Butler built a castle at Kerak. On a long spur of rock, it was to prove a redoubtable stronghold. Here there were ramparts, enclosing the town below the castle, and ditches, but the rectangular towers along the inner wall were of relatively slight projection and belong to an early stage of defensive planning. At the same time as these military works, queen Melisend founded and built a convent at Bethany. It was fortified by a strong tower, as it lay on the far side of the Mount of Olives, but the possibility of siting a convent here showed, as William puts it, 'a fairly satisfactory state of tranquillity'.

51 The castle of Kerak, south of the Dead Sea. It was built by Payan the Butler in 1142 but the keep is the work of Saladin's brother, al-Adil.

52 Caring for the sick: an illustration from the *Cántigas de Santa María*, a lively account of the miracles of the Virgin, compiled for Alfonso the Wise of Castile.

53 Scene of twelfth-century warfare, here representing that of the Maccabees, from the Winchester Bible, second half of the twelfth century.

HOSPITALLERS AND TEMPLARS

The Hospitallers were entrusted with Beth-Gibelin. In 1144 they received a greater responsibility. Raymond II of Tripoli ceded to them all rights over Rafaniyah and Montferrand, should they be recaptured, and the castle of Le Krat with three other castles in the same area. Le Krat, the Hisn al-Akrad of the Arabs, had long been a fortified post, controlling from its high hilltop the fertile meadows on the northern slopes of the gap between Homs and Tripoli. William le Krat, from whom Raymond purchased it, had no doubt worked on the irregular polygon of walls that enclosed its central courtyard, and additions were now made by the Hospitallers, particularly after the severe earthquake of 1157; but the great rebuilding belongs to a later phase, when the splendid walls and towers were erected that in the nineteenth century were to earn for it the romantic appellation of Krak des Chevaliers.

The Hospital had preceded the coming of the crusaders. In the twelfth century, legends were current tracing it back to the Maccabees and giving a place in its early history to Zacharias, father of John the Baptist, the patron saint of the order. Even without such improbable embellishments its beginnings are obscure, but there is reasonable certainty that some time in the mid-eleventh century Amalfitan merchants were supervising a hospice for pilgrims in the monastery of St Mary of the Latins, to the south of the Church of the Holy Sepulchre. At the time of the first crusade the man in charge of it, probably a lay brother of the monastery, was a certain Gerard. He survived the siege, and received some grants from Godfrey of Bouillon, and further patronage from Baldwin I. In the

first decade of the twelfth century, grants of lands in Italy, Spain and France testified to its repute. Before his death in 1120, Gerard had obtained a papal bull, recognizing the Order of the Hospital with control over its European dependencies. It thus became an early instance of an international order, with a centralized headquarters in Jerusalem. Gerard must have had considerable organizing ability, as well as a saintly and persuasive personality. Care of the sick was a very real need, and in the Rule, which was promulgated by his successor, Raymond of Le Puy, this and the collection of alms for the poor are still the prime obligations on members of the order, whether clerics or laymen. Military functions were only gradually introduced, but in this country of continuous border warfare the use of arms was unavoidable, and already in the hallowed warfare of the crusade even priests had sometimes been active participants. Beth-Gibelin might, despite the proximity of Ascalon, be considered a landed endowment, but claims over Rafaniyah and Montferrand involved reconquest, and the holding of Krak gave the order a strategic position.

Of the complex of buildings in which the Hospitallers worked in Jerusalem, little remains today, and there has been much controversy as to the site of St Mary of the Latins and of St Mary the Great, the church of the Benedictine nuns who provided female labour for the Hospital. The former, a foundation that dated back to Charlemagne, may fragmentarily exist in the German church of the Holy Sepulchre, with its re-used doorway, Romanesque signs of the Zodiac and charming cloister. The museum of the Greek patriarchate contains some carvings that probably come from this site, and, if so, prove that work of high accomplishment was being carried out here during the middle years of the century. Two much-battered capitals have scenes from the life of the Baptist, which would have particular appropriateness for a Hospitaller building. An angel from the castle of Belvoir, in Hospitaller hands from 1168, is further proof of the skilled Romanesque carvers available to them. These great buildings, necessary as they were for the large numbers of the sick and visiting pilgrims as well as the knights who resided there, did not go uncriticized. 'Before the very doors of the Church of the Holy Resurrection', wrote William of Tyre, 'to show their insolent contempt for the church itself, they began to erect an edifice far higher and more costly than that church which had been consecrated by the precious blood of our Saviour.' They even, William adds, rang their bells to drown the voice of the patriarch when he was preaching. William is expressing the grievances of the clergy against an exempt body supported by papal privileges, and standing outside the ordinary ecclesiastical discipline, in particular in the matter of payment of tithe.

54 Carved angel, found in excavations at the chapel of the castle of Belvoir which was built by Fulk and sold to the Hospitallers in 1168.

55 Crusader capital re-used in the façade of the al-Aqsa mosque, rebuilt after Saladin's capture of Jerusalem.

56 Seal of the Templars, 'the knights of Christ'.

57 Knights riding out of a forti-fied town from a wall-painting of crusaders fighting Saracens in the chapel of the Templars at Cressac (Charente): c. 1170–80.

The origin of the rival order, that of the Temple, was more recent and more casual. A Champagnois knight, Hugh of Payens, with some com-panions undertook to protect pilgrims on the perilous route from Jaffa to Jerusalem, where there was, as in many later times, much local banditry. In 1118 Baldwin I gave this small contingent, about nine knights, quarters in the royal palace, then occupying the mosque of al-Aqsa. In 1128 Hugh, on a visit to France during which he made contact with Fulk of Anjou, obtained from the pope a rule for a new order, composed of knights, all of whom had to be of noble birth, sergeants, squires who might become knights, and clerks as chaplains. All were to take the three monastic vows. At first the order seems to have made little headway, and about 1132 Hugh approached St Bernard of Clairvaux for his support. In response, Bernard composed his treatise, the *De laude novae militiae*. This glorification of the

84

Militia Domini uses many of the arguments already current in crusading propaganda, the just war replacing the civil strife between Christians, salvation achieved through it, and the merits of martyrdom leading to immediate bliss. Old Testament examples are quoted, and the knights are to purge Christ's lands, as Christ himself purged the Temple. Clad in St Bernard's lyric eloquence, this is another stage in the Church's attempt to permeate the feudal world. Already new ideas of knighthood were developing an ecclesiastical ritual of initiation with vigils, symbolic baths of purification, and white raiment, applicable quite apart from crusading activities. But in the *De laude* it is the extreme example, the warrior monk, with which Bernard is concerned. There is here a harsher, more fanatical element than in the origins of the Hospital, where care of the sick and the association with nuns in the work give a very different ethos.

58 Dome of the Rock, looking down on the rock, sacred to Christians as the altar of David and to Moslems as the place of Mohammed's ascent to heaven. Under the crusaders it was covered over with a marble floor.

59 The Dome of the Rock or Qubbet es Sakhra. It was built between 687 and 691, but the dome was rebuilt after an earthquake in 1022. It has recently undergone very drastic restorations.

It is not, however, till 1139 that we hear of any very active participation of the Temple in the military projects of the Kingdom, and then it was, under their grand master, Robert the Burgundian, a singularly rash and disastrous raid in the neighbourhood of Hebron. It was only in 1149 that a considerable castle was put in their charge, when Gaza, then an uninhabited ruin, was rebuilt and assigned to them. The exact relationship of the order to the buildings on the platform of the Haram, the Temple platform from which they took their name, remains far from clear and likely enough was never closely defined. Godfrey of Bouillon had installed Augustinian canons there, and the Temple itself, the Dome of the Rock, remained in their control. It was consecrated by the papal legate, Alberic, bishop of Ostia, in 1140, by which time it had been converted to Christian use. Much of the great Arabic mosaic was fortunately preserved, but below it were added scenes of the Gospel, and the rock was paved with marble and surrounded by the great iron grill which, though removed in the alterations of the 1950s, still, at least in part, exists in the museum of the Haram. A cloister was also built. The Templars had their own chapel by the al-Aqsa mosque, which, when the royal palace moved to the new buildings round the Tower of David, probably shortly after the dedication of the church, became entirely theirs. The Temple, though the mother church of the order, was never their responsibility, but they must have played some part in the building activities that continued there until the loss of the city. Usamah, when he visited Jerusalem, used

86

to go and pray in the former al-Aqsa mosque, and the Templars, 'who were my friends', encouraged him to do so. When a Frankish pilgrim protested at seeing Usamah praying towards Mecca, the Templars apologetically explained that this was a stranger who had only recently arrived. 'Those who come freshly from the Frankish lands', wrote Usamah, 'are ruder in character than those who have become acclimatized and have held long association with the Moslems.' This observation underlines a basic crusading problem that was often to be disastrously illustrated. The tolerant courtesy of the *poulains* was far removed from the committed fervour of St Bernard's Christian knight.

The building of the castles and the establishment of the two orders did much to strengthen the defences of the Kingdom. Furthermore Zengi's path southwards was barred by Fulk's alliance, even if not always closely honoured, with Damascus. Then one day in the autumn of 1143, while he and the queen were at Acre, Melisend wished to visit 'a place in the suburbs where there were many springs'. Riding out, the king spurred his horse in pursuit of a hare, was thrown when the horse stumbled, and was carried back to Acre to die after three days, without recovering consciousness. Melisend gave way to all the traditional Oriental forms of grief, tearing her garments and her hair, with loud wailings. She was left as regent with a young son of thirteen, Baldwin III.

60 The walls of Jerusalem and the al-Aqsa mosque: the building goes back to the eighth century, but alterations were made at many periods. The crusaders knew it as the Palace of Solomon, and it became the headquarters of the Templars.

61 The death of Fulk, when his horse stumbled as he pursued a hare; the start of the riding party with Melisend is shown above: from William of Tyre's *History*, probably illustrated at Acre.

62 St Bernard preaching the crusade. A late thirteenth-century rendering of the event from a volume of his sermons.

63 Christ in Majesty, detail from the tympanum of the inner doorway at Vézelay, showing Christ surrounded by all the races of the world: c. 1140.

THE SECOND CRUSADE

The regency was soon to be put to a severe test. On Christmas Eve 1144, Zengi's troops stormed through the walls of Edessa and occupied the town. Ibn al-Athir, in writing of it, quotes the Koran: 'When your Lord seizes a wicked city, he takes it with severity and violence.' The Latins were massacred, but the other Christian sects, after the first days of riot, received tolerant treatment. Joscelin II of Edessa waited for reinforcements at Turbessel, on the far side of the Euphrates, and dared not intervene. The news in September 1146 that Zengi had been murdered by some of his own servants induced him to make an ill-planned bid to recapture the city. Raymond of Antioch wisely refused to join him and instead went to Constantinople to seek aid from the young emperor, Manuel Comnenus, a humiliating and unsuccessful attempt. Joscelin's Edessa venture, though he succeeded in entering the town, only led to further massacres. Zengi's son, Nur-ad-Din, was installed in Aleppo and, colder, more fanatical, without Zengi's full-blooded, sometimes drunken zest, was an even more formidable foe than his father.

Edessa was a proud city with its rock-cut ditch and great Byzantine walls, the city that under Greeks, Armenians and Franks had been Christian for some two centuries. Europe heard the news with horror. In remote Melrose, the abbey chronicler noted that 'the noble city of Edessa, in Mesopotamia of Syria, was taken by treachery on the night of the Nativity of our Lord, while the people were engaged in divine service, the archbishop being cruelly beheaded by the Saracens.' On 1 December 1145 the pope, Eugenius III, issued a bull (*Quantum predecessores*) to Louis of France and the French nobility. Under Urban II no formal bull of crusading privileges had been set out, though it is clear from contemporary writings that the protection of the goods of absent crusaders, absolution

64 The Virgin appears to St Bernard, while behind him clerks chant the office: from an altarpiece in Palma, *c.* 1290.

of sins for all who sincerely took part in it, and the immediate entry into paradise of those who died on it were completely accepted. Eugenius's bull provides the classic definition: 'Whoever will undertake this holy journey with devotion and will follow it to the end, or shall find his death in it, shall obtain absolution from all the sins which he shall have confessed with contrition and humility, and will receive the fruit of eternal recompense from Him who remunerates all men.' Amid the more secular motives that drove men eastward, this remained a predominant and unquestioned inducement, and the requirement of confession was constantly adhered to. The immediate entry into eternal bliss was probably more eagerly received by the popular mind than explicitly defined. The doctrines of purgatory and of the scope of papal indulgence were to be much more closely examined in the following century. St Bernard who, in contradistinction to the papal bull, uses the term 'indulgence', stated elsewhere than in his crusading propaganda his personal views about the inevitability of purgatory, and it is doubtful that he would have endorsed the current theories of crusading martyrdom, though one of his correspondents, John of Casa-Maria, assured him that in a vision the apostles John and Paul had told him that the slaughtered crusaders were now 'a multitude of angels'.

92

It was, however, St Bernard who launched the new crusade. The reply to the papal bull, though it moved the French king, Louis VII, had little general response till, at papal command and somewhat reluctantly, Bernard preached at Vézelay on 31 March 1146. His passionate eloquence roused a wide response and from France he moved to Germany, winning over the emperor, Conrad III, to the crusading cause. As author of the *De laude novae militiae* Bernard could be regarded as an authority on crusading theory, and we know fairly fully his views about it. Above all it was to him an opportunity for contrition and penance. The worse the crime, the greater need for this 'occasion of salvation'. Among those urged to join the crusade were 'homicides, rapists, adulterers, perjurers, and all other criminals'; there was little regard for suitable recruitment. Odo of Deuil, who accompanied Louis, complains of how 'the weak and helpless are always a burden to their comrades and a source of prey to their enemies'. A Würzburg annalist wrote that 'different men had different purposes'. Some, he thought, went to see strange lands, others driven by poverty at home, others evading punishment: there were only a few who had not 'bowed the knee to Baal' and were guided by devotion and ready to shed their blood 'for the Holy of Holies'. Whatever the motives, the means of salvation could not be denied: the crusades remained pilgrimages.

Bernard was almost too successful with his propaganda. The Christian war once more caught men's imagination, and not only did considerable forces depart for Syria under Louis and Conrad, Amadeus of Savoy and Alfonso Jordan of Toulouse but crusading privileges were also extended to the wars in Spain, an effort to which the Genoese directed their fleet, and to a war against the pagan Wends on the eastern borders of Germany. An Anglo-Flemish fleet played a decisive part in the capture of Lisbon, before continuing to the Holy Land. And from Sicily, though without crusading privileges, which his relations with the papacy would hardly allow for, Roger was gaining ground on the North African coast. Never before, even in the days of the first crusade, had Europe thus exploded against the infidel.

It was all the more bitter that little came of it. The journey through Asia Minor took a heavy toll, and it was with much depleted forces that Louis and Conrad reached Syria, the former at Antioch, the latter at Acre, brought there in the end by a Byzantine fleet. For an attempt to regain Edessa and curb the growing power of Nur-ad-Din Antioch was the obvious base, and Raymond of Poitou was urgent that this policy should be attempted, enlisting, perhaps unwisely, the aid of his niece, Louis's wife Eleanor, in his pleas. There were rumours, that grew with time, that there had been more than councils of war between them, but there was to be a steady trend of blackening of characters to account for the failure of the crusade. Whatever the reason, Louis insisted that he must visit Jerusalem and marched south. At Tripoli also there were sorry intrigues. Alfonso Jordan, count of Toulouse, and son and successor of the Raymond who had played so prominent a part on the first crusade, sailed from Constantinople and arrived at Acre with his forces intact. It was an embarrassing visit for Raymond II, the then count of Tripoli, a great-grandson in a doubtfully legitimate line; and when Alfonso Jordan suddenly died at Caesarea, there was much talk of poisoning. Raymond II, whatever his part in these doings, took no part in the crusade and his wife, Hodierna, the sister· and confidante of queen Melisend, may well have been a disturbing influence in the councils that now took place in Acre and Jerusalem, where these mighty European figures met with the local figures of the Kingdom. It was agreed to undertake a campaign against Damascus, throwing away the peaceful relations that Fulk had established. It was a diplomatic blunder, whoever pressed for it. If not Aleppo and Edessa, then Ascalon was the obvious objective. No doubt Damascus was a compromise to make some use of this great crusading force. In the end, after arguments as to who should hold Damascus were it conquered, the army withdrew from the siege with nothing accomplished. Some said that the local Palestinians, the Templars being named, had been bribed by Damascene gold. The master of the Templars, Everard of Barres (1147–49), had accompanied Louis's march through Asia Minor, and had 'furnished his army an honourable example'. He later became a monk at Clairvaux, and it is unlikely that this pious and courageous man should have lent himself to treachery. But the Templars were already a target for suspicion. Louis and Conrad returned to Europe, amid deep heart-searchings as to how God should thus have deserted His chosen.

Much of the blame fell on St Bernard whose words had fired the original enthusiasm. 'This judgment of God', he wrote to pope Eugenius, 'is such an abyss that happy is he who is not scandalized thereat.' Moses, he argued, three times had to rally the Israelites in the wilderness, because they were stiff-necked and opposed the Lord. The Israelites persevered though frustrated. 'We said "peace" and there is no peace; we promised good things and lo! perplexity.' Bernard implies that, as with the Israelites, so with the crusaders, their sins were responsible for God withholding the victory, but his main theme is that man cannot seek to understand the ways of God. 'I had rather men murmured against me than against God. It is good for me if he condescends to use me as a shield.' To Christendom as a whole, it seemed that the failure must be due to the evil living of the crusaders. Some, like Otto of Freising, Conrad's half-brother, consoled themselves

65 Manuel Comnenus
and his ill-fated wife,
Maria of Antioch
(daughter of Constance
and Raymond of Poitiers),
whom he married in 1161.

with the thought that, 'If our expedition was not good for the extension
of boundaries or the comfort of our bodies, it was good, however, for the
salvation of our souls.' Others, Louis VII among them, blamed, unjustly,
the treachery of the emperor.

Manuel Comnenus had in 1143 succeeded his father, John, killed by a
chance arrow-shot while hunting in the mountains of Cilicia. The new
emperor was a young man about twenty years old, of powerful physique
and considerable personal charm. He aimed, with all the vigour of his
youth, at the restoration of the Byzantine empire in its full extent, but
was ready to use diplomacy as well as force. Shortly before the arrival of
Louis and Conrad, he had made a truce with the sultan of Iconium, a
sensible step in view of the imminence of crusading forces but one easily
misconstrued by Westerners still full of Bernard's exhortations against the
unbeliever. 'Constantinople', wrote Odo of Deuil, who was with the
French crusade, 'is arrogant in her wealth, treacherous in her practices,
corrupt in her faith: just as she fears everyone on account of her riches, she
is dreaded by everyone for her treachery and faithlessness.' It was the
superficial judgment of a foolish man, but it stands for a growing Western
tradition that was to have dire results.

95

The main result of these failures and conflicting policies was to encourage the Moslems, who saw such vast preparations come to nought. 'Our enemies', wrote William of Tyre, 'saw that the labours of our most powerful kings and leaders had been fruitless and all their efforts vain; they mocked at the shattered strength and broken glory of those who represented the very foundations of the Christian people.' In the West, he adds, there was enduring suspicion of the leaders of the Kingdom and the treacherous dealings at Damascus, so that 'fewer people, and those less fervent in spirit, undertook this pilgrimage thereafter'. Nur-ad-Din at once began to increase the pressure on Antioch, and in the summer of 1149 Raymond was defeated and killed. A man of great courage, unusual physical strength, and not devoid of some diplomatic sense, Raymond's loss, leaving only a young son to succeed him, was a hard blow to the Christian cause. His skull, set in silver, was sent by Nur-ad-Din to the sultan of Baghdad. The following year Joscelin II of Edessa was surprised by a band of Turkomans, having turned aside on a journey to relieve the needs of nature. Hated by the Moslems, with whom he had constantly broken his pledges, he was taken in chains to Nur-ad-Din, blinded and thrown into prison, where he died nine years later. William of Tyre had little sympathy for him: 'Wasted by mental and physical sufferings, he reaped the result of his dissolute ways and came to a wretched end.'

THE ARTS IN THE KINGDOM

Despite these many disasters, the Kingdom itself was not unprosperous. On 15 July 1149, some three months after Louis had left Jerusalem, the Church of the Holy Sepulchre was formally consecrated; it was the fiftieth anniversary of the capture of the city. The building must by then have been completed, with the elaborate carving of the southern façade in place, for when shortly afterwards it was decided to add a bell tower, the new building cut across the splendid string-courses. The same masons' yard was also busy elsewhere. The church of St Anne has in its façade a modest reduction of the scheme of the Holy Sepulchre and very similar ornamental motifs. The princess Yvette had been a nun there, before the building of the new monastery at Bethany, and certainly by 1150 St Anne's was a large and prosperous community. Apart from work on the neighbouring buildings of the Hospital, where they must have been employed, and on the Armenian church of St James, where their influence is evident, the masons were also working on the church of the Tomb of the Virgin, a site growing in significance as theories of the corporeal Assumption came more and more into prominence, and one that queen Melisend had chosen for her own burying-place, perhaps not unmindful of its close association through its former abbot, Gilduin, with the House of Le Puiset. Jerusalem stands on rocky ground; stone was readily available and on the whole, though there are many different strata, easily worked. There was also much already worked stone at hand among the ruins of previous buildings, and Byzantine capitals were frequently re-used. The workmen carrying out this considerable enterprise were drawn largely from the local Christian inhabitants and possibly some Moslem prisoners, but some Western master-masons must, from the general plan of the work, have been employed. Fulcher, previously archbishop of Tyre, was patriarch at the time of the completion. When he first came to Jerusalem in 1145, the church had been struck by lightning and the work endangered. Its completion must therefore have been one of his immediate cares. Strangely, William of Tyre tells us nothing of the consecration service, but in the calendar of the Holy Sepulchre from then on the dedication of the church is coupled with the capture of the city in the entry for 15 July.

Not only in building, but in other arts, there was much activity. The great screen of the Dome of the Rock testifies to the skill of metal-workers,

66 The grille set up by the crusaders round the rock in the Dome of the Rock. It is one of the greatest surviving pieces of twelfth-century ironwork.

and wall-paintings, unfortunately surviving only in fragments, were certainly carried out. Something of their quality can be assessed from illuminated manuscripts that still exist. Of these, three on 15 July commemorate the capture of the city only, and therefore can with some probability be assumed to precede the dedication of 1149. One of them is a sacramentary now divided between the Biblioteca Angelica in Rome and the Fitzwilliam Museum in Cambridge; it includes an obit in its calendar for Warmund Patriarch, on 27 July. This is Gormond, 'of precious memory' according to William of Tyre. He held office from 1118 to 1128 and during the captivity of Baldwin II took an active part in the affairs of the Kingdom. His successor, Stephen, held the office for only two years, dying in 1130, and it is tempting, as he is not commemorated, to place the sacramentary between the two deaths. Another, a missal (Bibliothèque Nationale, MS. lat. 12056), has no obits to aid in dating it, but it uses for many of its initials the same formulas as that employed in the sacramentary. The two *Vere dignum* illuminations, for instance, each show Christ with upraised arms between two angels. He blesses in the Greek manner with only one finger bent, a custom that James of Vitry was later to note with some disapproval, and the type of figures also suggests a Byzantine prototype. The scripts are very distinct, and in the missal the pages are numbered in Armenian. Dr Buchthal, the authority on miniature painting in the Kingdom, has proposed an English copyist for the sacramentary, a south Italian for the missal. This can hardly be more than a well-based supposition, but it suggests the cosmopolitan nature of so many crusading products.

The missal, however, shows the clear influence of another work that has come down to us, the manuscript known as the Melisend Psalter (British Museum, MS. Egerton 1139). In it the prayers are illustrated by figures of standing saints, and a seated Virgin and Child. Three of these, the Virgin, the Baptist and St Peter, are used in the missal to provide busts set in roundels, so closely and in places clumsily copied that they must be dependent on the psalter, or some common pattern book, for their model. Its date can be placed in the period 1131–43, for it contains the obit of Baldwin II (died 1131) and his wife, Morfia, who predeceased him, but there is no obit for Fulk (died 1143). It is a very splendid and lavish work, prefaced by twenty-four full-page illuminations of the life of Christ, the last of which, the Byzantine theme of the Deesis, is signed *Basilius me fecit*. These full-page scenes are a Western practice, and notably an English one, but the treatment here shows strong Byzantine influence, and prototypes of most of the scenes were available in the scattered illustrations of Byzantine lectionaries. In the scene of the Presentation, Anna holds a

67 and 68 Vere Dignum initials from the sacramentary
(above) and missal (below) illuminated in the Church
of the Holy Sepulchre, *c.* 1130–40. The latter is probably the slightly later work.

69 The missal has several initials with figures in
roundels, which seem adaptations of the standing figures
in the Melisend Psalter (*ill. 71*).

70 An initial from the
Melisend Psalter, designed
in black and gold and
using the Eastern motif
of the winged dragon.

scroll inscribed in Greek, and Greek names are inscribed on the Deesis. On the other hand, in the scene of the Marys at the tomb, there are three women (according to St Mark), whereas the Greek tradition only shows two (according to St Matthew). The decorative black and gold initials to the Psalms, works of striking originality and skill, show a mixture of Western and Islamic motifs: the figures illustrating the prayers are by a different hand from that of the full-page scenes, and, though based on Byzantine examples, much more Western in character. The apostles give the Latin blessing, whereas in the Deesis Christ uses the Greek gesture. To complete this medley of inspirations, the calendar contains the feasts of numerous English saints. William, the prior of the Holy Sepulchre, who in 1128 became the first archbishop of Tyre, was an Englishman: so also was Ralph, royal chancellor in the forties and 'most acceptable to the king and queen', who tried to obtain the archbishopric of Tyre for him, and, failing there, later secured for him the bishopric of Bethlehem. English communications were not lacking.

71 Virgin and Child from the Melisend Psalter. The caption Mater Dei is in Latin but the design conforms to a well-known Byzantine type.

ORATIO AD SCAM MARIAM·

The scriptorium that could produce such works was obviously a place of importance and some considerable organization. Three Latin gospels, whose illumination shows some common features with the preceding manuscripts and the same signs of Western use of Byzantine models, can be with some security attributed to the same source. These survivals can only be a small part of the output, and at the same time artists were at work on the paintings and mosaics for the Church of the Holy Sepulchre, of which only a fragment, the much-damaged figure of Christ in the vault of Calvary, remains.

THE REGENCY OF MELISEND

It is tempting to suppose that queen Melisend patronized and encouraged this considerable artistic activity. The giving of her name to the psalter, the most splendid of all these works, has much to support it. It is clear from the prayers that it was written for a woman, but there is no suggestion that she was a religious. St Mary Magdalen is treated with some

72 Ivory cover of the Melisend Psalter: acts of mercy performed by a king. The covers are the only surviving examples of work in ivory from the crusading kingdom.

prominence; her cult was connected with the abbey of St Mary of Jehosha-phat, where there was a confraternity to which the queen may well have belonged. Her younger sister, Yvette, for whom the obits of their parents would be equally appropriate was abbess of the convent at Bethany, over the tomb of Lazarus, which Melisend had built for her, and previously had been in the convent of St Anne: but Bethany was not founded till 1144, after Fulk's death and neither St Anne nor St Lazarus receive any special prominence. The final royal magnificence of the book is its ivory covers, still preserved and showing on one side the life of David and a very Western psychomachia, and on the other the works of mercy. These are performed by a crowned king with, at the top, a falcon inscribed Herodius, its common bestiary title; but it was also known as Fulcia and it may be a rebus suggesting that Fulk is the king whose acts of charity are commemorated.

There is ample evidence in William of Tyre that the queen was interested in the arts. To the convent at Bethany she gave sacred vessels adorned with gems, and silken stuffs for vestments. The church of the Tomb of the Virgin had her interest and support. At Monte-joie (Nebi Samuel) she established, as a result of correspondence with Bernard of Clairvaux, a Premonstratensian monastery. No doubt in Nablus, her dower town, some of the building was due to her, but it remains one of the least explored of crusading sites. Nor was it only churches in which she was interested. In Jerusalem she took an active part in town-planning, removing in 1151 a mill adjoining the Tower of David in order to open up the gateway. This was followed by the building, negotiated by the queen, of a new street, the vaulted Suq al'Attarin, to provide better quarters for the Syrian and Latin money-changers (nummularii); here and there on the walls the inscription 'Sca Anna' recalls Melisend's care for one of her favourite foundations.

In these developments her support of the indigenous populations played a large part. In 1140, the Armenian patriarch attended the Council held by the papal legate, Alberic of Ostia; and doctrinal differences between his Church and Rome were amicably discussed. The Armenian church of St James in Jerusalem was being built at the time and by 1162 John of Würzburg describes it as completed. Melisend, with her Armenian blood and her interest in ecclesiastical affairs, must have been involved in this undertaking. Her mother's home town of Melitene had a large Jacobite community, and the Jacobite patriarch in Jerusalem, Ignatius, himself from Melitene, was in frequent touch with the queen. The loss of Edessa brought an influx of Armenian and Syrian refugees into Jerusalem. A colophon in a lectionary in St Mark's, the twelfth-century Syrian church

103

73 Syriac psalter from Edessa. Later by some eighty years than the Melisend Psalter, it shows the continuous influence of the Byzantine tradition, and is also a reminder of those Christian communities surviving in lands retaken by the Moslems.

in Jerusalem, written in the convent of St Mary Magdalen in Jerusalem in the year 1149 by 'a sinful and humble monk from Edessa', praises Ignatius for all he had done for these unhappy survivors, and also king Baldwin and his mother, queen Melisend.

Reflections of these interrelations are shown in the art of the time. Gadroons, the characteristic voussoirs of the Church of the Holy Sepulchre, appear on doorways at Jacobite St Mark's and Armenian St James. A Syriac lectionary (Bibliothèque Nationale, MS. Syriac 355), inscribed as painted by Joseph of Melitene under bishop Mar-Joannes (1193–1200), has in its full-page scenes, of which only eight out of the listed twenty-four remain, strong recollections of the Melisend Psalter or some other allied work, though here treated by a powerful and very individual artist. Codex 28 in St Mark's, Jerusalem, dated to 1222 and written in Edessa, has similar relationships.

74 The Presentation in the Temple from the Melisend Psalter. The dome recalls the Temple as the crusaders knew it. Anna carries a scroll inscribed in Greek, 'this Child created heaven and earth'.

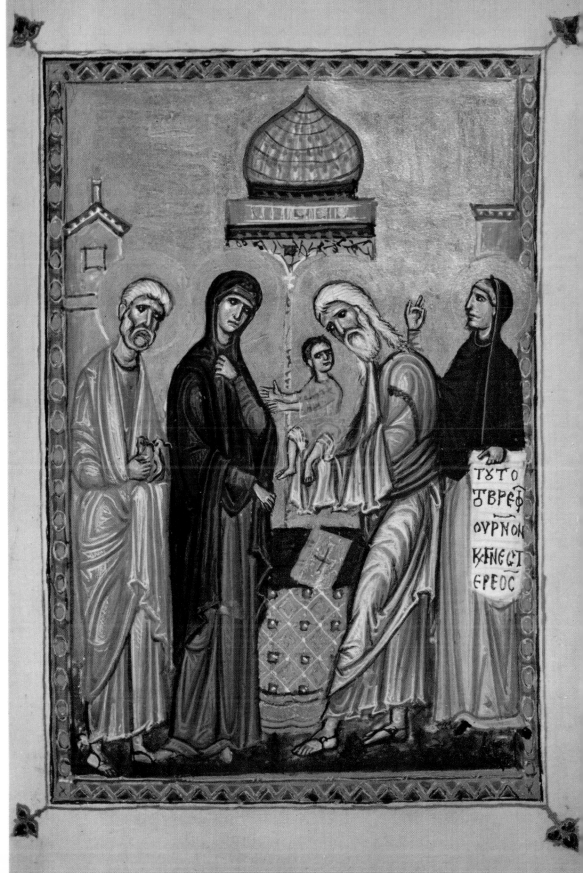

ΤΥΤΟ
ΤΒΡΕΦ
ΟΥΡΝΟΝ
ΚΑΓΝΕΣΤ
ΕΡΕΟΣ

75 The Church of the Holy
Sepulchre. In this illustration,
from the fifteenth-century
Book of Hours of René of
Anjou, the buildings have been
elongated, particularly the bell-
tower, but there is a careful
attempt at accuracy.

76 Bevelled voussoirs (gadroons) from the Church of the
Holy Sepulchre. The gadroon
was much used by the Arabs,
constantly employed by the
crusaders, but it seems never to
have gained popularity in
Western Europe.

77 Window in the Martorana
Tower, Palermo, built in 1143
and showing the Moorish
influence on Sicilian art by its
use of gadroons.

In the wider policies of the Kingdom, the control of the baronage, the support of Tripoli and Antioch and the defence against Islam, the queen shows to less advantage. These were matters where her sex told against her, and the strong ties between her and her sisters could cloud her judgment. She relied also too much on one man, Manasses of Hierges, whom she made constable. His mother was Baldwin II's sister, so that once again a close relationship was involved. He had married the widow of Balian of Ibelin, who brought him lands and wealth, and his arrogance alienated the barons and the young king, who in 1151 had reached the age of twenty-one, whereas the legal age for taking up the kingship was fifteen. Melisend clung to power. In the Kingdom hers was the hereditary right, and Fulk had always issued his writs 'by the assent of his wife Melisend', adding after 1138 'and of his son Baldwin'. On Fulk's death she had been crowned along with her son, and clearly intended to maintain a joint rule. Baldwin, however, had a strong following. In the end he had to lay siege to his mother, defending herself in the Tower of David. Manasses was banished from the Kingdom and Melisend withdrew to her estates at Nablus. She appears, however, to have borne no lasting grievance. Within a year she was accompanying Baldwin to Tripoli, where her sister Hodierna was in matrimonial troubles with her jealous husband, Raymond II. These seem to have been smoothed over, but it was agreed that Hodierna should return for a time with her sister to Jerusalem. As they set out Raymond accompanied them to the town gates: as he re-entered, 'between the barbican and the wall', he was assailed by some Assassins and mortally wounded, an unexplained assault, though there are dark and ambiguous passages in Raymond's life that may have given the fanatics cause. Hodierna remained in Tripoli as guardian of her twelve-year-old son, who, as Raymond III, was to play a great part in the closing days of Jerusalem.

This was the first murder of a Latin by the Ismailian sect to whom the crusaders gave the title Assassins. 'Neither Christians nor Saracens', wrote William of Tyre, 'know whence this name is derived.' Almost certainly it comes from the Arabic hashish, a drug whose uses were well known in the East. There is no contemporary evidence that the Assassins used it to inspire their desperate emissaries, but it clearly had some special association with them. From 1162 to 1194 the Syrian branch was controlled by a remarkable man, Sinan Ibn-Salman, whom the crusaders knew as the Old Man of the Mountain. The exact obedience obtained by him from his followers, sent out as they were on suicidal missions, excited the imagination of the West. 'I am your Assassin, who hopes to win paradise through doing your commands,' wrote a Provençal troubadour to his lady. The crusaders for a time regarded them as possible allies, and even, hearing vaguely of their mystical beliefs, as potential converts to Christianity. Raymond of Poitou had an alliance with them, and when, in 1173, the Templars, with their usual disregard for the general policies of the Kingdom, killed an Assassin envoy returning from an embassy to king Amalric, William of Tyre regarded it as an affair 'fraught with dire consequences for the Kingdom'. The Templars, it is true, were at the time receiving tribute from the Assassins and knew that this embassy was an appeal for its abolition, but Amalric was so incensed that William thought he might, had he lived, have taken up the whole question of this independent and arrogant order.

To Nur-ad-Din the Assassins were a constant menace. In 1148, he had prohibited the Shiite call to prayer in Aleppo, and his rigidly orthodox adherence to Sunnite tenets made him intolerant of religious divisions in Islam, all the more because of the new impetus he gave to the preaching of the Jihad, the Holy War against unbelievers. For the time being, however, his immediate aims were the consolidation of the territories round Edessa and the establishment of his control over Damascus. In the first of these undertakings he was faced only by a woman. Beatrix, the widow of Joscelin II, was a lady of high courage, a very different character from her husband. Her attempt to defend Turbessel, the last of her husband's strongholds, is a gallant moment in the sorry history of Antiochene affairs. It also makes some link with one of the most striking of all the crusading castles, that of her first husband, William of Saone.

78 The stone-vaulted hall in the great crusading keep of Saone. For the exterior see *ill. 87*.

It has no history till Saladin took it in 1188 after which it was never re-gained; its buildings, bar a few Moslem additions, remain unchanged. It is one of the mysteries of crusading history how, in what is almost a by-road, a never greatly used route from Latakia to the Orontes valley, this massive fortress came to be erected. The Byzantines had previously built there, and their keep and some of their walls still stand: where the spur of hillside joins the main mass, a great ditch has been cut some 90 feet deep, leaving at one point a pillar of rock to support a drawbridge. Who undertook this immense piece of rock-cutting cannot be decided. The probability seems that it is a Byzantine ditch enlarged by the Franks. Along its edge, on the further side from the main hill, the Franks erected a keep and walls with carefully planned round towers. Today it still remains one of the great spectacles of medieval defence work, a fitting background to the last lady of Edessa.

Turbessel, however, could not be held. Constance of Antioch ceded it and some other fortresses, equally indefensible, to Manuel Comnenus, but the Byzantines made no serious effort to occupy them, and they were soon in Nur-ad-Din's hands. Baldwin came north and evacuated the inhabitants from them and the surrounding district and in a well-conducted march brought them safely back to Antioch, a demonstration both of generalship and of a care for the local inhabitants that had often been lacking.

BALDWIN III

Baldwin III has some claim to be the most successful of the kings of Jerusalem. In 1153, after some desperate fighting, when the rashness of the Templars prejudiced the whole undertaking, Ascalon was at last captured. It had long been a main preoccupation of the Kingdom, and the ring of forts round it had recently been increased by the fortification of Gaza and its cession to the Templars. Now raiding-parties from the Egyptian base no longer needed the same watchfulness. The fertile plain of Sharon could be developed with a new security and food supplies for Jerusalem became more certain. 'For fifty years', wrote William of Tyre, 'through fear of hostilities, the fields around Ascalon had lain without cultivation. But during the years following its capture, the land was under the care of the farmer, and the people of the district, relieved from fear of the enemy, could cultivate the ground. Hence the entire kingdom enjoyed such abundance that all former years, in comparison with the present, might with justice be called sterile and fruitless.' Manors rather than castles could be built in the villages and the predominantly urban nature of the Latin settlement varied by country pursuits. On a column in the cathedral of

Barletta, the port that had seen so many crusaders depart, an inscription proudly records the taking of Ascalon.

In that same year, 1153, a disastrous character intruded himself into crusading history. Reginald of Châtillon was a younger son who had come crusading with Louis of France. Without prospects at home, he had stayed on to make his fortune in Syria. His bluff, buccaneering swagger pleased the undiscerning fancy of Constance of Antioch, who married him, having obtained a hasty consent from Baldwin, occupied with the siege of Ascalon. Manuel Comnenus had not been consulted, and sent forthwith to demand, as the price of his recognition, assistance against Toros II of Armenia. Cilicia had a particular place in Manuel's interest. In 1142 he had campaigned there with his father, the emperor John, and it was there in the following year that John had been killed, pierced with a poisoned arrow possibly discharged by an Armenian hand. The father and brother of Toros had both died as prisoners in Constantinople, whence Toros himself had escaped or been liberated in some mood of leniency. He was young, vigorous and able, with all the tenacity of his race. Manuel could not tolerate this resurgence of Armenian revolt. The Antiochene and Armenian forces met on the plain of Alexandretta, near the site of a far greater battle where Alexander had defeated the army of Darius. The result was inconclusive, but Toros thought it wise to cede the castles of the Beylan pass to Reginald, who entrusted them to the Templars. It was the beginning of a long involvement of the order in Armenian affairs, and also of a close relationship with Reginald. This was hardly what Manuel had intended. The expenses of the campaign had been promised to Reginald but were now withheld. To recoup himself the lord of Antioch made an alliance with Toros, by which the two of them, collecting a fleet between them, raided Cyprus, surprising the Byzantine garrison and for three weeks plundering the inhabitants, robbing the churches and mutilating the priests. It was a gloomy entry of that island into crusading affairs. William of Tyre quoted from his favourite Ovid, 'Booty wickedly acquired brings no good result.' But before Manuel's vengeance could come down on him, Reginald had another opportunity of dislocating policy. Thierry of Flanders, the most determined of crusaders, whose wife, Sibylla, was a daughter of Fulk of Anjou by his first marriage and a devoted friend of queen Melisend, arrived on his fourth visit to the Holy Land. With the help of his forces, Baldwin carried out an attack on Shaizar. The castle that summer (1157) had been almost totally destroyed by an earthquake, in which the Munqidhite family had all perished. It seemed impossible that the ruined fortress could resist, but Reginald claimed that if it was, as Baldwin intended, handed over to Thierry, the latter must do homage for it to Antioch, that is to himself. Thierry, not surprisingly given their respective status, indignantly refused, and the dispute grew so tense that Baldwin had to abandon the siege, and with it the chance of gaining the powerful count of Flanders, of proved devotion to the cause of Outremer, as a permanent settler at a strategic point of the northern defences. That Reginald had recently, after the most brutal handling, driven the patriarch of Antioch, Aimery of Limoges, into flight to Jerusalem, did little to reassure the king about Antiochene affairs. He now sought to move in advance of Manuel and sent to Constantinople asking for a bride for himself. Manuel sent him his niece, Theodora, a beautiful girl of thirteen, to whom Baldwin quickly lost his heart. This, while improving relations with the Kingdom, boded little good for Reginald.

79 The patriarch of Antioch, Aimery of Limoges, exposed on the tower of the citadel by Reginald of Châtillon. According to William of Tyre, Reginald forced 'the venerable man to sit in the blazing sun, his head smeared with honey to attract the flies'.

In the following autumn Manuel arrived in Cilicia with a large army. Toros fled to a secret refuge in the mountains; Reginald hastened to Manuel's camp and grovelled before him. Pardon was given on condition that the citadel of Antioch was entrusted to a Byzantine garrison, a Greek patriarch substituted for the Latin, and an Antiochene contingent provided for the Byzantine army. Baldwin arrived in the course of these discussions, and proceeded to charm Manuel. The terms seem to have been modified, at least no Greek patriarch was appointed and Aimery, no doubt as an effective check on Reginald, was re-established in his see. Baldwin, with much good sense, interceded also for Toros, arguing that he was a Christian who had battled hard against the infidel; he too was allowed to come to the camp and make submission to the emperor.

Manuel made an elaborate state entry into Antioch, his horse led by the humbled Reginald. But instead of a campaign, Manuel now entered into a truce with Nur-ad-Din in return for his help against the Selchukids of Roum. Nothing could have more clearly indicated the peripheral place of the crusading states in the emperor's schemes. It also demonstrated to the Franks that if active help was little likely, Byzantine prestige could still protect them. Baldwin was shrewd enough to grasp the fact, and carefully guarded his relationships with Constantinople. Fortunately, in November 1160, Reginald was ambushed while raiding some herds on their autumn migration, and passed into sixteen years' captivity, from which no one except the faithful Toros was anxious to see him released. After various intrigues, the young Bohemond III took over power, and Manuel, recently a widower, married his sister, Maria, despite previous negotiations for the hand of Melisend, sister of the young Raymond III of Tripoli who vented his sense of injury by raiding Cyprus without bringing down on himself any immediate retribution.

The capture of Ascalon was counterbalanced by the entry, in April 1154, of Nur-ad-Din into Damascus. Unur, lord of Damascus in everything but title, who had governed so adroitly, balancing Franks against Moslem emirs, had died in 1149, and Mujir ad-Din, in whose name he had ruled, was left to his own ineffectual devices. On this final occasion his appeal to the Franks, whose support had incidentally roused Islamic feeling against him, was sent too late. The union of Aleppo, Homs and Damascus under one hand at last gave a united frontier against the crusading invaders. With Nur-ad-Din, Baldwin obtained a two years' truce, which he then shamelessly broke. Plunder had become an economic necessity to both sides, and was the cause of many of these fluctuating and apparently feckless happenings. In the spring of 1157, the nomads in the security of the truce were bringing their flocks into the well-watered

80 The marshy country of Lake Huleh, north of the Sea of Galilee. The area was much used as grazing ground by the Bedouin, whose flocks were frequently raided by the crusaders. It is now largely drained.

plain north of Lake Huleh, when Baldwin suddenly fell on them, driving off their beasts. It was useful replenishment for the Kingdom, but it was a final breach with Nur-ad-Din, who retaliated by attacking Banyas, the fortified town controlling the route between the Kingdom and Damascus, and protecting the lands round Galilee. If Ascalon was the gateway to Egypt, Banyas was that to Damascus. It was strongly fortified, and on a hilltop above it, an hour's march to the east, was the castle of Subeibe, at that time a typical crusading keep in a rectangular enclosure. The sieges of Banyas are complicated by the uncertainty as to whether the citadel was part of the town defences or this somewhat distant castle: almost certainly the former, and Subeibe, where the main and impressive work is Arab, probably had at this time little importance. Never as yet excavated, it provides a classic example of the problems of crusading archaeology. In 1157, Nur-ad-Din's forces stormed the lower town of Banyas with ease, but the town citadel held out till relieving forces arrived, and it was not till seven years later that Nur-ad-Din secured this key position.

In 1163, Baldwin III had died unexpectedly at Beirut, aged only thirty-two. He was a vigorous and healthy man, but he had been taken ill at Antioch, then journeyed south to Beirut, and his end was more likely due to faulty diagnosis than to the poison that was generally suspected. Two years earlier, in 1161, the queen mother had died. Wasted in body, she had had a lingering illness, and was cared for by her two sisters, Hodierna and Yvette, and her sister-in-law, Sibylla of Flanders. The king, despite their differences, was for long inconsolable. 'A woman of unusual wisdom and discretion', was William of Tyre's final judgment on her.

Upon Baldwin's death and the succession of his brother Amalric, Egypt, to which the capture of Ascalon had opened the way, became the dominant concern of the Kingdom. Amalric had previously been count of Jaffa and Ascalon, with his interests particularly directed to the south, but even earlier Baldwin had taken preparatory steps, by attempting to prohibit the export of wood, iron and other military necessities to Alexandria, and in 1161 obtaining a payment for his non-intervention in the internal disputes of Cairo. Now events seemed set for further schemes. Amalric was a tall, powerful man, of rather ungainly build, stammering at times, a loud and hearty laugher: behind this misleading exterior he was a shrewd schemer and a skilful manipulator of legal niceties. His hereditary claim was unimpeachable, but there had been some bargaining at his accession, possibly to safeguard the vague baronial right of election, and he had been forced to separate himself from his wife, Agnes of Courtenay, on the grounds that the lady had been pre-contracted to Hugh of Ibelin, as well as being the new king's third cousin, well within the prohibited degrees. More probably Agnes herself was a cause of opposition. The daughter of Joscelin II of Edessa, widow of Reginald of Marash, who was killed along with Raymond of Antioch in 1149, she had none of the sterling qualities of her mother, Beatrix, but had rather the treacherous, dissipated nature of her father. Along with her brother, Joscelin III, whose ransom from a long captivity she eventually achieved, she was the centre of a group of Edessan refugees, impoverished and anxious for new lands and posts, and therefore suspect to the baronage of the Kingdom. It was a clique that, even after the annulment, retained some influence over Amalric, and was to play a fatal part in the last years of the Kingdom.

Amalric soon showed his quality. He had retained Jaffa and Ascalon in his own hands, continuing his brother's policy of extending the royal domain; and within a few months of his accession an opportunity occurred of showing his firmness. A vassal of Gerard of Sidon appealed to the king against his lord, who had dispossessed him of his fief. In face of Gerard's opposition, Amalric had the case brought before the High Court, and promulgated an assize, the *Assize sur la ligesse*, by which it was laid down that all holders of fiefs, from whomsoever they held, owed allegiance to the crown, and that, if any case between a vassal and his lord could not be settled by a court of his co-vassals, the case could be brought to the High Court and tried there by judges appointed by the king. In the sparse and constantly moving life of the Kingdom, the barons could not rely on regular courts of complaisant vassals, and this assize under Amalric strengthened the centralized power of the crown, as was almost certainly

Amalric's intention. The growing power of the greater barons and the consolidation of their lands by marriage threatened both the political and financial standing of the crown. The lands of the Church remained inviolable, increasing rather than diminishing as pious bequests were made to them. More and more land was passing under the control of the military orders. It is unfortunately not possible to make any real assessment of the royal revenue, but it was very limited, and bound in by exemptions of all kinds. The Italian cities had a large share of commercial profit; even in Jerusalem the crown, in its desire to maintain a contented and increasing community in the Holy City, had granted the citizens freedom from customs dues. The new prosperity of the coastal plain was parcelled out among many landowners. The *Assize sur la ligesse* was a warning against too great landed independence. It could, however, if there were any weakness in the central power, be used the opposite way, and in later times it was to become the bulwark of the baronage against imperial claims.

In the north, affairs seemed reasonably settled. At Antioch, Bohemond III had, at eighteen, taken over the government and wisely exiled his troublesome mother, Constance, to Latakia, following the footsteps of her own equally wilful mother, Alice. Bohemond's sister Maria was the second wife of Manuel Comnenus, who approved his brother-in-law's rule. Antioch seemed, despite troubles in Armenia, well bulwarked by Byzantine support, and in 1163 and again in 1164, as the Fatimid caliphate of Cairo fell into more and more internal disputes, Amalric felt free to lead expeditions into the Nile valley. It was a glittering bait, likely to solve many financial problems. The riches of Cairo were proverbial, and when Latin envoys were introduced into the caliph's palace, they were amazed not only at the buildings and stuffs, but at the menageries of animals and birds. William of Tyre had received trustworthy accounts of it all from this embassy, and chronicles it in detail. 'The very aspect of the place gave indisputable proof of the opulence of the Monarch.' In Christian hands Alexandria and Cairo would have controlled the caravan routes from the south, and made the eastern Mediterranean seaboard a line of Christian ports. Political reasons were even more urgent, the need to prevent the union of Damascus and Cairo, and the consequent encirclement of the Kingdom. Nur-ad-Din understood the position as clearly as Amalric. On the latter's second expedition, the crusaders found their way blocked by an army from Damascus, that had thrown itself into Bilbais. Its general (Shirkuh) was a Kurd, part of the new blood that Nur-ad-Din had drawn into his dominions, and with him was his nephew Saladin. They were hard-pressed by Amalric when news of an urgent diversion compelled the crusading force to withdraw. Nur-ad-Din had struck at Antioch, and once again a rash pursuit by the Franks had led to disaster. Bohemond, Raymond of Tripoli, Constantine Coloman, the imperial governor in Cilicia, Joscelin III, titular count of Edessa, and a visiting crusader, Hugh of Lusignan, were captives, and Antioch defenceless. Nur-ad-Din, however, would not risk bringing in Byzantium against him by taking the city. He readily negotiated ransoms for Coloman and Bohemond as Byzantine vassals, and, while Amalric was in Antioch, suddenly turned on the Kingdom and occupied Banyas. Bohemond, released from bonds, hurried to Constantinople and at last a Greek patriarch was installed in Antioch. Amalric, particularly after a third expedition to Egypt had proved inconclusive though on the whole successful, was anxious to bring in Byzantine support, and Manuel sent him as his bride a grand-niece, Maria Comnena, a lady of some character and good sense. William of Tyre was then dispatched to Constantinople to arrange for a combined attack on Egypt.

This marriage, in 1167, marks the closest union of Byzantium and the Latin Kingdom. It was commemorated by a series of mosaics in the Church of the Nativity at Bethlehem, some of which still survive; an inscription stated that they were completed by the hand of Ephraim the monk, painter and mosaic-worker in the reign of Manuel and the days of king Amalric and Ralph, bishop of Bethlehem in the year 1169. Even the unscrupulous wanderings of Manuel's cousin, Andronicus Comnenus, who had seduced Philippa of Antioch, sister of Manuel's wife, and had then carried off the youthful queen dowager, Theodora, seeking protection both against Manuel and Amalric in Damascus, failed to disturb the new relationships. Amalric, however, did not wait for the Byzantine fleet. The barons of the Kingdom were determined to use a contingent of crusaders that had arrived under count William of Nevers and would not delay for Manuel's slow-moving preparations. They wished also all the wealth of Egypt for themselves. The master of the Hospital, Gilbert of Asseilly, in particular urged immediate action and carried the day. Bilbais was captured, but the troops from Nevers, their count having died, got out of hand and, with their inexperienced piety, massacred the inhabitants. It was a fatal blow to Frankish hopes of Egyptian support, and the end of the undertaking saw Shirkuh and a Damascene force in control of Cairo. Supported at last by a great Byzantine fleet, Amalric made one more attempt, and attacked Damietta, the fortress town that from now on was to be one of the great crusading objectives. But the allies worked ill together and the siege was abandoned. On Shirkuh's death in 1169, his nephew Saladin took over control, and still held it when in 1174 first Nur-ad-Din and then Amalric died. That autumn, amid the disputes between Nur-ad-Din's successors, Saladin entered Damascus, and the encirclement of the crusading Kingdom became a fact.

It had been a period of hope and endeavour. The third quarter of the twelfth century saw the crusading states more settled and prosperous than could have seemed possible in the dark days of the forties. In Egypt they had been the attackers; the alliance with Manuel had provided a constant check on the activities of Nur-ad-Din; the conquest of Ascalon had brought peace to the southern coastal plain. Building activities matched this new mood. In the Temple area a masons' yard of notable and very individual skill was carving capitals and friezes of deeply cut coiling acanthus leaves. So pleasing was the work that much of it was re-used by the Moslems after their capture of the city. The reading platform (*dikket*) of the al-Aqsa mosque is entirely composed of such pieces, and elsewhere they were used for prayer niches and for an outdoor pulpit. Within the Dome itself, the doorway to the cave below the rock, the most sacred spot of the whole site, still has sprays of acanthus with a central cone, a typical product of this workshop. Even some unfinished capitals, only partially blocked out, were re-used and completed with the bulbous decoration used by Moslem carvers. The Temple craftsmen must have been employed on them in the fatal year of 1187. Elsewhere, at the Templars' castle of Latrun, on the foothills of Judaea, whose ruined walls still testify to its strength, the same masons were at work, and six small capitals, linked in triplets, were found there, and were carried off by the Germans in 1917. They are now in the museum of Istanbul, as fresh as when they were made, with even the birds and animals in the coils, which elsewhere have been mutilated.

These capitals belong to the high Romanesque style of Italy and southern France, but they have their own character, unmistakable and not easily linked with Western examples. It is a very different matter with another great group of capitals, found in 1908 hidden away in a pit at Nazareth. They are not completely worked: the figure scenes are carved with great refinement, but the backgrounds had not been smoothed. Here, too, work must have been in progress when, in 1187, the Saracens overran the town and these masterpieces were hidden away to save them from the iconoclastic mutilations that would certainly have been their fate. Unweathered, they are, save for a few chips, in mint condition. The museum of the Greek patriarch in Jerusalem has two heads, life-size, that also come from Nazareth, and stylistically belong to the same workshop. More recent excavations in 1955 produced the torso of a standing figure. These must have been designed for a great doorway, which would in quality have ranked high with anything in France. The subjects of the

118

81 and 82 Re-used carving of the Templar workshop on an outdoor pulpit on the platform of the Dome of the Rock (right) and on the reading platform of the al-Aqsa mosque (below).

83 Triple capital found at the Templars' castle of Latrun, now in the Archaeological Museum at Istanbul. These splendid carvings, unsurpassed by any Romanesque foliage in the West, must have been carried out under a master mason of the highest skill.

capitals are the miracles and legends of the apostles Peter, Thomas, James, Matthew, and Bartholomew. Peter and James are Palestinian subjects, the other three are traditionally the missionaries of India and the East. The programme clearly was thought out with some real appreciation of this Christian crossroads. The feathered devils, sharply featured faces, and architectural canopies are found, unmistakably by the same hand if any reliance can be placed on stylistic affinities, in some carvings at Plaimpied, close to Bourges. It is hard to think that they are not by the same artist, and that he was one of those who took 'the way of the Sepulchre'.

Between Nazareth and Jerusalem, there was building also at Sebastia, and here too the church does not seem to have been completed. The arches rise on composite piers of splendid masonry joined without mortar, with shafts for rib-vaulting that may never have been added. The capitals of the piers are stiff leaf and the transition to the Gothic style is evident. Four capitals from here are in Istanbul, scenes of Herod's feast and Salome's dance, where the figures are somewhat heavy but the eyes still have their inlay giving a curiously vivid expression to the faces. These were examples that have survived. The fallen columns of the great cathedral at Tyre have recently been re-erected by the Lebanese government. Beirut has its fine Romanesque triple-apsed eastern end, Saffuriyah the remains of the church that celebrated the home of St Anne, Mount Tabor the ground plan of the great church of the Transfiguration. Elsewhere, 'The voracity of time', as Henry Maundrell was to write in his travels of 1697, 'assisted by the hands of the Turks, has left nothing but a few foundations remaining.'

In painting and mosaic there is even less preserved. Wall-painting has survived only in fragmentary and shadowy patches: the crude votive paintings on the columns at Bethlehem, a head and a piece of drapery from the chapel at the Damascus Gate, the faint outlines at Abu Gosh. A fine section of a fresco, showing the figure of Simeon from the scene of the Presentation, was found recently in restorations on the outer wall of the chapel at Krak des Chevaliers and is now in the museum at Tortosa. It seems to be, as would be expected from its position, twelfth-century work by an artist of some ability. In the chapel on the ground level of the medieval campanile at Bethlehem there is a Deesis painted above the altar, and figures of saints on the walls and vault. Heavily restored in 1950, it is now difficult to judge their quality, but fortunately pre-restoration photographs exist. Iconographically, the figures follow Byzantine formulas and they have a competence that is very different from the column figures. They may well be associated with the large-scale decorative work carried out in 1169, commemorated by the inscription of

84 Capital from the church of
the Annunciation, Nazareth:
miracles of St Bartholomew.
The Nazareth capitals, found in
a pit in 1908, are wonderfully
preserved examples of the work
of a Western master whose
highly individual style can be
recognized in some carvings at
Plaimpied, south of Bourges.

85 Capital from the abbey of
Plaimpied (Cher), France: the
Temptation.

Manuel and Amalric. This inscription, originally in Latin and Greek, is in the apse and applies with certainty only to the scenes of the lives of Christ and the Virgin, of which the Incredulity and the Entry into Jerusalem survive in reasonable completeness. Earlier accounts show that before this date the church was decorated with mosaics, and the series of decorative panels on the north wall of the nave, showing by a series of altars, divided by foliage, symbols of the seven provincial councils, from Carthage (254) to Ancyra (314), inscribed in Greek, could well be Byzantine work of the eighth century, stylistically not far removed from the Umaiyad mosaics of Damascus and the Dome of the Rock. The absence of any human figures would make them tolerable to the Moslem conquerors. On the south wall there are similar but simpler designs, one of which has the inscription in Latin, that of the second Council of Nicaea (787) restoring the use of images, and therefore of a particularly Latin acceptability. Some twelfth-century modifications are evident here, and the busts of the ancestors of Christ on the south wall seem work of that period, as are also the angels between the windows of the nave. Six of these survive, full-length figures of considerable distinction, moving, with their hands open in adoration, towards the eastern end of the church and the place of the Nativity. Under one of them in Latin script is the name Basilius Pictor, the same that appears under the Deesis in the Melisend Psalter. It is tempting to think that the same man, now advanced in years, took part in this great co-operative work of Franco-Byzantine art, the brilliant affirmation of the new relationship between the two powers.

86 The prophet Elijah: painting on a column in the church of the Nativity, Bethlehem. The paintings on the columns of the church are varied in style and may well have been votive offerings from pilgrims. Elijah has the oval folds of drapery popular in Western art of the time.

87 Saone, of which there is little recorded history, remains one of the most spectacular of crusading buildings. The great rock-cut ditch, in which a stone pillar was left to support a drawbridge, is a remarkable feat of engineering but whether Byzantine or crusading work is not known.

tur quã uolũtatẽ inamicicia que
rere. Certe confident dicã. et multos hu
ius opis testes citabo me nihil dũ taxat
sciẽtẽ de hebrea ueritate mutasse.
Sicubi g̃ editio mea á ueterib' discrepa
nt. interroga quelibet hebreos. et liq
do p̃uidebis me. abemulis frustra lace
ran! q̃a malunt contẽpnere uidere p̃
clara. quã discere. puersissimi homi
nes. Hã cũ semp nouas expectant uo
luptates. et gule eorũ uicina maria
ñ sufficiant! cur insolo studio sc̃ptu
rarũ. ueteri sapore contenti sunt? Hec
hoc dico q̃ p̃cessores meos mordea. aut
quicq̃m dehis arbitror detrahendũ.
Quox̃ tñslationẽ. diligentissime eñ
data. olim mee lingue hominib'. de
derim! sed q̃d aluid sit inecc̃lia xp̃i cre
dentiũ psalmos legere! aluid uideis.
singula uerba caluniantib' responde
re. Q̃d opusculũ meũ. si ingrecũ ut pol
licens tñstuleris. ANTIPHONICON. TOBA
TA. SYPOYSIN . et impericie mee doc
tissimos q̃sq̃ uiros. testes facere uoluer!
dicã tibi. illud oratiõnũ. In silua ne
ligna feras! nisi quod hoc habebo solã.
si in labore cõmuni intelligã. et mihi et
laudẽ. et uitupatiõnẽ tecũ esse cõmune.
Y ale in domino ih̃u! cupio te memi
nisse mei.

EXPLICIT·P̃FACIO·SCĪ

IEROHIMI·PBRI·

The great defeat 4

Of all his acts of patronage the most important for Amalric's future fame was his dealings with William of Tyre. It was at the king's command that the latter undertook both his history of 'deeds done beyond the sea' and also a history of the Arabs from 'the time of the false prophet Mohammed' down to the year 1184. For it Amalric provided him with various Arabic texts, which it is tempting to think came from the confiscated library of Usamah. Whether or not William's work had this ill-omened source, fate was against it and the *Gesta orientalium principum* has not survived, though a copy of it was in England, in the library of St Albans, in the thirteenth century, and known to Matthew Paris, as was also the surviving work, the History of the Kingdom, of which the manuscript now in the British Museum may well be the actual St Alban's copy, brought by Peter des Roches, bishop of Winchester, from the Holy Land in 1231.

William had many qualifications for his task. He was a trained Latinist, familiar with many of the classical authors; he also knew Greek and some Hebrew. In common with many of the *poulains* he spoke and read Arabic fluently; for the later part of the history he had, as archbishop of Tyre and chancellor of the Kingdom, a considerable part in the course of events, and contacts with older men of longer memories than his own. Such advantages, however, could not by themselves have produced this remarkable work that has many claims to be the most impressive piece of Latin twelfth-century historiography. Begun as an account of the reign of Amalric, and read in sections to the king himself, William broadened the scheme, opening his first book with an account of the emperor Heraclius and the restoration of the True Cross, of Charlemagne's interventions in the East and of al-Hakim's destruction of the Holy Places. He thus builds up the setting for the great epic of the crusades. He closes it in deep

125

88 Twelfth-century instruments (chime bells, recorder, shawm, citole, viol and harp).

foreboding in 1184, 'for now every source of glorious renown is taken from us, and the only subjects that present themselves are the disasters of a sorrowing country and its manifold misfortunes'. He was being persuaded to continue, and had decided to do so, 'for examples of misfortunes patiently endured may render later generations more cautious'; but kindly death intervened and spared him the task of chronicling the loss of Jerusalem.

Underlying William's philosophy of history is the conventional Augustinian view of failure as due to sin and success as due to divine grace. But his own shrewdness often transcends this basic concept. He had great interest in human nature, and his characters are living people, whose motives he criticizes and whose acts he analyzes. He was well aware of the problems that confronted them, and he has a surprising grasp of the complex construction of the Kingdom, the Church, the baronage, the merchants, and the native communities. He is interested in all that touches the 'sweetness of his native land', its geography, archaeology and agriculture, and he has a wide tolerance that can see good in men of all races and creeds. Only in Church affairs does a certain bitterness and also prolixity intrude. Here he is the defender of ecclesiastical authority, and stands too near the issues. Otherwise he holds wonderfully consistently to the words he quotes from Cicero's *De Amicitia*: 'Truth is troublesome, since verily from it springs hatred which is poisonous to friendship; but compliance is even more disastrous, for, by dealing leniently with a friend, it permits him to rush headlong to ruin.'

He was born in Jerusalem and, according to an autobiographical passage preserved in only one manuscript, went to Paris about 1145 when he was fifteen years old. For twenty years he studied there and in Bologna, returning to Outremer in 1165. He was therefore not an eyewitness of much that he recounts, but he had the training to assess the versions of those 'he spoke with'. In 1167 he was appointed archdeacon of Tyre. It was the year in which Amalric had selected him to write the history of his reign, and three years later, William, with some reluctance, was appointed tutor to Amalric's son, Baldwin, for whom he soon had considerable affection. In 1174, with his pupil now on the throne, William was given the office of chancellor, and within a few months was elected to the archbishopric of Tyre. In 1168, while still archdeacon, he was sent as an envoy to Constantinople, and in the following year he was in Rome at the Curia, answering charges arising from 'the urgent enmity of my archbishop, Frederick', of whom William writes that he 'was a Lotharingian, noble according to the flesh. He was an extremely tall man. He possessed little education but was inordinately devoted to the art of war.' In 1179 William was once more in Rome at the third Lateran Council, and in the following year he was being strongly supported as a candidate for the vacant patriarchate. Owing, however, to the intrigues of the Edessa party, Heraclius, a favourite of the disreputable Agnes of Courtenay, was elected. William chronicles this without comment, though it must have been a sore disappointment and a sore blow too to the welfare of the Kingdom. Late in 1184 or early in 1185 he died, possibly in Rome, poisoned, some thought, by an emissary of Heraclius. The readiness with which poison was assumed, though no case of it is proven, is a sad indication of the violence of rancour and jealousy in Outremer; almost certainly poison is here an unnecessary piece of melodrama clouding the end of a career that stands for nobler things. Important as had been his active part in the affairs of the Kingdom, it is as a leading intellectual figure that he has his first importance. His skill in language and his classical learning may have been the products of his European studies, but his training is devoted to the understanding of his homeland: 'An insistent love of my country urges me on . . . that those things which have been accomplished by her be not buried in silence.' But he also has a clear view of the unique position of the Kingdom for the exchange of views between East and West. William tells us how Amalric loved to converse with men from distant lands. It was a social milieu that at its best was alert, inquiring and cosmopolitan. William may mourn, as he begins the final and unfinished book of his History, that there is no longer 'in the acts of our princes anything which seems to a wise man worthy of being committed to the treasure house of memory', but he himself is ample evidence of the crusading achievement.

William had had predecessors, of some of whom he made considerable use. The capture of Jerusalem thrilled the West into an unprecedented activity of narration. The demand for news of the crusading achievement was widespread, and many felt the urge to record it. Even a knight, perhaps a younger son originally trained for the Church, could vividly record his experiences as in the anonymous *Gesta Francorum*. Raymond of Aguilers, the chaplain of Raymond of Toulouse, wrote of the siege of Antioch and the capture of Jerusalem, with a Provençal bias and a liking for miracles. His account, dedicated to the bishop of Viviers, was written particularly to counteract the false stories brought back by deserters from the crusade, and, he tells us, he undertook it at the request of a knight, Pons of Balon, who was killed at the siege of Arqah by a stone from a *petraria*. Stephen of Blois, withdrawing from the camp at Antioch, and the rope-climbers, who let themselves down the walls when Kerbogha besieged the city, were the unwarlike and frightened (*imbelles et pavidi*) Raymond had in mind; with some sense of the dramatic he also used their cowardice

auanc· leue lerim tei ouz ʒ regate ve la pui
fance vou tor ton fauuierre te uient vefu
er vou lien vont tu es luee.

erutez
eft que
la faite
cure ve
ierim
fuer en
tre ij·
moitta
ignief·
vont vi
tuo li
profe

tef vuft el fautier· Li fonverhz ve luu font
ef fais moʒ· ve uerf folau cochait li eft la
mer· ʒ la tir ves phuuftues· ʒ oluuer fi a yr·

89 The crusaders arrive outside
Jerusalem and pitch their camp, while
the defenders gaze at them from the
towers of the city: a thirteenth-
century version of the scene.

90 The crusaders attack
Constantinople from the harbour on
9 April 1204; after three days of
assault they entered the city. This
continuation of William of Tyre's
History mistakenly dates the event in
1201.

and lack of faith to throw into greater relief the divine mercy of the discovery of the Holy Lance. Raymond himself and also Pons of Balon were
present when, after much digging, the lance thought to be that which had
pierced Christ's side, was found in the church of St Peter at Antioch. This
episode, along with the ordeal of fire that was later undergone by Peter
Bartholomew whose visions led to the discovery, is the central episode of
Raymond's chronicle. His handling of it is the most complete example of
crusading credulity in the potency of relics. Raymond had one difficulty,
he knew that the legate, Adhémar of Le Puy, his own bishop and a 'man
dear to everyone, whose death soon showed how useful he had been to
God, the army and the princes', had doubts about the lance. A few days
after his death, Adhémar had conveniently appeared in a vision to
Bartholomew, explaining that he was suffering special rigours in purgatory on account of his scepticism. Raymond has the fierceness as well as
simplicity of the fanatic. Fulcher or the anonymous author of the *Gesta
Francorum* can boast that 'at the taking of Jerusalem there was no spot
where the Saracens escaped the sword'. It is only Raymond who depicts
for us with pious glee the streets filled with heads, arms and feet. Few

128

Ensi fu prise la noble cite de costantinople
a·vij·iorz dauril par un mardi· en lan de
lincarnacion de nre seignor· m·cc·j·

1201.

E uos di
rai q li
francois
& li uene
cien fi
rent dis
q il as
saillisset
la cite· il
furent· i·
coman

derent· que des mostier ne prendroient
nule riens· & les auoirs que len prendroit
en la cite· len le metroit touz ensemble
& partiroit adroit· q li uenecien deuoiet
auoir la moitie par tout en quel terre
q ce fust· Apres come il orent establi ce
fait· si firet escomenier a·iij·euesques
qui la estoient· li euesques de soissons
& li euesque de troies· & un euesq dalema
igne· E il escomenierent toz ceauz qui tres
destorneroient· & qui naporteroient ce quil
trouueroient la ou len establiroit por par
tir· Apres ce si escomenia len· toz ceauz q
en mostier prendroient nule chose· ne

129

documents are more vivid than his narration, but it is hard to like him. Fulcher of Chartres has already been considered. William depended much on his narrative, and the lack of it is at once apparent when he comes to the reign of Fulk. Ekkehard, abbot of Aura, came to Constantinople with the German contingent in 1101, and fortunately for himself went by sea from Constantinople to Jaffa, arriving there at the time of the battle of Ramla; he caught the plague at Jaffa (he says that 300 people a day were dying in Jerusalem). Despite this he took a favourable view of the new settlement: 'the holy places are purified from the filth of the pagans, the destroyed churches are restored, bishoprics and monasteries are established in their former sites, cities and castles are fortified, ports and markets, formerly desolate, rejoice in populous gatherings; to the farmers, wine growers and shepherds their duties are conceded, and what excels all temporal benefits, the heavenly fire on the Resurrection of Christ provides an annual blessing on human needs.' Raoul of Caen, who came to Antioch after Bohemond's Epirote campaign of 1107, wrote his *Gesta Tancredi* in a high-flown, learned style, occasionally breaking into verse. It is tedious reading on the whole, but has some unique information and occasional reflections that reveal the reactions of an educated man to these new circumstances.

Very different is the account *De Bello Antiocheno* of Walter the Chancellor, who held that office in Antioch around 1113 to 1119 under Roger, and was present at the fatal Field of Blood when the latter was killed. Walter observed military events with a practised eye, and we owe to him not only the sole account of Antiochene affairs during these critical years, but many details that have wider significance for crusading history.

These were eyewitness accounts, eagerly seized on and written up in the West, either in sections of chronicles or in histories of Jerusalem such as those of Robert the Monk, possibly the deposed abbot of St Remigius at Rheims, with time on his hands; Baldric, archbishop of Dol, who improved the Latin of the *Gesta Francorum* for a friend who had made the journey to Jerusalem; and Guibert, abbot of Nogent, a pupil of St Anselm and a prolific writer, whose title *Gesta Dei per Francos* was to have considerable success.

Of all these narratives that of Albert of Aix (almost certainly Aix-la-Chapelle) was the most widely read. He aimed to tell 'how they left their fatherland, their relatives, their towns, their castles, their fields and all the pleasures of life, how they made the journey to Jerusalem and triumphed so many times over Turks and Saracens, how they opened the way to the Holy Sepulchre, and how they freed all pilgrims thither from any dues or tax'. It was a story that came home to many, and the crusades opened a new era in Western desire for communication. Albert, however, was weak in critical sense and his work includes much that is legendary stuff – hence its great popularity – but it also embodies passages based on first-hand information from returning crusaders. It was much used by William of Tyre, who, in his attempts to reduce its information to consecutive plausibility, was tackling what has remained one of the great problems of crusading historiography.

Soon verse took over from prose. In the genesis of the crusade the *chansons de geste*, passing from verbal tradition to written word in the second half of the eleventh century, were a formative influence on opinion. Warriors were already beginning to think of their fame in terms of the minstrels' praise. Lambert of Ardres, writing at the beginning of the thirteenth century, relates a story of Arnoul II of Ardres told by his grandson: at the siege of Antioch, a singer refused to include Arnoul's deeds in his *chanson*, because the latter had denied him a pair of scarlet slippers. Some such singer, whom his later compiler names as Richard the Pilgrim, composed a *Song of Antioch*, dealing with events in which he had

91 The attack on Antioch, June 1098. This vivid illustration is an example of work of the Acre school shortly before the loss of the city in 1291.

participated. *The Chanson of Jerusalem*, written after 1130, contributes little to our knowledge of the conquest, but much to our knowledge of life in the Kingdom: the growing admiration for Moslem civilization, the cult of St George of Lydda, the importance of the part played by women. In the *Chansons des Chétifs* romance has the upper hand. There is little that has historical value, and several of its heroes may well be entirely fictional. It is an adventure story of Christian prisoners in Moslem hands, with escapes, fights with wild beasts and dragon-like serpents. At one point the author (his work, as we have it, has had much Western alteration) mourns for the death of Raymond of Antioch, and states that Raymond had rewarded him for his *chansons* by giving him a canonry at St Peter's, the cathedral of Antioch. This, then, is a cleric writing epic verse. Philip of Novara tells us how, as a page at the siege of Damietta, he used to read verses to Ralph of Tiberias. Such vivid songs were a real part of the life of Outremer. What tunes they were sung to, and how Western and Eastern music met in Jerusalem, is a subject as yet hardly explored, perhaps unexplorable on existing material. That choral music of another kind was practised is shown by the beautiful notation of the sequences in the Angelica Sacramentary, which was presumably in use in the Church of the Holy Sepulchre. That the manuscript retained its musical interest for some time is suggested by the fact that some 150 years later seven pages of the *Dies Irae* with neumes were added to it, but there is no indication where, when the great thirteenth-century hymn had come into common use, the manuscript had been taken.

BYZANTIUM WEAKENED

While disputes over the inheritance of Nur-ad-Din gave the Franks a temporary breathing-space, his death, in 1174, had wide repercussions elsewhere. In Asia Minor, Nur-ad-Din had supported the Danishmendids against Kilij Arslan II of Iconium, always seeking a balance of power among his Selchukid neighbours. By the end of 1174 Kilij Arslan II had retaken Caesarea from the Danishmendids, and ousted his own brother, Shahinshah, from Ankara, which he held from the emperor. Twelve years earlier, in 1162, he had been received in Constantinople as an honoured but vassal guest; now he seized the opportunity to regain much that he had then lost. On 7 September 1176 Manuel, with his army at full strength, met the forces of Kilij Arslan on the hillside by the fort of Myriokephalon and was completely routed. The great Byzantine army was destroyed, and never again was to be so fully organized. Manuel himself recognized it as a second Manzikert. 'From that day', wrote William of Tyre, who visited Constantinople shortly afterwards and knew and admired the emperor, 'he is said to have borne, ever deeply impressed upon his heart, the memory of that fatal disaster.' It was a lasting blow to the prestige of Byzantium, and no longer could its protecting shadow fall on northern Syria. Manuel turned to a revival of earlier Italian schemes, but here he had added to his enemies by a breach with Venice. There had been growing friction between Byzantium and the Venetians, and Manuel, now financially hard-pressed, needed the revenue which, through their exemptions, passed into the hands of these arrogant foreigners. In 1171 all the Venetians in the empire were arrested and their goods confiscated: in Constantinople alone more than 10,000 were said to have been imprisoned. It was a shock to Venetian commerce that was long remembered and was to be terribly avenged. There were many dangers threatening when Manuel died in 1180, leaving the empire to his young son, Alexius, under the regency of his mother, Maria of Antioch, whose own mother and grandmother had been poor examples of women regnant.

THE BATTLE OF HATTIN

Baldwin IV, the beloved pupil of William of Tyre, was a leper. The historian tells us how, when he watched some of the boys of the court testing their endurance by sticking nails in their flesh, he saw that the prince had no reaction. This led to the discovery of the fatal disease, and when Amalric died in July 1174, it was this stricken boy who succeeded to the throne, to face Saladin, a greater opponent than either Zengi or Nur-ad-Din. In the Kingdom there was little time to think of Byzantine affairs, however much repercussions from them might increase its perils. By 1174, Saladin had joined Egypt and Damascus under his own rule and was preparing to absorb the Frankish settlement. It was no longer to be a war of raids and retreat, but one of final conquest; and the leader had appeared who could provide the personal ascendancy to unite, if only for brief periods, the discordant Arab aims. About Saladin we are well informed. Imad-ad-Din of Isfahan has left in profuse and rhetorical language an account of his life, and as he was Saladin's personal secretary from 1175 he was well qualified to know both the man and his actions. Baha-ad-Din, his other biographer, only met Saladin in 1184, but from 1188, when he became Judge of the Army, he was on terms of close personal friendship with him. These two men wrote as admirers and colleagues, but their intimacy provides convincing details of a man who, though he had many defects, and seemed at moments to fall below his own standards, had unquestioned greatness. His power to dominate his times was based on deep, heart-searching religious faith, and if at times he was austere and

133

harsh, he was always unsparing of himself and his often sickly and harassed bodily frame. His compassion to the people of Jerusalem moved even his enemies and was a reproach to their own doings. To later minstrels he became 'the best prince that ever was in pagandom'. Among the Arab authors, Ibn al-Athir gives a more critical account. His *History of the Atabegs* was written in 1210–11 for a young prince of Mosul, 'to set out the merits of his ancestors', much as William of Tyre wrote for Amalric's son. The work has as its two heroes Zengi and Nur-ad-Din, and though, born in 1160, Ibn al-Athir had no personal knowledge of the earlier events, he, again like William, had many contacts with those who had participated in them. He writes with some tolerance and can recognize the bravery and devotion of the Franks. It is only against the trickery and broken faith of Joscelin II of Edessa that, with good reason, he writes bitterly. Amid the intrigues of the time he finds a sure path, and can write a vivid description of the clash and noise of battle. When, however, he comes to Saladin, the supplanter of the Atabegs, he twists the words of Imad-ad-Din, on whom he often relies, to less favourable interpretations. But Saladin can abide his questioning.

Faced with this adversary, it was ill luck for the Franks that Reginald of Châtillon was once more with them. He had been released in 1176, when the Franks were in alliance against Saladin with Gumushtigin of Aleppo; no longer having any claims to Antioch, where Bohemond III now ruled, he soon married Stephanie, the heiress of the lordship of Kerak. In 1182 he had ships carried overland from this new possession to the Red Sea and raided the coasts of the Hejaz. It seemed, for a moment, as if even the sacred city of Medina might be threatened. It was a stirring piece of daring, but nothing could be better calculated to fan the zeal of the Jihad. The raiders were captured; some were sent to be sacrificially slaughtered at Medina, others brought bound to execution at Cairo. Saladin ordered that none should survive, that 'no eye should remain capable of seeing nor any man of knowing and indicating the Red Sea route'. Then, in 1184, he appeared before Kerak to exact vengeance. It was a dramatic moment, for the castle was full of guests come to celebrate the marriage of Isabella, daughter of Amalric and Maria Comnena, to Humphrey of Toron, Stephanie's son by her first marriage. The sultan, with one of those gestures that won the reluctant admiration of the West, ordered his mangonels not to fire against the nuptial tower. However, the castle held out, and when there was news of a relieving force, Saladin withdrew.

The leper king, who had shown courage and spirit in his adversities, was nearing his end. Seeking to ensure the succession, he had married his

92 The citadel of Aleppo, the city the crusaders never captured. The entry bridge across the paved slopes of the mound is Aiyubid work of the late twelfth century, restored after the Mongol sack of the city in 1260.

sister Sibylla, Amalric's daughter by Agnes of Courtenay, to an Italian nobleman, William of Montferrat, but William had forthwith died, and his posthumous infant son became heir as the fifth Baldwin. The king designated as regent his cousin, the experienced Raymond of Tripoli, and it was planned that Baldwin of Ibelin should marry Sibylla. He was at the time a prisoner in Moslem hands; when he was released, however, Sibylla stated she could not marry him till the ransom was fully paid. Manuel Comnenus, very shortly before his death, generously paid the sum for Baldwin, but meanwhile Sibylla's wandering fancy had fixed on a handsome newcomer, Guy of Lusignan, whose brother Aimery was now constable and, it was said, the lover of Agnes of Courtenay. In 1180, backed by her mother and her uncle, Joscelin of Edessa, Sibylla forced her brother to consent to her marriage to the young Lusignan. At last, with his disease in an advanced and paralyzing state, the leper king died in March 1185. In August of the following year, the child, Baldwin V, followed his uncle. It was at Acre that he died, and Raymond of Tripoli misguidedly allowed Joscelin of Courtenay to take the body to Jerusalem for burial.

There he was joined by the patriarch Heraclius, Reginald of Châtillon, and the newly elected master of the Templars, Gerard of Ridefort, who nourished an old grudge against Raymond, claiming that the latter had promised him a rich marriage and then disposed elsewhere of the heiress. Gerard had turned to celibacy and the order of the Temple, becoming seneschal and then master. (A strange relic of his tenure of the office exists in a letter written by him about one Robert of Sourdeval, an Antiochene family, who was to be brought a prisoner to Acre. This was found in one of the joints of a pillar in the al-Aqsa mosque and is still preserved in the museum of the Haram.) Gerard's influence was now predominant, and is illustrated by the arrangements for the child king's funeral. A drawing preserves for us the elaborate design of the tomb of Baldwin V as it existed until the disastrous fire of 1808 in the Church of the Holy Sepulchre; in the Greek restorations, the tombs of the Latin kings were wantonly destroyed. It was an elaborate work with linked columns and the deep undercutting of the Temple masons. A very similar piece of work can still be seen converted into a *mihrab* in the cave under the Temple rock. The Templars were clearly in charge of the arrangements, and under their influence a coronation soon followed the funeral.

Raymond and the Ibelins were gathered at Nablus, where there was talk of setting up Isabella, the child of the Comnenian marriage, as queen; Sibylla after all came of a divorced and dissolute mother. But Isabella's husband, the gentle, handsome Humphrey of Toron to whom she was devoted, would have none of it and stole away to make his peace with Guy and Sibylla in Jerusalem. There Sibylla was crowned by the patriarch Heraclius, and then she herself crowned Guy as her consort. Raymond retired to his county of Tripoli: the rejected Baldwin of Ibelin refused to stay in the Kingdom and went north to Antioch.

Despite a truce with Saladin, Reginald of Châtillon, operating from his castle at Kerak, chose this moment of civil tension to plunder a large Moslem caravan, in which Saladin's sister happened to be travelling. Bohemond of Antioch and Raymond of Tripoli both sought to secure their own lands by new treaties with Saladin; but the end was at hand. The folly of Gerard of Ridefort, attacking in Galilee a Moslem reconnaissance under Raymond's safe-conduct, broke all hope of further treaties. Raymond, in this last emergency, came to join Guy at Saffuriyah; though Guy's march there had been originally directed against him. Saladin was besieging Tiberias and held the hills above it on the west side of the Sea of Galilee. Even though his own wife was besieged in Tiberias, Raymond urged that they should maintain a defensive position at Saffuriyah, where there was water and where they were in communication with Acre as a supply base. It was the traditional crusading strategy, to avoid exposing themselves to a march on which their forces could be surrounded and split into detachments. It was clear that a battle now must be a decisive one, and also that, if they held firm, Saladin's troops, having taken Tiberias, would gradually disperse to their various localities. Raymond's advice was accepted, but during the night king Guy, persuaded by the grand master of the Temple, changed the orders, and next morning, across the waterless uplands, the march proceeded. Ernoul, a squire with Balian of Ibelin, left an account of the fatal battle, when, on 4 July 1187, the crusading muster of about 30,000 was completely routed and destroyed at Hattin. The True Cross was captured; king Guy was a prisoner. Reginald of Châtillon was executed by Saladin's own hand, and all the Templars, except the grand master, and the Hospitallers, as men pledged to the Holy War, were handed over to the victorious troops to be slaughtered. Raymond of Tripoli, Balian of Ibelin and Reginald of Sidon broke their way through the Moslem encirclement and escaped.

93 The Battle of Hattin: Saladin and Guy of Lusignan struggle for the True Cross. The defeat of Hattin was an unforgettable disaster in Western Europe to which the chroniclers gave much space.

eumons li prin
ces danioche
⁊ Reymons li
cuns detriple
enterent el reg
ne agrant com
paignie de chis
li rovs en fu
mlr espoentes. car il auda qul
le nofissent uair ou chacier de la
terre poz retenir le reyaume aleur
eus carla maladie le roy se desce
utoit ⁊ apertoit la lepre ront aper

94 The marriage of Sibylla, daughter of Amalric, to William Longsword of
Montferrat. Within a year of the marriage the bridegroom was dead.

THE FAMILIES OF LUSIGNAN AND MONTFERRAT

The Lusignans had been a family of baronial freebooters, whose ruined castle still crowns a hilltop between Niort and Poitiers. Hugh VI of Lusignan had joined the crusading forces led by William IX of Aquitaine, and was killed in 1102 at the battle of Ramla. Hugh VIII of Lusignan was in the contingents of Louis VII, and returned to the Holy Land in 1164 when he was captured by Nur-ad-Din and led bound amidst the jeers of the crowd through the streets of Aleppo. He had left five sons in Poitou, of whom Geoffrey, the eldest, was involved in constant risings against the duke, Richard of England. Two of the other sons, Aimery and Guy, the youngest, found their way to Palestine. Geoffrey was to join them later in the camp at Acre, sent there as a penance for his misdoings. They were adventurers to whom Palestine offered opportunities, as the central power closed down upon their lawlessness in France.

A very different family was now to play a part on the same stage. William of Tyre, writing of the marriage of Sibylla and William Long-sword of Montferrat, states that 'his worldly position was exalted – few if any could claim to be his equals'. Through his mother, he was nephew to the emperor Conrad and first cousin to Frederick Barbarossa, and through his father first cousin to Louis VII of France. The Montferrat genealogy is a puzzling business, but William the Old, father of William Longsword, was married to Giulita, daughter of Leopold III of Austria and Agnes, the daughter of the emperor Henry IV and the widow of Frederick of Hohenstaufen: Giulita was therefore a half-sister of Conrad III and aunt of Barbarossa; Leopold IV, Henry of Austria, and the chronicler Otto of Freising were her brothers. William the Old's father, Rainier, had married Gisela, widow of Humbert II of Savoy, by whom she had a daughter, Adelaide, who married Louis VI of France and was

95 The emperor Frederick Barbarossa with his sons, Henry (king of Germany since 1169) and Frederick (duke of Swabia); painted about 1180.

mother of Louis VII. William the Old was therefore uncle of the king of France. It can be easily understood that to the crusading Kingdom, William Longsword seemed satisfactorily well connected, though the intricacies of twelfth-century marital schemes must often have been too elaborate to secure lasting political aims.

Nothing could be more characteristic of the times than the impact of this vigorous family, or more significant of background motives and circumstances. William the Old, in the hill-country south of the curve of the Po between the new town of Alessandria and Turin, had been forming Monferrato into a somewhat vaguely controlled district. He had joined with the forces of Amadeus of Savoy in the second crusade, though later transferring his contingent to Conrad's army and sailing with him from Constantinople to Acre. The accession of Barbarossa and his Italian campaigns gave the marquis of Montferrat new opportunities; but with the defeat of Frederick at Legnano in May 1176, the year of Myriokephalon, a bad year for emperors, the marquis had been forced to come to terms with the Lombard League and make peace with his neighbours. His sons began to look elsewhere for new openings. A few months after Legnano, William Longsword sailed for Syria, where within forty days of his arrival he was married to Sibylla. His death at Jaffa in June 1177 was inevitably attributed to poison, but was more likely due to a young man's heedlessness of new dietary and climatic conditions. His father, William the Old, came to Jerusalem for his grandson's coronation as Baldwin V; then almost immediately to assist at the child's funeral and, shortly after that, to become Saladin's prisoner at Hattin.

CONRAD OF MONTFERRAT

Conrad, the second son, had been forming new policies for his family in Italy. In the years preceding Legnano he had been attached to Frederick's delegate in central Italy, Christian, archbishop of Mainz, and seems to have held some office in southern Tuscany; but in 1179 the Montferrat family were directing their interests towards the Eastern rather than the Western emperor. While Barbarossa sought to restore his prestige by being crowned king of Burgundy, Manuel revived his earlier Italian plans, and offered a marriage alliance to the Montferrat family. The second and third Montferrat sons, Conrad and Boniface, were married; the fourth, Frederick (or Otto, the name is uncertain), was a cleric. The youngest son, Rainier, was only seventeen years old, but this seemed no impediment to his marriage with the thirty-year-old Maria, Manuel's daughter. Rainier reached Constantinople in the autumn of 1179 and the wedding was celebrated in February 1180. The young man was given the title of Caesar. William of Tyre who had officiated at the funeral of the eldest Montferrat was now on an embassy to Byzantium and attended the marriage of the youngest. Conrad was preparing to join his brother in Constantinople, when Manuel's death on 24 September 1180 changed the whole situation.

His heir, Alexius II, was a young boy under the charge of his mother, Maria of Antioch, Manuel's second wife, a foolish and frivolous woman who soon roused opposition against herself and her favourites. Maria Comnena and Rainier were involved in a revolt, but the decisive step was taken by Andronicus Comnenus, who, returning from the banishment to which his wild deeds had subjected him, seized power for himself, accompanying it by a terrible massacre of the Latin merchant community. Maria of Antioch, the young emperor, Maria Comnena and Rainier all fell victims to his purges. Another page of horror was added to the history of Constantinople, when, in 1185, Andronicus was overthrown, and the mob lingeringly tore him to pieces in the Hippodrome. The new emperor, Isaac Angelus, who had been driven into revolt to save himself from threatened arrest, soon also had to face a rising. One of his generals, Branas, led his forces on the capital. It was at this moment that Conrad of Montferrat reached Constantinople, probably on his way to Jerusalem. He was now a widower, and Isaac, wishing to enlist his help, offered him the hand of his sister, Theodora. This second marriage did not, however, serve to keep Conrad in Constantinople. His brother's fate may have served as a warning of Constantinopolitan uncertainties, or news from Palestine may have roused his crusading ardour. Having distinguished himself in crushing the revolt of Branas, he quietly boarded a Genoese ship and arrived off Acre on 13 July 1187, knowing nothing of the defeat at Hattin nine days previously. When a Saracen ship came from the harbour, Conrad claimed to be a Genoese merchant, still covered by a treaty with Saladin, and then with a favouring wind made for Tyre.

In its great Phoenician days, Tyre had been an island, but when in 332 BC Alexander laid siege to it, he broke its seven months' resistance by building a causeway giving approach from the land side. The crusaders had fortified this causeway with a ditch across it, three walls and twelve towers. Ibn Jubair, visiting it in 1184, some three years before Conrad reached it, wrote that 'he who seeks to conquer it will meet with no surrender or humility. The Franks prepared it as a refuge in case of unforeseen emergency, making it a strong point for their safety.' The harbour was surrounded by walls on three sides and two towers controlled the entrance, which could be closed by a chain stretched between them. The Venetians, whose fleet had aided its capture in 1124, held a third of the town, and regarded it as their main emporium on the Levantine coast.

96 View of Tyre in the mid-nineteenth century, seen from the mainland side of the causeway. Classical ruins lie in the foreground.

When they and the Franks had occupied it after a five months' siege, it had been crowded with Moslem refugees from the crusading conquest. Now fortunes were reversed and the limited island site was crowded with Christians, many of them women and non-combatants. Provisions were short; Reginald of Sidon was in command, and in treaty with Saladin for the surrender of the town. Acre, Sidon, Beirut and Gibelet had fallen. In Tripoli, count Raymond was sick and near his death. Balian of Ibelin, allowed by Saladin to go to Jerusalem to bring his wife, Maria Comnena, and his children to Tyre, had broken his pledge to spend but one night in the city, and was organizing the scanty garrison there. Reginald, knowing that Saladin's word could be trusted, had decided to avoid further bloodshed.

The locally bred, orientalized lord of Sidon, and the career-seeking, adventurous marquis represented opposed viewpoints and temperaments. Reginald shared to the full the confusing blood and marital relationships of the Kingdom. Great-grandson of Eustace Garnier, the first lord of Sidon and Caesarea, and Emma, niece of the patriarch Arnulf, his family had been closely involved in state affairs and intrigues. He himself had married Agnes of Courtenay, divorced wife of Amalric and mother of Baldwin IV and Sibylla. As with other of Agnes's numerous marriages, this was of brief duration, and ties of kinship were once more invoked to secure an annulment. Consanguinity was held to cover relationship to the seventh degree, and as husband and wife were one flesh this applied to both their families. It was easy to overlook such intricacies, and only to raise them when some better marital alliance presented itself. In the inbred crusading states hardly any marriage could have been strictly canonical. Reginald's second marriage, probably later than the disasters of 1187, was to Helvis, daughter of Balian of Ibelin and Maria Comnena. In politics he had sided with Raymond of Tripoli, but he had shown himself ready to compromise, and already, before his escape from Hattin, he had been suspected of overcaution in warfare. He spoke and read Arabic, and no surviving document indicates any patronage by him of the Christian Church. He understood the need to come to terms with his neighbours and for him the age of fanaticism was past. He was described as grimly ugly and very wise ('durement lait et moult sage').

The vigorous Western adventurer, whom the citizens of Tyre now hailed as their deliverer, had none of Reginald's Eastern expertise; but he had confidence, untarnished by defeat, and an unflagging determination to make a name for himself. 'He was distinguished', Baha-ad-Din wrote, 'by his good judgment, the energy and decision of his character, and his religious zeal.' This last quality may seem doubtful, but compared to the tolerance of the native baronage, Conrad stood for the traditional crusading outlook. To rally the forces of Outremer was a challenge and an opportunity that he was very ready to take. Reginald, aware of his commitment to Saladin and that it could not now be carried out, prudently withdrew by night. Sidon was in Moslem hands, and he made his way to Tripoli, and eventually to his castle of Beaufort, above the Litany valley, one of the few strong points that still held out. The standards sent by Saladin to Tyre, that Reginald was to have placed on the walls on the day following the marquis's unexpected arrival, were defiantly flung by Conrad into the city's ditch.

It was the first check in the tide of Moslem conquest. Saladin at once appeared before Tyre, bringing with him his captive, William the Old, Conrad's father, whom he offered to exchange for the town. Conrad's reply hit exactly the temper of the time and was much appreciated by the chroniclers. Not the least stone of Tyre would be given for his father, and if Saladin bound the old man to a stake before the walls, he, Conrad, would be the first to shoot at him, for the old man had lived too long, he did not wish him to suffer more, and he would glory in being the son of a martyr. Saladin did not take him at his word; he spared his captive, and withdrew from Tyre. Going south to Ascalon, he was more successful in his bargaining; Guy of Lusignan, made of less stern stuff, persuaded the city to surrender, in return for a pledge that he would be released at a later date. In September, Saladin turned on Jerusalem. His own deep religious feeling and the general morale of his troops required this final triumph. Jerusalem was short of defenders, but Balian of Ibelin put a bold face on the negotiations, and the liberality of Saladin's terms set a new example of clemency to the Western world. The ladies of Jerusalem published abroad 'the kindness and honour which Saladin had done to them'.

On Friday, 2 October 1187, the Holy City, the heart of the crusades, was lost. It was the day kept by Islam as the anniversary of the Prophet's ascent to heaven from the rock of the Temple. The huge cross that had been placed above the Dome was thrown down and throughout the city the Friday prayers were celebrated. The Armenian patriarch, looking back on the years of Frankish occupation, wrote an elegy on the loss of the city. 'Where are the fêtes and dances, the clapping of hands and applause, where are the young gamesters, the guests who drank in their reunions, the singers of praises to the lute, the singers of farces in the assemblies and the players on the lyre.' It had not been altogether the Holy City of pilgrim longing.

If, however, the patriarch could look back, a little regretfully, on the urbane gaiety of Jerusalem, it is also from Armenia that the most balanced,

97 Frankish prisoners, carrying their chains, are released from captivity: from a mid-thirteenth-century drawing by Matthew Paris.

tolerant view of the Latin settlement came. While the West could find the readiest explanation of the great débâcle in the sins of the orientalized *poulains*, St Nerses of Lampron, bishop of Tarsus from 1176 till his death in 1198, proclaimed his admiration for Latin piety. This remarkable and attractive man was the leader in a movement towards a new oecumenical approach to ecclesiastical divisions. In 1179, at a synod in Hromgla, the monastery that, since its cession by Beatrix of Edessa to the Armenian Catholics, had become the church centre of Cilician Armenia, Nerses urged Armenian reunion with the Greek church, despite the long tradition of hostility towards it. From the Latins he borrowed rituals for his own diocese, in this following the example of Leon II's Westernizing innovations in secular affairs. Leon, a less sincere, more politic man, aiming at kingly rule in Armenia, was alarmed at Nerses's enthusiasms, and warned him not to push matters too far. Already, based on the Armenian churches still surviving in the old homeland of north-east Asia Minor, there was a strong reaction against these changes and deputations of protest about them. The rugged nationalism of the Armenian Church was easily aroused. In a letter to Leon, written shortly before his death, Nerses compares the church life of Armenians and Latins, praising the devotion of the latter: 'Marash, this great and rich city, which under the Armenians

145

had neither an episcopal see nor a church, and which, fallen to the Franks, was provided with a large church.' He compares their church buildings, their rich vestments and seemly rites, with the rough and crude asceticism of old Armenia, though, he admits, services there had often to be held in secret by itinerant priests. 'When an Armenian enters a church with a Frank, the Frank bursts into tears as he prays, the Armenian stands beside him as a beast without reason.' He remarks also that 'if now I declare myself the partisan of one nation, how can I be in communion with others'. Little was to come of it. Nerses was enlightened beyond his fellows, and Latin-Armenian church unions were to be of a superficial, political nature, but, if it is a lone voice, here, from close observation, is testimony that there was still religious fervour in the battered and hard-pressed Kingdom.

Saladin's preoccupation with Jerusalem had given Conrad in Tyre a brief respite, an opportunity to strengthen the fortifications and to bring in supplies. There had been some Pisan ships in the harbour when he first arrived, and he now secured Genoese and Provençal help in return for confirmation of trading privileges in the town. Other refugees were arriving, though not all of military use. Among them were Balian's wife, Maria Comnena, and her children, for whom Saladin, despite Balian's breach of faith, had provided an escort from Jerusalem before he laid siege to the town. Maria's friendship with Conrad was to play an important part in later events.

The respite, however, was brief. On 1 November Saladin's forces arrived before Tyre, and now he brought up ships from Acre to blockade the town. Some ships from Tripoli, trying to slip past the blockade with supplies, were dispersed in a storm, but Conrad succeeded, by spreading a false report that the garrison was to attempt an escape by sea, in luring the enemy ships into the harbour, where they were captured and destroyed by the Italian vessels. Today the harbour of Tyre, with the ruins of its outer breakwater still visible, seems strangely cramped for such stirring happenings. It was a battle of small ships, such as those that still sail among the islands, but it was decisive. The blockade was broken, and on 31 December Saladin withdrew to winter quarters.

The two months' siege of Tyre was the most prolonged incident in Saladin's subjugation of the Kingdom, and its duration shows how rightly he appreciated the significance of this point of resistance. When summer campaigning began in 1188, his first aim was Tripoli, but the Sicilian fleet, under the great admiral Margaritone, was off the coast, a rare instance of Sicilian intervention, and one that could well cause Saladin to hesitate. His policy of offering favourable terms of surrender, and the confidence placed in his word, had been for him economy of time, even though it meant leaving forces that could fight another day. Now he had other regions to consider.

It was only in June 1183 that Saladin had brought Aleppo directly under his own control, only in 1186 that Mosul had finally recognized his overlordship. In the policies of his wide dominion, it was essential that some demonstration should be made against the northern Christian princes. The Orontes could not be indefinitely neglected for the Jordan; stronger barriers were needed to impede the flow of crusading reinforcements along the land route. Richard of Poitou, the heir to the English throne, had taken the cross at Tours as soon as the news of the loss of Jerusalem reached him, and on 27 March 1188, Frederick Barbarossa followed his example. German forces had always favoured the land route, and there was every reason for Saladin to make preparations.

The logistics of the northern campaign had their problems. Tyre and Tripoli still controlled a long stretch of the coastal route, and Raymond III of Tripoli, at his death towards the end of 1187, worn out by disasters, had left his county to his godson, Raymond of Antioch. Bohemond III of Antioch had in fact retained his eldest son, Raymond, for the defence of his principality and consigned Tripoli to his second son, another Bohemond. This union of the two northern states must have seemed a new menace to Saladin, more pressing even than Conrad's occupation of Tyre. Homs was to be the base for this northern campaign and obviously the capture of Krak des Chevaliers would have immensely facilitated movement along the lines of supply. In June Saladin encamped within sight of it, but he never attempted to storm it. Krak was then a smaller fortress than it was to become and so strikingly to remain. It was only the present inner circuit that Saladin viewed from the opposite hill. It is a tribute to its twelfth-century design that he decided to by-pass it as he struck through to the coastal road. This meant, however, that his supply route must run through the mountainous land between Homs and the Orontes valley, the territory of the Assassins.

Saladin had come to terms with them in 1176 after laying siege to their chief stronghold of Masyaf. As the dispossessor of the Shiite dynasty in Egypt, the sultan had been deeply suspect to the Ismailians. Twice at least, their emissaries had come near killing him, and this secret threat was ever present. The treaty that ended it now served another purpose. While Saladin struck at the coast route, capturing Tortosa and Latakia, supplies and reinforcements could follow inland paths to the great bridge crossing of the Orontes at Jisr-ash-Shogur. Once more Saladin was following his policy of leaving the greater castles untaken. The Templar fortress on the sea front of Tortosa had withstood attack, and the Hospitaller castle

of Marqab, overlooking the coast road between Tortosa and Latakia, he left unassailed. Speed was essential, for his campaigns had already taxed the patience of his troops and allies. It was also an indication of the castles' functions. They provided no strategic barrier, and a campaigning army could all but neglect them. Once the campaign was over, these garrisoned points became effective again, preventing any settled hostile occupation.

The news of the loss of Jerusalem had reached Rome as pope Urban III was dying. Henry of Albano, the first choice as his successor, declined the office in order to devote himself to preaching the crusade, and it fell to the newly elected Gregory VIII to deal with this great catastrophe of Christendom. His appeal echoes the apologia for the failure of the second crusade. It is the sins not only of the Kingdom but of all Europe that have brought this disaster upon them. It is men's unworthiness that is defeating God's purpose. Repentance for sins, and the restoration of peace in Europe are the first obligations. But it seemed that the old response was lacking. Richard of Poitou was rebuked by his father for precipitately pledging

148

98 Masyaf, the chief castle of the Ismailians, on the eastern slope of the Ansariyah mountains.

99 Marqab: the hall in the Hospitaller castle which stands on the hills overlooking the coast road from Tortosa to Latakia.

himself to the crusade. Henry of England and Philip of France took the cross the following year but continued their warfare. Henry of Albano was not a preacher to enflame men's hearts; rather he was a negotiator working steadily to an organized and possible plan. Finance had to be dealt with. The Saladin tithe was levied in France and England, though some cried out that to oppress the poor was not the way to assuage God's wrath. The crusading vow itself became marketable, from which suitable payments could buy release. Here and there the old enthusiasm survived. Baldwin, archbishop of Canterbury, preached in Wales and western England, and his own simple, straightforward devotion to the cause, which he was to seal with his death in the sickness-ridden camp at Acre, brought crowds to hear him. But it was trained men and money that were needed, as Richard, now come to the throne, well knew.

It was from Germany that a fresh impetus came. Barbarossa was past his sixtieth year, a veteran of the second crusade and of his own Italian wars. To retake Jerusalem seemed the fitting climax of his career. Old, for those days, he might be, but he was still able. He conducted what was probably the largest and best organized of all crusading armies across the land route, overawing the feeble Byzantine emperor. Then, when he had crossed Asia Minor, he was accidentally drowned, bathing in or rashly fording the River Saleph. The eyewitnesses, who were shocked and confused by this misfortune, give accounts which do not make clear how the accident occurred. The great army, now leaderless, was largely dispersed; it was a much-reduced force that bore the emperor's corpse to Syria, burying the flesh in St Peter's of Antioch but carrying the bones down to Tyre to leave them in the cathedral there.

It was hard news for Conrad, but he was much busied with other plans. On 27 August 1189, Guy of Lusignan, released by Saladin but disregarding his pledge not to fight against him, appeared with a small force before Acre. Conrad had refused him admittance to Tyre. This small encampment became the nucleus of crusading reinforcements, and, thanks to the cross-bowmen arrived from Europe, it was able to repel Saladin's first attack and gradually to encircle the town, while Saladin in turn surrounded the Latins from the hills beyond the sea plain. Throughout 1190 the camp grew, but it was a hot, fly-ridden summer with much sickness, and among those who died was queen Sibylla and the two daughters she had borne to Guy of Lusignan. Guy was thus deprived of any claim to the kingship, a fact that well suited his enemies. The Ibelins, with the help of the queen dowager, Maria Comnena, and against the protests of the worthy Baldwin of Canterbury, obtained from the papal legate the annulment of Isabella's marriage to Humphrey of Toron; the poor heiress to the throne, much against her will, was married to Conrad, whose deserted Byzantine wife was never mentioned. It was a complex dynastic problem for the kings of France and England to unravel, and needless to say they took, when both had reached the camp at Acre, opposite sides. Richard supported the Aquitainian Guy, who shrewdly had come to his assistance in Cyprus. Leopold V of Austria naturally urged the claims of his Montferrat cousin. For the time being, however, the capture of the town was the main priority, overriding disputes.

On 12 July 1191 Acre was taken, and on 31 July Philip sailed for France. In the interval Richard had agreed to recognize Conrad, leaving to Guy the town of Acre and the county of Jaffa, whither early in September the English king proceeded to march, having embittered the war by massacring the garrison of Acre. Saladin, it is true, had failed to complete the terms of the peace by the fixed date, and Richard had no means of feeding or guarding the prisoners, but this cold-blooded execution of some 3000 men, who had distinguished themselves by a valiant and prolonged defence

150

of the city, stands out grimly even in the callousness of the time. Strangely it did not entirely dispel Saladin's admiration for Richard. He was still ready to treat with him, and even to propose a settlement based on a marriage between his brother al-Adil and Richard's sister Joan, the queen dowager of Sicily. That this extraordinary proposal was ever seriously regarded as more than a diplomatic move, must be open to question. Certainly it was discussed, though the lady herself, with the vigour that might be expected from a daughter of Henry and Eleanor, furiously opposed it. In the end little was accomplished. There was a three years' truce; the coast from Tyre to Jaffa was left in Christian hands, but Ascalon, that had been refortified by Richard, was once more dismantled and handed back to Saladin. On 28 April 1192 Conrad of Montferrat, with the preparations for his coronation finally in hand, was killed in the streets of Tyre by Assassin emissaries. His vigorous career came to its violent conclusion, leaving many suspicions behind as to the instigator of the deed. Conrad had played no part in Richard's crusade, and had been treating independently with Saladin. The English king was naturally suspected, and was openly accused by Leopold of Austria, but no evidence supports the accusation and there are many improbabilities, of character and opportunity, against it. Conrad had confiscated the merchandise of an Assassin ship in the harbour at Tyre, and this comparatively trivial act, of a piece with his grasping nature, was undoubtedly the reason he never wore the crown for which he had so fiercely striven.

151

Isabella was once more married, this time more happily, to Henry of Champagne, young, handsome, wealthy, the son of Richard's half-sister, Marie of Champagne, 'the gay countess'. Richard himself sailed for England on 9 October 1192, but fell into the hands of his enemy, Leopold of Austria, to the great prejudice of all crusading privileges.

On 4 March 1193 a much greater man died. For a month Saladin had been sore sick in Damascus. The faithful Baha-ad-Din watched by his bedside: often the sultan's mind wandered, but all wondered at his patience. Then, 'while the Sheik Abu Jafr was reading from the Divine Word – "There is no God but He, in Him do I trust" – the sick man smiled, his face grew radiant, and he went in peace to his Lord.' To Western chroniclers he had seemed 'the hammer of the faithful' and early accounts invented discrediting tales: that he was an illegitimate son of Nur-ad-Din, that he had seduced Nur-ad-Din's wife (he married his widow for dynastic reasons) and that he was 'instructed in a thousand arts of doing ill'. To William of Tyre, at nearer hand, he was 'a man of keen and vigorous mind, valiant in war, and liberal [*liberalis*] beyond measure'. By the mid-thirteenth century, Matthew Paris could suggest that his mother was a Christian captive and an Englishwoman.

BONIFACE OF MONTFERRAT

New figures and new problems were emerging. Guy of Lusignan died in the autumn of 1194 and Tancred of Sicily the same year, leaving a son who could make no headway against the claims of the new emperor, Henry VI. In the spring of 1195, Isaac Angelus was deposed and blinded, and his brother, Alexius III, ruled in Byzantium. Henry VI was planning a crusade the scope of which remained threateningly undefined. His death from a fever in September 1197 brought confusion and uncertainty. A German expedition already in Syria was busied with the reoccupation of Sidon and Beirut, linking Tyre once more with the county of Tripoli. When the news of the emperor's death reached these men they forthwith began plans for their return journey. How far Henry had been prepared to push crusading matters must remain an open question. He had secured recognition of his suzerainty from Cyprus and Armenia; with the conquest of Sicily he had inherited the traditional Norman hostility to Byzantium; and for his brother, Philip, he had arranged a marriage with Irene, daughter of Isaac Angelus, and widow of Roger of Apulia of the dispossessed Sicilian line. His control of the eastern Mediterranean was being steadily consolidated. But with Henry's heir, Frederick, a child only three years old, and the empire in Germany disputed between Philip and Otto of Brunswick, the imperial crusade was at a standstill.

The new pope, Innocent III, elected in January 1198, was well aware that the third crusade had failed in its full achievement through disputes among the various princes involved. His aim now was a crusade organized and planned from Rome and accompanied by papal legates. He sought to inform himself thoroughly on the situation in the East and wrote to the patriarch of Jerusalem demanding a detailed survey, particularly of the strength of the various Moslem leaders. Alexius III wrote to Innocent urging the need for unity and the recognition of the supremacy of Rome. But he knew that spiritual enthusiasms, as well as practical considerations, were necessary. Advised as it seems by Peter le Chantre, the eminent Parisian master, he authorized a simple parish priest, Fulk of Neuilly, whose eloquence was rousing much enthusiasm, to preach the crusade. The vigour of the vernaculars was affecting sermons as well as poetry. After the fine rhetoric of St Bernard, Fulk's emphasis on the abandonment of usury, so that money should be used to feed the poor not breed of itself, and his call to prostitutes to leave their way of life, reveal an ingenuous view of moral reform, of the purification that would produce true crusading aptitude. Contemporary sources, however, agree that his words found their hearers. He also collected considerable sums of money to help poorer crusaders, a fact that Robert of Clari, himself a knight of no great holding, particularly stresses. In 1202, when news of Fulk's death reached the crusading army in Venice, the barons and all the people grieved much for this good and holy man.

It was not, however, to be a popular crusade, but rather a baronial one. Theobald of Champagne was the first to take the cross; a brother of Henry of Champagne, he had close associations with the Holy Land. Baldwin of Flanders, his brother-in-law, also took the cross; the grandson of Thierry and Sibylla of Anjou, the nephew of Philip who had campaigned in Palestine in 1177, Baldwin came of a family with long crusading traditions. But Theobald of Champagne died, still a young man, in May 1201, and it was then that the last of the Montferrat brothers, Boniface, stepped into the leading place. He was now a man of about fifty, who had successfully maintained the estates that his father had secured, and had skilfully remained on good terms with both Henry VI, for whom he had campaigned in Sicily, and with the papacy. He had the goodwill of the troubadours, not a minor factor in the public relations of the times; Peter Vidal and Rambald of Vacqueyras, noted poet-singers, had both enjoyed his patronage. When the French crusading leaders met at Soissons, Geoffrey of Villehardouin proposed the name of Boniface as master of the host: 'there was much said one way or the other, but the end was that all agreed'. Baldwin of Flanders, later to be Boniface's successful rival for the

101 Fulk of Neuilly, 'a right worthy man and a right good clerk', preaching the crusade in France in 1198.

102 The crusaders attack Constantinople by land and sea; a fourteenth-century version of the event.

empire, was present, but no claim seems to have been put forward for him: though the relationship between the royal house of France and the Montferrats was by now a somewhat distant one, Philip Augustus gave his approval.

Negotiations with Venice for the transport of the crusading army had already been agreed. Boniface went to France to take over command, and from there went to Haguenau to visit his cousin Philip of Swabia. At Christmastide, when he arrived, the young Alexius, son of the deposed and blinded Isaac Angelus and brother of Philip's wife, Irene, was already there. He had recently escaped from the hands of his usurping uncle, Alexius III. Discussions as to the plots and influences that led to the final diversion of the fourth crusade to the capture and sack of Constantinople are as involved as were the events themselves. Boniface, through his brothers, Rainier and Conrad, had vague claims on some position in Byzantium; in particular the former had been granted by Manuel Comnenus a title in Thessalonica, which Westerners could easily interpret as a feudal holding. The chance of restoring the young Alexius as rightful heir of the deposed Isaac Angelus must have seemed a tempting one, arguably of advantage to the crusading project. The Venetians, ever since they had been expelled by Manuel Comnenus in 1171, had been seeking payment of damages for their losses, and a new footing in the city.

154

Under Isaac Angelus agreement had been reached, only to be disowned
by his supplanter, Alexius III, then, in 1198, confirmed but little acted on.
Against this weak, indolent and superstitious ruler there was a concentration of Western grievances that made his removal a pious and
justifiable aim. The failure of the crusaders to concentrate all their forces
at Venice, and their consequent inability to meet the numbers and payment
stipulated in their agreement with the Republic resulted in the diversion
of the crusade to Zara and its recapture for Venice from the king of
Hungary, not only a Christian ruler but one who also had taken the
crusading vow. The inhabitants of Zara had hung crosses on their walls,
but the holy sign had not stayed the crusaders' assault. 'Evil angels',
wrote pope Innocent, 'have induced you to pay your debt with the spoils
of Christians.' The papal predicament was to become more and more
difficult. In a series of letters Innocent seems to be arguing with his own
conscience as much as with the leaders of the diversion, and it is impossible
to assess his knowledge at any time of what they intended. Constantly he
draws back from extreme measures. Sanctions would destroy all hope of
any succour to the crusading cause. Later, horrified as Innocent was when
he received details of the sack of Constantinople, he had to qualify his
reactions with the aim of at last achieving a union of the Greek and Latin
Churches.

From Zara the crusaders sailed for Constantinople, all except a few, among them Simon of Montfort, who withdrew from an undertaking they could no longer approve. The blinded Isaac Angelus and the young Alexius once restored, the feebleness of the first and the incapacity of the second soon produced not only their deposition and death, but a situation in which the taking of the city and the establishment of a Latin emperor were the only steps that would secure any of the advantages for which the crusaders had been looking.

The sack of Constantinople, with its brutalities, profanities and pillage, ranks high in the annals of destruction. Perhaps too high: Constantinople had been often plundered in its own riots. Many buildings of the city, including the Great Palace, were sad ruins when the crusaders found them. But an ignorant fanaticism was let loose on the great statues of Greek art, which no doubt seemed idolatrous works tolerated by a schismatic people. Venice saved much: the bronze horses, the porphyry group of kings, the enamels in San Marco's Pala d'Oro. The colossal bronze of an emperor shipped to Italy was wrecked off Barletta, and when brought ashore remained there, ironically erected in front of the church of San Sepolcro. But to the Westerners, works of art were nothing compared to sacred relics. Throughout France and Germany, church after church received its portion of holy booty, a last and most ungracious twist of crusading piety. As far afield as East Anglian Walsingham, these pious fragments were for some 300 years to stimulate the faith of simple folk who knew nothing of the blood-stained pillage from which they came. But the event has lain heavy on the European conscience.

The diversion of the fourth crusade to Constantinople has provided a fascinating and much-exploited study in motives. Rarely has an historical event involved so many and so varied impulses. But the basic facts were the crumbling weakness of Byzantium and the determination of Venice to rid itself of this shadow of former greatness that lay across its eastern trade routes. Among the leaders concerned, doge Enrico Dandolo had a consistency of purpose and clarity of aims that gave him an overriding control in all discussions. In the debates of the campaign he was the expert. An old man, with failing sight, he drew energy from his memories of Manuel's expulsion of the Venetians and Andronicus's massacre of the Latins. The involvement of Philip of Swabia in the imperial disputes in Germany left Dandolo with no great rival in prestige, and in Boniface's vague fraternal claims he had a useful theme on which to play. The bargain by which the crusading army should capture Zara for Venice was an adroit piece of policy. An inroad on Christian Hungary, it broke down the last vestiges of crusading prejudices, and was a calculated defiance

LOOT FROM CONSTANTINOPLE

103 A view of Venice, painted about 1400, showing the bronze horses from the Hippodrome in Constantinople in the position they still hold above the porch of St Mark's.

104 Byzantine pillar at the southern corner of St Mark's, Venice, taken from the church of St Polyeuktos.

105 Colossal bronze figure of an unidentified emperor; traditionally said to be Heraclius (610–14) but almost certainly the work predates his reign. In the thirteenth century the figure went down in a shipwreck off Barletta. It was erected, in 1491, in front of the church of San Sepolcro.

of the papacy, a break with the one man, Innocent III, whose strength of character and diplomatic skill Dandolo might well fear as thwarting obstacles. He now prepared to take full advantage of his schemes.

Boniface clearly assumed that he would be elected emperor. He had occupied the Bucoleon palace, and was already arranging his marriage with Margaret of Hungary, the widow of Isaac Angelus. Against him, however, were many Venetian prejudices. He was a former ally not only of the Hohenstaufen but also of the Genoese. His Italian blood and back-ground were here against him, and the Venetians carried the election in favour of Baldwin of Flanders, a younger, more malleable and certainly less capable man. It was proposed that the unsuccessful candidate should be assigned the Byzantine lands in Asia Minor and the Peloponnese. In Asia Minor the Lascarid family were already establishing a Greek empire in exile at Nicaea and the Peloponnese was as yet unconquered. Boniface, mindful of his brother's association with it, claimed the establishment of a kingdom at Thessalonica, which would have the added advantage of proximity to the territory of his wife's Hungarian kin. After negotiations almost leading to warfare, this settlement was agreed, and Boniface occupied his new dominions.

Byzantine hold on its Greek territories had been steadily weakening, and under Alexius III a brigand adventurer, Leo Sgourus, had seized

106 The walls of Thessalonica. In the main they date from the sixth century AD but they have been continuously maintained by Byzantine, Latin and Turkish rulers.

Nauplion, Argos and Corinth; Athens had been saved from him only by the determined defence led by the metropolitan and historian Michael Choniates. Boniface led a force down into Attica, and drove Sgourus into the citadel at Corinth, which he was to hold for another three years. When the emperor Baldwin was captured and killed by the Bulgars, in 1205, Boniface married his own daughter to Henry of Flanders, Baldwin's brother and successor, whose eleven heroic years of rule gave some hopes of permanence to the Latin empire. With the refugee Greek empire at Nicaea he secured a treaty, and the Bulgarian threat was for a time in abeyance owing to the death of the Bulgar leader Kalojan. Boniface, however, had no part in this brief time of hope and success. He was killed in 1207 in a minor battle with Bulgar forces.

THE FATE OF THE LATER MONTFERRATS

For some fifteen years Thessalonica remained in Latin hands, the scene of constant disputes between a group of Lombard nobles, who sought to lure William VII of Montferrat, Boniface's son by his first marriage, from his marquisate, in opposition to the regency of Margaret of Hungary for her own infant son, Demetrius. In the end it fell to a new power, the despotate of Epirus, established by a Greek officer, Michael, calling himself, with no adequate right, Angelus. From his capital at Arta he occupied Durazzo and Corfu, and thereby controlled the Via Egnatia leading from the Adriatic to Constantinople. Michael was murdered in 1215 and it was his brother Theodore who captured Thessalonica in 1224, extending the despotate from the Adriatic to the Aegean. Demetrius, Boniface's young son, passed into a dreary life of exile and solicitation for help, dying in Pavia in 1227. His uncle, William the marquis, sailed with a small expedition in 1225, part of Frederick II's designs, but died early in the course of it. Maria, the daughter of Isabella and Conrad, was to marry the elderly soldier John of Brienne, bringing with her the crown of Jerusalem; dying in childbirth she left a daughter, Yolanda, who was to marry Frederick II and leave disturbing claims to the Kingdom to her son Conrad and ill-fated grandson Conradin. Boniface II of Montferrat accompanied Frederick II on his crusading venture, and one of his sisters married Henry of Cyprus and died in one of the many sieges of Kyrenia. A granddaughter of Boniface II, Yolanda, married (though it was a stormy union) the emperor Andronicus II, and through her a branch of the Palaeologi became in 1305 lords of Montferrat. Medea, a daughter of this line, married John II of Cyprus in 1440, but died only a few months later. She was the last transient intrusion of this family whose name had once meant so much in Eastern lands.

107 The walls of the castle of Clermont, the chief castle of the Villehardouin family, in Elis.

THE FRANKISH STATES IN GREECE

When Thessalonica fell to the despot in 1224, the Epirote forces turned southwards towards Boeotia and Attica, but their advance was checked by Guy Pallavicini, one of Boniface's companions, from his castle of Bodonitsa above the famous coastal route of Thermopylae. Athens, where Boniface had plundered the Parthenon, not of classic marbles but of the great treasure of the Orthodox Church of the Holy Wisdom, had been given to one of his followers, Othon de la Roche, and, when Boniface's own kingdom fell, Pallavicini's success in holding the pass preserved the Frankish settlement in Attica. Further south, the Franks had achieved one of their most remarkable conquests. While Boniface and Henry of Flanders were fighting their grim struggles against Bulgars and Lascarids, some Latin bands, mainly dispersed from the fourth crusade and led by Geoffrey Villehardouin and William of Champlitte, had occupied the Peloponnese, the Morea, as the Franks called it. Michael of Epirus, alarmed at the remarkable success of these small and scattered forces, crossed the Gulf of Corinth with an army of between 4000 and 6000 men, at least three times as many as the Franks could muster. He joined with the local Greek resistance in the central Peloponnese, and in the olive groves of Koundoura, in northern Messenia, the Franks met him and routed him with a fierce cavalry charge. As the Chronicle of Morea put it of another incident, 'one Frank on horse was worth twenty Romans'. It was the one pitched battle of the Franks' conquest, and after it the castles of Arcadia (Cyparissia), Nauplion and Argos, even Corinth after its long siege, passed into Frankish hands. Only Monemvasia and the hill-country of Lacedaemonia remained out of their control, while in the south Modon and Coron were handed over to the Venetians to become 'the eyes of the Republic', guarding the northward turn to the mouth of the Adriatic.

For the past two centuries Greece had been a place of little history. In 1018 the emperor Basil II had celebrated at Athens his triumph over the Bulgars, and this marked also the highpoint of a Byzantine reorganization of Greek territory. The eleventh and twelfth centuries seem to have known a modest prosperity, evinced by the growing interest of Italian traders in the ports of the Peloponnese, but in the later part of the twelfth century, here as elsewhere, Byzantine control declined. In 1141 the Normans from Sicily raided and sacked Corinth, a first demonstration that was to have a more drastic sequel in 1185 when, turning aside from the needs of the Holy Land, they sacked Thessalonica. These were preliminary sketches of Western occupation, and the crusading barons found a land of little organization, with strongly localized interests, unprepared to make any stand against them.

Geoffrey of Villehardouin, prince of the Morea, and Othon de la Roche, lord of Athens, the two main creators of this new sphere of Frankish influence, worked together in unusual amity. The Villehardouin capital was at Andravida, in fertile Elis, and close to it, overlooking the ports of Clarentsa and Katakolo, Geoffrey built his main castle, Clermont or Khloumoutsi. It is today the most impressive surviving monument of Frankish Greece. A hexagonal enceinte crowns the summit with an outer enceinte stretching down the north-west slope, the only easy means of access. Within the hexagon were the living quarters, including a hall with high-pitched barrel-vaults. In its polygonal design, which shortly was to be used so splendidly in Frederick II's Castel del Monte, it is an example of new trends in defence work, on which it may well have had some influence; but in decorative work it is severely plain.

No Gothic masons have left distinguished works in Greece, as they had in Syria and were contemporaneously doing in Cyprus. The Morea had first been conquered by a contingent of 100 knights and 400 sergeants. Though it became an attractive resort for ambitious warriors, it lacked the element of pilgrimage that appealed to simple folk, the lesser burghers and artisans. Building traditions that had survived elsewhere seem to have lapsed in Greece and the Franks did little to renew them. After some early troubles, the Greek Church was reasonably tolerated in its former sites, and the Latin Church has left few memorials. The much-dilapidated eastern end of St Sophia still stands at Andravida, but can never have been an impressive church, and its capitals show Gothic foliage in its simplest form. In sloping fields above the Alpheus river, where it bends westward to Olympia, the ruined Gothic church of Our Lady of Isova still seems a curious anachronism in these classical sites, but its windows and vaulting ribs suggest that here some Western masons may have been employed. At the Cistercian monastery of Zaraka, near Stymphalia, a mass of fallen masonry has vaulting ribs among it, but other of the stones seem re-used earlier material; at Geraki some carved decorations must be Frankish work. When at Daphne the Cistercians added a western porch of pointed arches to the Byzantine church, the planning of it ran into difficulties and compromises. Of adaptations, the most notable was that of the Parthenon. Already the eastern pediment had been partially destroyed by the Byzantine apse, and little new work was needed, but the Latin rite, under the great frieze still in position and fortunately difficult to come at, was one of the strangest confrontations of the time.

Castle-building is equally unimpressive. Much of it was on earlier foundations, Byzantine or classical, and, where not left to fall into complete ruin or plundered for building-stones, it has been subjected to haphazard Catalan, Turkish or insurgent alterations, or to more competent Venetian reconditioning. In the hills above the pass of Thermopylae, Bodonitsa, which held the boundary against the Epirotes in Thessalonica, is still reasonably complete and, with its upper double bailey, and lower

108 The central keep of the Frankish castle of Bodonitsa in the hills above the plain of Thermopylae.

line of walls encircling the hillside, has some merits as a defensive scheme. The central keep is built on a wall dividing the upper circuit into two parts. The flat lintel of its doorway is in a Byzantine tradition that must have been familiar to local builders. On the western route into Attica, the castle of Salona, now in ruins, is an amalgam of various building periods. The great castle of the St Omer family at Thebes, built about 1260 by Nicolas II with the dowry of his wife, Mary of Antioch, daughter of Bohemond VI, was the most celebrated of all these castles, with 'dwellings within it fit for an emperor' and its walls covered with paintings 'depicting how the Franks conquered Syria'. Thebes, the centre of the important silk trade, was the richest town in Frankish Greece, and here the arts flourished most. But this castle was destroyed in 1332 by the Catalans and today only a solid tower, with walls 9 feet thick, remains, surrounded by the busy traffic of the modern town. On the Parthenon, at some uncertain date, a tower was built, and finally removed only in 1874. Argos has four round towers that seem Frankish work; Arcadia a round tower of small, rectangular stones, very distinct from the Byzantine blocks near by. Karytaina is a marvellous silhouette on its hilltop, but the walls are rough work, remade in many later occupations. On the route between Arcadia and Kalamata, the castle of Androussa, the Druges of the chroniclers, is better built than usual, and on the whole well preserved.

109 Karytaina, perched on its rocky hill above the river Alphaeus, was an important Frankish stronghold. This nineteenth-century drawing hardly exaggerates the romantic nature of its setting.

110 The hill at Mistra is crowned by the castle built by William of Villehardouin between 1248 and 1261. On the slopes below are the palace and churches of the Palaeologan despots.

The reign of William of Villehardouin, prince of Achaia from 1246 to 1278, saw both the greatest triumphs and the decline of Frankish power. In 1248 he established his hold over the hill-country between Laconia and Monemvasia, an area in which a population of Slav extraction lingered, and thus he controlled the whole Peloponnesus. To supervise this new area he built a castle at Mistra, near ancient Sparta. When Louis IX set out, in 1248, on his ill-fated crusade, William joined him in Cyprus with twenty-four ships and 400 mounted men. He and his followers shared the misfortunes of the king, and only returned when, released from Egypt, Louis sailed for Acre. From the French king William obtained the right of minting coinage, and Franco-Greek tournois were added to the Mediterranean currency and seem to have circulated freely. At Andravida or Mistra, it was a French culture that drew the chivalry of Europe to this new school of warlike manners, and the songs sung were mainly French, though Greek also was in use, particularly among the *gasmouloi*, the children of the mixed marriages that became frequent here, as in Palestine. But in this world of courtesy new dangers were at hand. On the death of Theodore II Lascaris at Nicaea, his leading general, Michael Palaeologus, had assumed the regency and virtual control of the reviving Greek empire. In 1259, under his brother, he sent a considerable force into Thessaly. William of Villehardouin and Michael, the despot of Epirus, to whose

165

daughter William was married, met the Byzantine forces on the plain of Pelagonia in Macedonia. At the crucial moment the Epirote forces left the battle, and the Franks were surrounded and captured or slain. For two years William was a prisoner, and when eventually he had to come to terms, yielding up Mistra and Monemvasia, it was with a Greek emperor once more resident in Constantinople. The defeat of Pelagonia had cleared the way to the great city, and Michael Palaeologus now took for himself the imperial crown. The greatest Eastern attempt of the Latins was over.

Faced with this restored empire, William of Villehardouin turned to a new Western power. In 1266 Manfred, the brilliant natural son of Frederick II, had been defeated and slain at Benevento by Charles of Anjou. Two years later the attempt of Conradin to regain the Neapolitan kingdom was likewise defeated, and he perished on the scaffold, to become a legend of ill-fated youth. Charles, adroit, hard and ambitious, inherited the Eastern aims of his new dominions. In 1267, William, without a male heir, made a treaty with him by which his daughter Isabella should marry Charles's son Philip, and they, on William's death, should hold the Morea from the Angevin ruler. If Isabella died childless, as in fact happened, the Morea should pass to the king of Naples.

It was not all defeat and diplomacy. The gaiety of these feudal courts comes to life in a collection of *chansons*, the so-called *Manuscrit du Roi* (Bibliothèque Nationale, MS. fr. 844), compiled for Charles of Anjou in the course of the years 1254 and 1270. Here, with the notations to which they were sung, are the ballads of the day, many of them by princely composers, Charles himself, John of Brienne, Theobald of Champagne, and the Prince of the Morea, who is most easily identified as William II Villehardouin. The noble *trouvères* are depicted mounted on caparisoned horses, holding their blazoned shields, but unfortunately the book has been mutilated and many of the miniatures removed, among them that of the Prince of the Morea. But these knights prepared for the tourney, over their songs of love and battle and the tunes composed for them, are a wonderful piece of the civility of the time, and one closely interwoven with the crusades in which so many of the singers participated. But now these days were ending, and it was in Byzantine Mistra that the arts were to find their new Greek home.

THE KINGDOM OF CYPRUS

While the attractions of Frankish Greece provided a new outlet for Western adventurers, the kingdom of Cyprus was slowly growing into prosperity. The island, an area of 3584 square miles, emerges into history when it was conquered by Thotmes III of Egypt about 1500 BC. The population at that time seems to have been a Mycenaean people, with a cult of Aphrodite centred at Paphos. The Phoenicians later had trading posts there; in 58 BC it was annexed by Rome and for a year was administered by Cicero. In 395, when Honorius and Arcadius divided the Roman empire, the island passed to Byzantium. From then on till 1191 it was an outpost of the Byzantine empire, Greek-speaking, Byzantine in its arts. The Arabs raided it, but did not settle. The crusaders raided it also, from Antioch and Tripoli, and in 1191, when the ruler, Isaac Comnenus, an unpopular tyrant, attempted to abduct Richard Coeur-de-Lion's betrothed, Berengaria, and her sister, Joan of Sicily, whose ship had been forced to take shelter at Limassol, the English king overran the island, sent Isaac a prisoner to Syria, and sold Cyprus to the Templars. They found it more than they could manage and handed it back. Richard then installed Guy of Lusignan, who had come to aid him in conquering the island.

This final stage in Guy's hitherto unfortunate career marked the establishment of the most successful of all these Latin dynastic schemes in the eastern Mediterranean. His death in the spring of 1194 left Cyprus without a ruler. He had held it from Richard for his lifetime only, but the English king, occupied in France, made no claim to its reversion and the Latins whom Guy had overgenerously installed in Cypriot estates, many of them men who had lost their lands on the Palestinian mainland, elected his brother Aimery, the former constable of Jerusalem, as their overlord. He had no exact title, and one of his first steps was to obtain from the emperor Henry VI, busy with his own crusading schemes, the recognition of Cyprus as a kingdom. In the autumn of 1197 Aimery was crowned in Nicosia by the imperial chancellor, Conrad, bishop of Hildesheim, the leader of the advance guard of the imperial crusade, and a politician of proven ability. It was his influence which now promoted Aimery to further honours. In the course of a conference with some Pisan emissaries at Acre, Henry of Champagne, the king (though never officially crowned) of Jerusalem, stepped back unguardedly and fell to his death from an upper window. With death so easily come by in the crusading states, this was a sad and trivial way to lose a leader of such promise and of such widespread European connections. Isabella, his wife, was still only twenty-six, and by the advice of the archbishop of Mainz, she was now given Aimery as her fourth husband, thereby uniting the kingdoms of Cyprus and Jerusalem. A fortunate victory celebrated the event. On 27 October 1197, with the help of the German crusaders and the complicity of some Christian slaves within the town, Beirut was recaptured. It was given to John of Ibelin, half-brother through his mother, Maria Comnena, to queen

Isabella and first cousin of Eschiva, Aimery's first and recently deceased wife. The Old Lord of Beirut, as John came to be called, stood at the centre of a network of relationships and for the next forty years was to be a dominant and noble figure in crusading affairs.

The taking of Beirut raised Christian hopes, even though co-operation with the German contingent presented the usual divergence of aims between settlers and Western reinforcements, particularly in this case with the vague threat of imperial supremacy in the background. But with the news of Henry VI's death, Outremer once more stood on its own. Nevertheless Conrad of Hildesheim carried out one more act in completion of his dead master's policy. With the papal legate, Conrad of Mainz, he moved north to Cilicia. At Tarsus, Leon of Armenia was crowned king with both papal and imperial agreement, and even the grudging assent of the Byzantine emperor, Alexius Angelus. It was the climax of a remarkable career. While the Kingdom of Jerusalem perished, Armenia had reached a new stage of prosperity. Leon was a skilled diplomat, who had aided Barbarossa's journey, joined Coeur-de-Lion in the conquest of Cyprus, and sent a contingent to the camp at Acre. Only with Antioch were his relations strained, despite the marriage of his niece to Raymond, son and heir of Bohemond III. Raymond's death, leaving a young son, Raymond Roupen, provoked a dispute over the succession. Conrad of Mainz now obtained from the court of barons at Antioch the recognition of this child's rights when his grandfather should die. To a Westerner this consolidation of Christian forces must have seemed an adroit and

111 Old Beirut, as it appeared in the nineteenth century, showing the ruins of the castle of the Ibelins. Today the only remaining crusader building in the town is the cathedral, now a mosque.

reasonable step, but it took no account of ecclesiastical suspicions between the Latin and Armenian Churches and the strong localism of baronial feeling; nor did it allow for Bohemond's second son, Bohemond the One-eyed, who had been count of Tripoli, and had wider ambitions. The German intervention had left many seeds of new discords.

Meanwhile there was a pause. The disputes among Saladin's sons kept back any renewed Moslem attack, and Aimery was able to organize a new area of Latin power in Cyprus. It had been an inauspicious start. Richard's rapid conquest, though it removed a tyrannical governor, had merely ravaged the island. From his hermitage on the rocks near the site of the old temple of Aphrodite at Paphos, St Neophytus wrote of 'the cloud of English' who had descended on his island, and of the pillage they inflicted, so that the rich fled away to Constantinople and the poor suffered endless tribulations. Under the Templars matters went from bad to worse. To raise 100,000 dinars, the price due to Richard for the island, they attempted to levy crippling imposts on the Cypriot markets. A revolt broke out in Nicosia at Easter 1192, with a total force of little over one hundred Latins, of whom fourteen were knights, to resist it. Such, however, was their desperate vigour that they dispersed the rioters, massacring them in the streets. Their brief rule left nothing but hatred behind them, or almost nothing. At the east end of St Sophia in Nicosia there is a doorway, clearly remade from different fragments, and on one side the capitals and impost have the characteristic foliage that was the hall-mark of the masonic yard in the Temple area in Jerusalem. The main construction of this great Gothic church dates from the archbishopric of Eustorgue of Montaigu (1217–50), but there had been earlier building on the site and possibly the Templars had already begun to work on it. It would have been a natural step, even with their insecure hold on the island, for the establishment of the Latin rite at the expense of the Greek schismatics was one last remnant of crusading apology in this occupation of a Christian island.

In the Kingdom of Jerusalem policy had demanded, and joint hatred of the infidel allowed, a certain tolerance of the native churches. In Constantinople and Cyprus there was less cause for such forbearance. To the former, the Greeks at Nicaea were the main enemy; to the latter, the sea, as yet, was a stronger frontier than any in Palestine. External danger and internal security both prompted a disregard of tolerance. One of Aimery's earliest acts was to establish an archbishopric at Nicosia with three suffragan sees, and the appropriation of Orthodox lands and tithes to finance them. The long tenure of the archbishopric by Eustorgue of Montaigu must have done much to consolidate the Latin position. He was an enthusiast for the crusade, who was at the siege of Damietta in 1217, and returned with St Louis, dying there on 28 April 1250 in the terrible days of defeat and surrender. To the people of Nicosia, the great Gothic cathedral rising above the buildings of the town must have seemed strangely foreign compared to their own small-domed churches, some of which still retain frescoes and mosaics of high quality dating from pre-Frankish days. A more terrible demonstration came in 1231 when thirteen Greek monks were martyred in Nicosia for refusing to recognize Roman authority in disputed matters of doctrine. The papacy had to intervene in 1260 with the *Bulla Cypria* laying down that the Latin archbishop should be the sole metropolitan, but confirming the rights of Greek bishops to administer the affairs of their co-religionists.

The diversion of the fourth crusade, regarded by many in the West as the great negation of crusading principles, allowed the joint kingdom of Cyprus and Jerusalem a period of comparative peace and reorganization. A series of truces with Cairo, Damascus and Aleppo, where the sons of Saladin were jealously watching one another, controlled only by the diplomatic skill of their uncle, al-Adil, was welcomed by the local baronage, even if at times they sought, particularly in the disputes over the succession in Antioch, infidel alliances. It is noticeable that when foreign reinforcements arrived, as in the crusade of 1217 led by Andrew of Hungary and Leopold VI of Austria, the latter redeeming his father's outrage against Coeur-de-Lion, some campaigning (often to the dislocation of existing treaties) had to be undertaken, if only to provide food and forage for the troops, who could not be supported on the limited resources of the coastal towns. Otherwise it was a pacific period. The patriarch of Jerusalem, Aymar, had reported to Innocent III in 1199 that another crusade was inadvisable and that more could be regained by diplomacy. Trade was in fact flourishing, and Venice in particular had satisfactory relations with Egypt and did not wish them broken. They much preferred al-Adil to the transient rulers of Constantinople and its xenophobic mob.

Aimery, therefore, before his death in 1205, had some opportunity of consolidating his control over Cyprus. With his decease, the union of the two kingdoms ended, and his wife, the much-tried Isabella, died soon after him. She was in her late thirties, had been four times married, happily and unhappily, and left five daughters to continue the marital intrigues in which she herself had so often figured. Hugh, the young king of Cyprus, married Alice, whose father had been Henry of Champagne. But the eldest and the heiress was Maria of Montferrat, daughter of Isabella's second husband, Conrad; she was married, after a search for a more prominent husband, to a comparatively obscure and elderly knight, John of Brienne, for whom the pope and Philip of France had to put up a dower of 40,000 silver pounds. Maria died in childbirth, leaving a daughter Yolanda, who was to marry Frederick II. John of Brienne, thus widowed, married a daughter of Leon II of Armenia, with whom everyone now was seeking alliances; in 1216, after a series of incidents of little credit to any of the participants, he had eventually established his great-nephew Raymond Roupen in the principality of Antioch.

Leon, himself a widower in the marriage market, in 1210 married Sibylla, daughter of Isabella and Aimery, and Raymond Roupen married, apparently after abducting her from an earlier husband, Sibylla's half-sister, Helvis. Cyprus had a large Armenian population, part of the wide scattering of the race after Old Armenia was overrun by the Selchukids, and geographically the Cilician coastline, only some forty miles distant, was the nearest mainland. A new factor, however, had brought an element of crisis into Cypriot-Armenian relations. The break-up of the Byzantine empire had led to new expansions in the old Selchukid dominions of Roum. In 1207 Kai-Khusrau, the eventual successor to the great Kilij Arslan who had died aged seventy-seven in 1192, occupied Antalya at the head of its wide gulf. His son Ala-ad-Din Kai-Qobad (reigned 1220–37) made this bay his particular interest, building a new town at Alanya and strongly fortifying a castle at Anamur. Ala-ad-Din's buildings still largely survive; his splendid minaret at Antalya, the docks for his ships at walled Alanya, the many towers of Anamur, all testify to the magnificence of his reign. A keen trader, he was ready to negotiate with Cyprus, as also with the Italian merchants. Cilician Armenia had reason to be alarmed at so able a neighbour and Leon II called in the Hospitallers to hold Silifke and Camardusium on his eastern frontier.

112 The castle of Silifke (Seleucia), for a time held by the Hospitallers, on the western boundaries of the Cilician kingdom of Armenia. It was in the swift-flowing river Saleph, below the castle, that Frederick Barbarossa was drowned in 1190.

113 The siege of Damietta as illustrated in a fourteenth-century version of Joinville's *Histoire de Saint Louis*.

114 Frederick II and his third wife, Isabella of England (daughter of king John). The marriage took place in 1235 and Isabella died in 1241.

Compared to the Selchukid and Armenian powers, Cyprus was as yet poor and unimportant. Above all there was no Cypriot fleet. This led, in 1218, to the grant of considerable privileges in the island to the Genoese. It was the beginning of a long and, in the end, disastrous connection. But new pressures of a civil nature now distracted the island and the period of comparative peace was to be wrecked, not by Moslem attack but by a war between Christians.

Pope Innocent III continued to have the plight of the Holy Land much at heart. Crusading propaganda still had an emotional popular appeal, even if the princes and barons regarded crusading projects in terms of self-interest. In 1212, the so-called Children's Crusade took place. Bands of young people converged on Marseilles or came down from Germany and crossed the Alps to embark at Genoa and Pisa. It was a protest of youth against the inaction and indifference of their elders, a representation in medieval terms of demonstrations very familiar today. Unplanned and unorganized, it petered out in disaster. The crusade that followed was a different matter. In 1217, urged by the papacy, a force, drawn mainly from France and England, assembled in southern Italy and from there sailed to join forces with an expedition from Acre led by John of Brienne, encamped in the Nile delta. The aim was Damietta, and beyond Damietta, Cairo. It nearly succeeded, but the papal legate, Pelagius, was a rigid,

Jmpator fretheie in uroze duar ysabellam
fororem h̄.
regis Angt.

fanatical man. To attack Egypt, ruled under al-Adil, was to destroy the balance achieved in Eastern affairs and to endanger the whole trading prosperity of the eastern Mediterranean. Strategically, it might be argued, though with little evidence, that Jerusalem could best be attacked from Egypt, and that it was only when Egypt and Damascus were under one rule that the Kingdom was lost. At one point of the campaign al-Adil actually offered the restoration of the Kingdom, except for the southern castles beyond Jordan, but Pelagius was opposed to any compromise, and the military orders argued that dismantled Jerusalem could not be held, and its surrender would prove a deception. Finally, the crusade dispersed, unable to hold Damietta, which had for a time been occupied. Hopes had been raised by the prospect that reinforcements would arrive under the young emperor Frederick II, but Frederick, more and more embroiled with the papacy, delayed, even though the heiress to the Kingdom, Yolanda, now sixteen years old, was sent to Italy as his wife. It was not till 1228 that Frederick set sail, landing first in Cyprus. By then Yolanda was dead, leaving an infant son, Conrad, in whose name the emperor claimed the Kingdom; and John of Brienne, her father, was warring against imperial troops in Italy and was shortly, indefatigable in his late seventies, to withdraw to much-harassed Constantinople as regent for the young Baldwin II, dying there at a ripe age in 1237.

In Cyprus, John of Ibelin, lord of Beirut, was acting as regent for another boy king, Henry I. Alice of Champagne, the queen mother and widow of Hugh, was now married to the future Bohemond V, the heir to Antioch. At a feast given by Frederick at Limassol, the emperor and the lord of Beirut confronted one another. Frederick had surrounded his guest with armed guards, and demanded that John surrender his estates to him and the revenues accrued while he was *bailli* in Cyprus. John's speech is reported to us by his devoted adherent, Philip of Novara, doubtless with some literary licence; but it was a famous utterance and one that must have been much quoted at the time. For his rights to his lands he appealed to the court of the Kingdom of Jerusalem; for his handling of the revenues to the court of the kingdom of Cyprus. 'But be certain', he concluded, 'that for fear of death or of prison will I not do more unless the judgment of the good and loyal court requires me so to do.'

It is to the Ibelin entourage that the great codification of laws and customs of the Kingdom was to be due. Now was the testing time for them. Frederick gave way, but never forgot or forgave. He demanded John's two sons as hostages: 'I well know', he said, 'that Balian is your very heart and that so long as I have him I shall have you.' John surrendered the two young men on the understanding that they should be freed when he had proved his right in the court of the Kingdom of Jerusalem and that meanwhile they should be treated honourably; but 'the emperor had them put in pillories, large and exceeding cruel; there was a cross of iron to which they were bound so that they were able to move neither their arms nor their legs'. Frederick, however, was anxious to get on with his crusading business, and did not wish to be held up in Cyprus. In the end he released the hostages and sailed for Acre, where he was received with acclaim, until some Franciscan friars arrived with news that the pope had excommunicated him. Al-Kamil, al-Adil's successor in Cairo, sent an embassy to him led by a man with whom Frederick was already acquainted, the sheik Fakhr-ad-Din, who had twice visited Frederick in Sicily; it is said that Frederick had knighted him and that he carried the emperor's arms. This crusading emperor, who spoke Arabic, had a Saracen bodyguard, and admired much in Islam, had qualities which, with more tactful handling, might have been understood and appreciated by the *poulains*. The alienation of the Ibelins was a disastrous mistake that marred his whole enterprise. Yet, by diplomacy and despite the smallness of his own contingent, he achieved the cession of the three holy cities, Jerusalem, Bethlehem and Nazareth, the *seigneurie* of Tibnin (Toron) in Upper Galilee, and the territory of Sidon still occupied by the Moslems. Balian of Sidon was one of Frederick's intermediaries and supporters, a

115 A Christian knight plays chess with a Moor: from a fifteenth-century Spanish manual on chess.

man who had inherited from his father, Reginald, a knowledge of Islamic ways, and who was much respected by all factions in the Kingdom (his mother was a sister of John of Ibelin, his wife's mother a sister of John of Brienne). The treaty no doubt reflects something of his interests as well as his skill. Jerusalem was, however, not wholly ceded. The Moslems retained the Temple area, and free access to it for their pilgrims. Frederick himself visited it, but rather as a friend of Islam than as a Christian devotee. It was a form of condominium, tolerant and practical, a rare incident in the history of that passion-evoking city. But it was achieved by an excommunicate ruler. In the Church of the Holy Sepulchre, where Godfrey of Bouillon had refused to wear a crown in the place of Christ's suffering, Frederick had to place the crown on his own head. The patriarch of Jerusalem, Gerold, lately abbot of Cluny, had placed the city under an interdict while Frederick remained there. The Templars had steadily been against him and were now indignant at the retention of the Haram in Moslem hands. Old crusading impulses lingered, and Frederick's disregard for the rights of the baronage did nothing to extinguish them. Leaving Jerusalem after only three days' sojourn there, the emperor returned to Acre to sail for Italy and the defence of his territories against papal troops. He confided the *bailliage* of the Kingdom on behalf of his infant son, Conrad, to Balian of Sidon and Garnier l'Aleman, an Alsatian

175

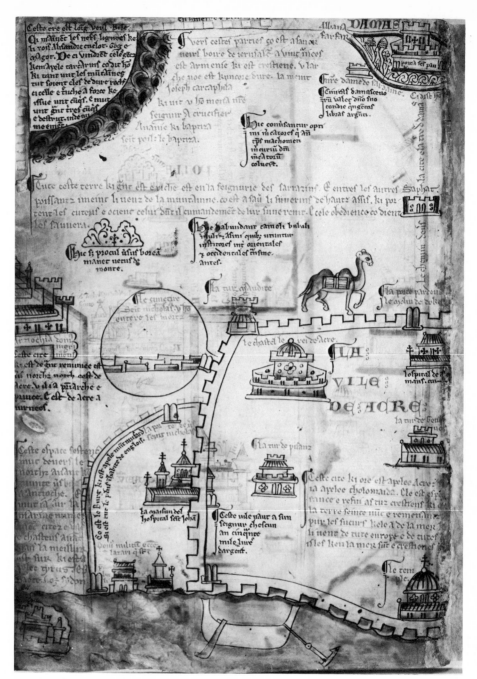

116 Matthew Paris's map of Acre, showing the main walls of the town. The outer suburb of Montmusart, here only weakly protected, was enclosed in new walls by Louis IX between 1250 and 1254.

who had recently by marriage established some position in the Kingdom. When the emperor embarked, the mob pelted him with dirt, and, a crowning indignity that must have been hard for him to bear, he was only extricated by John of Ibelin. Within a few weeks of his departure, some unorganised raiders from Nablus and Hebron entered Jerusalem, whose fortifications had been left unrestored; they were easily dispersed when the two *baillis* came with their forces, but it was a comment on Frederick's claim, made to pope Gregory IX, that he had reopened the way of pilgrimage.

Leaving Acre he paused in Cyprus for the marriage of the boy king Henry, to Alice of Montferrat, daughter of William VII of Montferrat, recently dead supporting his kin in the Latin empire. He also set up five *baillis* chosen out of the opponents of the Ibelin family, in particular Amaury Barlais, who had a long history of difficulties with them. It was not, however, simply a nomination of imperial officers. For the three years' *bailliage* Frederick demanded a payment of 10,000 marks of silver, and the raising of this led, as in the case of Richard and the Templars, to heavy taxes, which were especially directed against lands held by the Ibelins. In July of 1229 a pitched battle took place between a force sent from Acre under John of Ibelin and the imperial *baillis*, in which the latter were defeated. The war thus begun spread soon to the mainland, whither Frederick sent Richard Filangieri as his representative. Until 1243, the year in which Conrad came of age and Frederick's claim to the regency ended, there was almost continuous civil strife passing backwards and forwards between the mainland and Cyprus, centring on the constitutional issue of the baronial right to a hearing in the High Court for any questions concerning them, sometimes with condemnation, sometimes with support from the papacy, according to the fluctuations of the papal-imperial dispute.

In the history of Europe it is a small matter; for Cyprus it preserved laws that for better or worse remained valid for two centuries; for the crusading kingdom it was suicidal folly only rendered possible by Frederick's truce with al-Kamil. But by one of the chances of historiography, it leaps into a vivid life of its own through the account of it written by Philip of Novara. In his pages the characters take on recognizability. We can see the camp outside the castle of Dieudamour, above the pass between Nicosia and Kyrenia, which was later to be called St Hilarion. We know how Philip himself was wounded and the besieged shouted from the castle 'Your singer is dead', but that Philip made a new song and the following evening 'sang it loudly'. We know how the young queen, Alice of Montferrat, this shadow of a great name, died besieged in

Kyrenia, and a truce was made that her body might be carried out in all honour and buried in the cathedral church of Nicosia. Through it all there is the dominating personality of John of Ibelin, the Old Lord of Beirut, strenuous for baronial rights, standing on the law, but capable of generous acts and beloved by the lesser people, who, when a commune was formed at Acre, called on him to take charge over it. In the spring of 1236 John was crushed by his horse in a riding accident and soon after, having become a brother of the Temple, he died. Philip of Novara held the crucifix before him 'and if one believes that good souls go before God, one can be certain that his soul went there to paradise'.

Poet, satirist and historian, Philip of Novara was, to his contemporaries, above all a legalist. At the siege of Damietta, a young page, recently come from Novara in Lombardy, he was set to read romances to Ralph of Tiberias, the seneschal of the Kingdom, who was sick: 'Sir Ralph slept little and badly, and when I had read as much as he wished, he himself told me many things concerning the Kingdom of Jerusalem and the usages and assizes, and he said that I should remember them.' He could hardly have had a better instructor. Ralph had been consulted by Aimery when the latter wished to undertake a codification and clarification of the laws of the Kingdom. The scheme broke down through a personal quarrel. In March 1198, riding near Tyre, Aimery was attacked, and only rescued after being severely wounded. He suspected, it seems groundlessly, Ralph who had been an alternative suitor for the hand of Isabella. John of Ibelin had to intervene to calm the king, but Ralph thought it well to withdraw from the Kingdom during Aimery's lifetime. The outcome of these Damietta talks was a lasting interest on Philip's part. He consulted all the leading legalists of the day, though he found the Old Lord of Beirut 'never talked so willingly as Sir Ralph did'. His *Livre de forme de plait* provides an important section of the compilation known as the *Assizes of Jerusalem*, of which the *Assize of the High Court* by John of Ibelin, count of Jaffa, is an even more outstanding piece of jurisprudence.

The problems of the *Assizes* are not easily summarized. From Godfrey's time onwards there had been promulgations of laws with the consent of the High Court of Barons and these had been deposited in the Church of the Holy Sepulchre, whence they were known as the *Lettres du Sepulchre*. Both Philip and John of Ibelin state that they were lost when Saladin took the city, a surprising statement, but the obvious is sometimes overlooked; the patriarch Heraclius is known to have been busy with his own treasures, and there were few responsible nobles in the city. The *Assizes* as compiled by John Ibelin of Jaffa, shortly before his death in 1266, were therefore a record of enactments handed down verbally, though some written lists of fiefs seem to have survived. John, however, did not content himself with summarizing. His work is a learned treatise on the nature and purpose of the laws, a piece of highly intelligent expertise that reflects well on the intellectual life of the Kingdom, and also shows that the legalist stand of the House of Ibelin had not been entirely in vain.

Though little noticed at the time of these baronial disputes, some victims of the period's disturbances were to have a much longer destiny. About 1235 a group of hermits living on Mount Carmel were dislodged by the Saracens, and joined the flow of westward-moving refugees. Among them was, as seems most likely, an Englishman, Simon Stock. In 1242 he became general of this hermit order, whose first rule had been received from Albert, patriarch of Jerusalem, himself to be a canonized saint. From Simon's reforms grew the great order of the Carmelites, which was to play, and still plays, so considerable a part in the spiritual life of Europe.

Henry I of Cyprus, who was not yet a year old when he came to the throne in 1218, died in 1253. He had made little impact on his time. As a child he was dominated by the interventions of his much-married mother, Alice of Champagne, who did not die till 1246. Passing from hand to hand in the war between the Ibelins and the imperialists, debarred from any claim on the Kingdom of Jerusalem by the prior right of Conrad, Henry's greatest moment was probably the winter of 1248–49, when he entertained Louis IX of France, before the opening of the renewed attack on Egypt. For the crusade it was a disastrous delay: an epidemic raged in the French army, and any element of surprise was lost. But for the rulers of Cyprus it meant a close contact with the most advanced court of Western Europe. As the mainland became more and more hard-pressed, the island prospered. Louis's sojourn seemed to confirm its position as the new bastion of Christendom.

Henry had been three times married, but it was only a few months before his death that a son was born, and once more an infant in arms, Hugh II, became king, to die when he was fourteen. It was for him that St Thomas Aquinas began to write his *De regimine principum*, a tribute to Christian hopes of Cyprus, but little else preserves the boy's memory. He was succeeded by his cousin, Hugh III, who in 1268, when the young Conradin was executed by Charles of Anjou in Naples, reunited the kingdoms of Cyprus and Jerusalem. Hugh spent the greater part of his reign at Tyre and Acre, struggling courageously to organize defence and end the disputes among the Franks. But it was too late. His son Henry II, who succeeded him in 1285, after his elder brother John had reigned for only a few months, had on a night of May 1291 to depart in flight from Acre, as the last city of the Kingdom was falling.

117 Mongols besieging a city. In this early fourteenth-century manuscript, costumes and weapons are carefully depicted and a new realism is grafted on to the Persian tradition of illustration.

Mongols and Mamluks 7

Three years before Michael Palaeologus so easily reoccupied Constantinople another empire had fallen. In 1258 the Mongol leader, Hulagu, entered Baghdad with his army and overthrew the caliphate. The last of the Abbasid caliphs perished along with many of his Moslem followers; the Christian sects, protected by Hulagu's wife, herself a Nestorian, on the whole were spared. The Ismailians, of whom the Mongols seem to have had considerable wariness, had already been defeated and their great fortress of Alamut, with its famous library, destroyed. The campaigns of Genghis Khan had swept over China, Transoxiana and Khurasan; his sons had occupied Iran and crossed the Caucasus into southern Russia. In 1241 they were in Poland and Hungary, and it was only the death of their leader, Ogodai, that stayed their advance into Europe. Everywhere this great upheaval drove lesser tribes before it. In northern Europe, where in 1241 a German army had opposed the Mongols in Silesia and been completely routed, the heathen tribes were pressing westward away from the Mongol threat. Innocent III had sought to limit crusading privileges for these northern wars, privileges which St Bernard had allowed, but now the dangers were more pressing and eastern Germany ranked with Syria as a crusading field. The Teutonic Knights, this new order to which the wisdom and high character of Hermann of Salza, grand master from 1210 to 1239, had given prestige and importance, detached some of its knights from its headquarters at Montfort, near Acre, and sent them to establish a new base at Torun in Prussia which was from 1225 onwards to absorb much of their resources.

In the first half of the thirteenth century the sultanate of Roum, in Asia Minor, had reached its greatest period of power. The Danishmendid state that had so long rivalled it had been driven to submission, and the Latin conquest had reduced the remnant of Byzantium to a small area round Nicaea. Ala-ad-Din Kai-Qobad (1220–37) ruled over prosperous and expanding territories, maintaining friendly trading relations with Antioch, Cyprus and the Venetians. One threat to his power came from the appearance in Anatolia of a warlike people, the Khorezmians, driven by Mongol pressure from their home in Transoxiana. In 1230, Kai-Qobad succeeded in defeating them, and driving them south to new adventures in Syria, but other roving tribes, Turkomans displaced by stronger Mongol forces, plundered their way through Roum, and the sultanate, weakened by these ravages, could not resist the Mongols when their army at last appeared in 1243 as an invading force. From that defeat the Selchukid state never recovered.

Europe watched these events with deep if generally ill-informed interest. The Mongol advance into eastern Germany seemed to have brought the foe to their gates, and thrown crusading ardour on to the defensive. But there were also new hopes. It became known, as the world horizons widened, that in the Mongol dominions there were many Christian communities, hitherto unheard of and unimagined. Some of the Mongol leaders were themselves Christian or married to Christian wives. The legend of Prester John, the Eastern potentate who was to come to the aid of Christendom, was constantly repeated in varying forms and the Mongol subjection of the Christian kingdom of Georgia could not destroy it. Under its great queen Thamar (1184–1212), Georgia itself had been a land of legend, but it had kept to the business of self-preservation, and rarely figured in crusading history. To a period when apocalyptic visions were much heeded, these Eastern rumours were widely and wildly interpreted. Even Innocent III, distracted by his incompatible aims, could write of 'King David, vulgarly called Prester John, a Catholic and God-fearing man', and could quote prophecies based on the Book of Revelation that the era of Mohammed was drawing to a close. At the siege of Damietta the legate Pelagius had some letters translated from Arabic and dispatched to the West. James of Vitry, lately appointed bishop of Acre, and by no means tolerant of Christian sectarianism, wrote that 'King David most victorious in battle, whom the Lord raised up in our days that he should be the hammer of the pagan and the exterminator of their traditions and laws, is he who is commonly called Prester John.' Attempts were made by embassies and letters to make contact with these promised allies, and the Franciscan John of Pian del Carpine journeyed as far as Karakorum in Mongolia.

The baronage of Outremer, absorbed in their disputes with the imperialists, were less alert to these great changes. The years 1239 to 1241 saw two crusading contingents come to their assistance, the first under Theobald of Champagne, a better poet than leader, the second under Richard of Cornwall, brother of Henry III of England and brother-in-law of the emperor Frederick. This show of strength, coming at a time of civil troubles of his own, persuaded sultan Aiyub of Cairo to make various concessions and much of Galilee was once more ceded to the Franks. Then, in 1243, the baronage shook off the last imperial controls, and Richard Filangieri, Frederick's *bailli*, was driven from his final stronghold, Tyre. Aiyub was warring against his uncle, Ismail, in Damascus, and the latter was strongly supported by the Templars, to whom he had restored the Temple area in Jerusalem. Aiyub called to his aid the Khorezmian army. On its march south in August 1244, it took and sacked Jerusalem, pillaging the Holy Places. The Templars' reinstatement had been short-lived, and never again were the Franks to hold the city. An effort was made to retrieve the position. An army of about 6000 men, as great a muster as could be made, led by Philip of Montfort, lord of Tyre, and Walter of Brienne, count of Jaffa, both comparative newcomers to the Holy Land, joined the Damascene forces and near Gaza, on 17 October 1244, joined battle with the Egyptian and Khorezmian forces. For the crusaders it was a total defeat. The master of the Temple and the archbishop of Tyre were both among the slain. Walter of Jaffa was captured and paraded before the walls of Jaffa, but his life was spared even though the town refused to surrender. He was later to die in captivity in Cairo.

It was a disaster that recalled the débâcle of Hattin, with the merciful difference that the Egyptian sultan, Aiyub, still had to establish control over Damascus, a dispute internal to Islam and more urgent than the final liquidation of the Franks. These precariously held ports had, too, some trading advantages for him, and Christian depots had their place in the general marketing of the Near East. Ascalon was once again taken by him in 1247, but with that essential anchorage in his hands Aiyub seemed for the time satisfied.

The loss of Jerusalem and the defeat at Gaza were clear signs of impending doom. The bishop of Beirut was sent to France with appeals for assistance, and found there a situation of little encouragement. In 1245, Innocent IV fled from the Hohenstaufen menace in Italy to Lyons where, in June, he opened a general council. Its aim was the deposition of Frederick II, and the authorization of crusading privileges to any that fought against him. To his legate in Germany, Innocent wrote that the preaching of the crusade of Outremer should be discontinued, so as not to distract from that against the deposed emperor. Crusading vows could also be switched to this new purpose. Crusading tithes and fines for release

obligam. rpd uz
rcp fraz. Loð.

Rex fracoz
Lodollue?

ecce cruce dm

118 The Crown of Thorns, one of
the greatest Christian relics preserved
in Constantinople, was mortgaged by
the Latin emperor Baldwin II to the
Venetians and redeemed from them
by Louis IX, who built for it and other
relics the Sainte-Chapelle in Paris:
drawing by Matthew Paris.

119 Joinville offers Louis of Navarre
(Louis X of France) his *Histoire de
Saint Louis*, completed in 1309 when
Joinville was eighty-four years old.
He died in 1317.

from vows were diverted to the same end. 'The pope and the curia', wrote
Matthew Paris shrewdly and bitterly, 'sell crosses, give absolution for
money and hinder any from departing.' The ballad-makers, mostly
partial to the secularly minded Frederick, were quick to condemn the
wolves in sheep's clothing, who preached war against Christians so that
the Saracens no longer had any cause for fear. It was the climax of that
dilemma into which Innocent III had fallen, when in 1199 he had offered
'the same remission of sins that we accord to those who take the cross
against the perfidious Saracens to those who fight against Markward of
Anweiler [the imperial representative in southern Italy] because he
hindered Christendom from bringing succour to the Holy Land'. From
this standpoint it was almost inevitable that, when Philip Augustus
refused to intervene, the pope was forced into using the same privileges

against the Albigeois, those heretics of Languedoc 'who were worse than Saracens'. In the course of these operations, Innocent, mingling divine authority with problems of feudal confiscation, despoiled the great-grandson of the first crusader, Raymond of Toulouse, of his lands. If Urban II had thought of the crusade in terms of the exaltation of papal power for the peace of Europe, he had forged a weapon that his successors turned to a different purpose. 'Now', Fulcher reports Urban as saying, 'those who were formerly fighting against brothers and blood relatives, will rightly fight against the barbarians . . . here the enemies of the Lord, but there His friends.' Those were words sadly forgotten or forced into strained interpretations.

Innocent IV, however, could not entirely neglect the appeals from Outremer, particularly as they found a response in Louis IX of France, whose authority, personal as well as political, could not be questioned. In 1243 the king had been sore sick, 'in such extremity', Joinville tells us, 'that one of the ladies watching him wished to draw the sheet over his face saying that he was dead.' He recovered and took the cross, and now was busied with preparations. In him the old single-minded crusading fervour lived again, and his example fired something of the old enthusiasm. But once more a great expedition came to disaster in the network of channels in the Nile delta. Louis had directed his attack against Egypt as the heart of Moslem power, despite the complaints of the Venetians and the arguments of the Templars, urging him to diplomatic intervention in the disputes between Cairo and Damascus. Louis had come, as those of old, to fight the infidel, and it was only after his defeat and capture that he learned in the four years (1250–54) loyally spent in Palestine that much could be done by negotiation.

Joinville shared his master's captivity in the Egyptian camp, and describes one horrible and poignant incident with the vivid detail of an eyewitness. The sultan, Turan-Shah, a dissolute and incompetent young man, was murdered by his Mamluk guard, hacked to pieces as he flung himself from a burning tower into the river. He was the great-grandson of Saladin's brother, al-Adil, and it was a grim end to this dynasty, so eminent for its far-seeing policies, its great building schemes and its sophisticated tolerance. Power passed, at first nominally then completely, into the hands of the Mamluks.

Ransomed and released, Louis sailed for Palestine. Of his doings there, not the least curious, to contemporaries as to us today, was his exchange of gifts with the Assassin leader at Masyaf, to whom he sent the Dominican friar Yves the Breton, who spoke Arabic and often acted as the king's interpreter. The sack of Alamut by the Mongols had left the Assassins in Syria without their former support, and they had been paying tribute to the Templars and Hospitallers for their protection. Yves the Breton understood something of their beliefs, looked through their library and knew that 'they held to the law of Ali'.

Less conspicuous but all important was the control that Louis exercised over the local baronage. He always punctiliously respected the rights of Conrad, Frederick's heir, but his personal ascendancy even more than his royal rank held the local feuds in check. He reconciled Antioch and Armenia, arranging a marriage between Bohemond VI and the daughter of Hayton who, in 1226, began his long forty-four-year rule of the Armenian kingdom. When the Templars negotiated an agreement with Damascus without consulting him, Louis at once summoned the master to his presence and banished the marshal, Hugh of Jouy, who was responsible

186

for the negotiation, from the Holy Land. The Moslems realized the presence of a leader, and viewed him with respect. He, however, knew that his sojourn must come to an end. His chief aim was to leave the Christian towns repaired and refortified. Jaffa, Acre, Sidon were all worked on, and Louis himself at times took his place among the labourers, as Saladin had done in the rebuilding of the walls of Jerusalem. At Sidon his new castle on the landward side still stands; at Acre the walls were extended to include the northern suburb of Montmusart, which had spread beyond the earlier fortifications.

120 The sea-castle of Sidon was built between 1228 and 1229 after the crusaders had regained control of the town. It is on a rocky island linked by a causeway to the mainland.

121 Stone head of a youth, from the castle of the Teutonic Knights at Montfort. The blue paint of the eyes is still visible.

122 The castle of Montfort: ruins of the keep. The castle commanded the approach to Acre from the north-east.

Nothing is stranger in this history of civil dispute and external defeat than the continuous prosperity of these beleaguered towns. Acre was a mart and 'from the rising to the setting of the sun all kinds of wares were brought thither'. There were said to have been forty churches there in the thirteenth century, including those of the Franciscans and Dominicans, for whom Acre was their Eastern base. Of the cathedral of St Cross nothing now can be certainly identified. Of the church of St Andrew something more is known. Corneille le Bruyn drew it in 1681, a fine early Gothic building with five lancets in its western façade. Its doorway still survives, carried off by al-Ashraf and incorporated in his father's mausoleum at Cairo, where its mouldings and stiff leaf capitals are in a refined Gothic taste that shows Acre to have had high standards of craftsmanship. In the town museum a corbel carved with a young man's head has a sulky charm that well suggests these wilful, heedless youths, and a fragment of a tomb slab of an ecclesiastic bears the date 1290, only a year before the final catastrophe. A warrior's head from near-by Montfort, now in the Jerusalem Museum, has a lively vigour, and the eyes, still painted blue, recall its Teutonic occupants.

The greatest surviving example of thirteenth-century crusading churches is the cathedral of Tortosa. Considered to be on the site of the first church dedicated to the Virgin, and possibly incorporating it as a chapel. In the thirteenth century, when other Biblical localities were no longer accessible, it enjoyed considerable repute as a place of pilgrimage. 'A great resort of pilgrims', Joinville called it, and obtained leave from king Louis to visit it. In the mid-thirteenth century the cathedral was extended westward; the capitals take on a new freedom and naturalism, and the façade is a striking and carefully balanced piece of work. It stands on the land-side of the town, and there was talk of pulling it down in the desperate last years of the crusaders' occupation for fear of it aiding the besiegers. But instead it was partially fortified and most fortunately survives.

Castle-building, largely in the hands of the military orders, was carried on even more vigorously. The Templars had a great fortress on the sea front at Acre, and at Tortosa another strong point, where their treasure was kept, and where still today stretches of walls with the traces of vaulting arches loom up among the houses of the town. But their greatest thirteenth-century undertaking was the building of a completely new castle, Château Pèlerin, at Athlith. Placed on a small bay south of Mont Carmel, it strengthened the coastline between Acre and Jaffa, and secured the narrow passage at the mountain's foot. Two great towers overlooked and

123 The cathedral of Tortosa is the finest surviving Gothic church of the crusading kingdom. The opening under the pillar on the left possibly led to a small Byzantine chapel, thought to be the first dedicated to the Virgin Mary, but removed in the final Gothic rebuilding.

controlled the triple walls blocking the landward approach to the small peninsula. At one corner of the inner ward was a polygonal church, recalling the shape of the Temple, the Dome of the Rock, of which the order was now deprived. On the sea front was a vaulted hall, a pleasant place of cool breezes. It was never taken, but when Acre fell the garrison abandoned it and sailed for Cyprus. In 1837 Ibrahim Pasha despoiled it of stones for restoring the fortifications of Acre, but enough remains to show that it was not only a formidable defence work but also a noble and distinguished dwelling-place. The Templars had many other castles to keep in repair: Baghras, north of Antioch, at the entry of the Beylan pass; Beaufort, sold to them in 1260 by Julian of Sidon, grandson of the Reginald who had fled at Hattin; Safitha, visible from Krak des Chevaliers. But the only undertaking at all equal to that at Athlith was the rebuilding of Safad. The treaty secured by Theobald of Champagne in 1240 had restored it to Christian control, but the Templars lacked resources to rebuild it, and were only roused into activity by the bishop of Marseilles who led out a band of pilgrims to start work on it. Given this impetus, more skilled labour was certainly brought in, for the castle was a large and impressive one. Burchard of Mount Sion saw it shortly after it was 'betrayed and taken in shameful sort', and thought it 'the fairest and strongest castle I have ever seen'. Some ruins were described by the nineteenth-century archaeologists and very diversely interpreted, but little today can be traced among the buildings of the town. It fell to Baybars in 1260, but only after the knights were tricked into surrender. They were all massacred, and their skulls piled in heaps before the town, a token of the ferocity of the Mamluk ruler of Egypt.

The Hospitallers have been much more fortunate than their rivals in the survival of their buildings. Krak des Chevaliers, the grandest fortification of the Western world, is still almost complete. Its hilltop position allowed a partial view, through the gap between the Lebanon and Ansariyah mountains, of the road from Homs to Tripoli. North of it, paths led up through the Assassins' country, from whom in the mid-century the knights claimed and received a tribute of 1200 dinars and 100 mudel of wheat and barley. The slopes and valleys around it were fertile in crops and pastures. It was both a strategic emplacement and a rich landholding. To the original fortified courtyard, the Hospitallers added a second enceinte, with semicircular towers, and stirrup-shaped loopholes, which brought the base of the walls within bow-shot. On the west front, where the easiest approach lay, two round towers rose with impressive grandeur from a steeply pitched talus faced in stone, at the foot of which was a long water-tank. Given the difference in the nature of the sites, the general scheme has much in common with that of Château Pèlerin. And here too the interior had Gothic tracery and carving. From an inscription it seems that the last works were carried out under the command of Nicholas Lorgne (1254–59), who later as grand master of the order (1277–85) was to see its gradual Syrian decline, and busy himself with appeals for Western help. Krak surrendered to Baybars in April 1271. Marqab, the great Hospitaller castle that still looks down on the coastal road between Tripoli and Latakia, was taken by the Mamluk sultan Kalavun in May 1285, and the island fortress of Maraclea, held by Bartholomew of Gibelet with Hospitaller help, was surrendered shortly afterwards. By then only their buildings in Acre were left to them, and here, true to their lasting tradition, the main work was the actual hospital, used for the wounded and the sick. Its great vaulted hall, probably late twelfth-century work, has recently been cleared, and beyond it lies a complex of other rooms, still built over and not fully investigated; here something of the solid splendour of medieval Acre can still be experienced.

124 The castle of Athlith (Château Pèlerin)
was built by the Templars, in 1217/18, to
guard the pass south of Mount Carmel.

125 The hall of the Hospital in Acre is the
grandest medieval structure in the town. It
had been much built over and filled with
rubble and has only just been cleared.

126 Krak des Chevaliers: view from the
north. It was ceded to the Hospitallers in
1144. Their work on it in the next hundred
years made it the greatest surviving castle of
Christendom.

Other arts flourished: that of illumination had not been lost with the dispersal of the Jerusalem scriptorium. It is possible even that there was some return of painters to the Holy City after Frederick II's treaty, for a beautiful psalter now in the Riccardiana Library in Florence, datable to *c.* 1230, has strong associations with Jerusalem in its calendar and prayers. Stylistically it is a fusion of European, particularly German, and Byzantine motifs; the Latin scrolls held by the prophets in the splendid Beatus initial are translations from the Greek Septuagint, not quotations from the Vulgate. It is a brilliant product of the meeting of cultures.

Another psalter, in the Capitular Library of Perugia, has the entry on 12 July of *Dedicatio ecclesie Aconensis*, that is of the cathedral of St Cross. Though less accomplished in its illustration than the Riccardiana psalter, the characteristic features of its style make it a key piece for the identification of other manuscripts and their assignment to the Acre school. The finest of these, a Bible (Arsenal Library, Paris, MS. 5211), shows a lavish mingling of Byzantine and Western conventions, with the strongly marked facial types of the Paduan Psalter and some detailed knowledge of the dress and animals of the East. More arrestingly interesting from the point of view of text are three manuscripts of the *Histoire Universelle*, one now in Dijon, another in Brussels, and the finest in the British Museum, all showing typical stylistic features of the Acre school. The Brussels manuscript, which seems later than that of Dijon, has an inscription indicating that it was written by Bernart of Acre and there is no reason to doubt the statement. The *Histoire* is a compilation made from a variety of texts, setting out the relationship between Biblical and classical events. Here we are in contact with much that furnished the crusading mind. The lands in which they travelled had their own legends, and heroes with whom they felt akin. Geoffrey of Villehardouin before a battle exhorted his companions 'to remember these heroes who were before our time, and who are still recalled in the books of histories'. Robert of Clari in his *Conquest of Constantinople* writes how his favourite warrior, Peter of Bracieux, at an interview with the Bulgar leader, Kalojan, boasted that Troy belonged to his ancestors and those who escaped from it came to his country. In the illustrations to the *Histoire*, Achilles and Hector are in chain-mail, and the warriors carry blazoned shields as they ride their caparisoned horses. To the troubadours the deeds of their own time seemed worthy to compare with those of Alexander.

127 The entry to Jerusalem: an initial from the Riccardiana Psalter, illuminated between 1235 and 1237, possibly in Jerusalem. Internal evidence suggests it was made as a gift for Isabella of England, wife of Frederick II.

128 Joshua and Balaam: from the Arsenal Bible. Stylistically it is linked with the Acre school and with French influence dating from the time of Louis IX's visit to the Kingdom (1250–54).

129 Initial from a psalter at Perugia which includes in its calendar the dedication feast of the cathedral of Acre.

This medieval synopsis of history ranges from Genesis to the triumph of Pompey after his capture at Jerusalem. Three manuscripts of it were associated with the school of Acre. That in the British Museum is outstandingly splendid.

130 The finding of Oedipus: from the Brussels manuscript which was written by Bernart of Acre.

131 Scenes of the Creation: opening page of the British Museum *Histoire.*

132 Death of Hector: from the British Museum *Histoire.*

133 Pyrrhus fighting Penthesilea: from the British Museum *Histoire.*

Literary interest in the heroic was not confined to the legendary past. The translation of William of Tyre's History into French seems to have been first made in the West, but three manuscripts suggest by the style of their illustrations that they were produced at Acre. French continuations were written, whose interrelationships and authorship provide many problems, but which show a continuing interest in the chronicling of crusading events.

Thirteenth-century wall-paintings have not come down to us, though they are known to have existed. John of Ibelin, the Old Lord of Beirut, had in his castle mosaic floors and the ceiling painted with the signs of the Zodiac. Elsewhere there must have been other such works, successors to the twelfth-century paintings that still fragmentarily survive. And certainly panel painting was being done, for in the great collection of icons at Mount Sinai some have Latin inscriptions and stylistic affinity with the Acre school.

In these artistic manifestations some place must be given to the Latin empire in Constantinople. It has long been considered a period whose beginnings were marked by destruction, and whose course was undistinguished by creative art. Recent discoveries are, however, modifying this view. Illuminated manuscripts were still being produced by Greek artists, and their stylistic progress had some influence on the Acre school. In the churches of the Pantocrator (Zeyrek Cami) and the Saviour in Chora (Kariye Cami) fragments of leaded and figured window glass have been found that suggest the import of Western craftsmen and methods; and in a blocked-up chapel of the Kalender Cami, probably the church of the monastery of Akataleptos, a frescoed semi-dome has been found with scenes, unfortunately very fragmentary, from the life of St Francis, the earliest frescoed cycle of them known. The heads have unmistakably the features familiar in the Acre school, and there must have been some stylistic interchange between the painters of them and those of the Arsenal Bible. It may well be that the latter was a product of the Empire rather than the Kingdom, though the formation of the style comes from Acre.

Nowhere is the contrast between artistic excellence and the perils of the time more vividly apparent than in the Cilician kingdom of Armenia. Here leading figures such as Sempad the Constable and king Hayton I were writers and historians as well as patrons who had artists of rare distinction working for them. The Gospel book made for Sempad (died 1276) and bearing his autograph (Matenadaran, Yerevan, MS. 7644) has full-page paintings of great imaginative force and originality. The traditional Byzantine iconography is invaded by a new fluency of design

134 Icon from Mount Sinai: a Nativity scene much influenced by Western models. One of the kings is shown as a Mongol which suggests a reference to the Mongol general Kitbogha (d. 1260), who was a Christian.

and delight in realistic detail. A greater painter was to follow. Toros Roslin is, by any standards, one of the great figures of thirteenth-century art. Five manuscripts illuminated by him at Hromgla and claimed as his work in the colophons are now in the library of the church of St James in Jerusalem. One, written in 1262, includes a portrait page of prince Leon (later king Leon III) and his wife, Keran of Lampron; another (1268–69) was written for prince Hayton, later Hayton II and the colophon recalls the sack of 'great Antioch' by Baybars, and how 'we were in this great danger and trembling', but that peace returned when prince Leon was released from captivity in Egypt. The great Gospel book at Matenadaran (MS. 197), though unsigned, must also be Toros's work. His range of expressions and poses has a new humanity far removed from Byzantine formulas and his colours are vividly contrasted. Amid invasion and pillage, civilization was still in some of its branches being brilliantly maintained.

135, 136 Crucifixion and ordination: from a Gospel-book made, in 1287, for John, archbishop of Sis, brother of king Hayton I. Attributed to Toros Roslin.

137 Death and burial of John the Baptist: from a Gospel-book signed (1262) by Toros Roslin.

138 Portrait of prince Leo (afterwards Leo III) and his wife, Keran: by Toros Roslin, 1262.

Such achievements depended on trading prosperity. Venice, Genoa and Pisa, Marseilles and Barcelona are the chief names in Eastern commerce, and against their combined shipping Islam had only the Egyptian fleet based on the Nile ports of Alexandria, Rosetta and Damietta, of which Rosetta was kept closed to Occidental merchants. It was sea-power that preserved the crusading ports, and it was a power based on commercial policies little influenced by religious qualms. James of Vitry, knowing well the circumstances of his diocese of Acre, wrote of the merchants: 'They more often join battle against one another than against the treacherous infidels and have more to do with trade and merchandise than with warring for Christ; they whose bold and warlike fathers were greatly dreaded by the infidels now cause them to be of good cheer and fear nought.'

Whatever the temporary dislocations, the invasions of the Mongols opened up wider trading possibilities. Their tolerance, at times encouragement, of Christian emissaries made for new commercial contacts. One of the first to realize these new possibilities was Hayton I of Armenia (1226–70). This intelligent man had come to the throne through his marriage, despite her opposition, with Isabel, daughter of Leon II. Hayton was eleven, his wife, already a widow, was fourteen at the time of this marriage that ended an ancient feud between the two rival houses of Armenia, the Roupenides and the Haytonides; but maturity came early in these fierce and precarious times, and the boy bridegroom was soon to show adroitness and perseverance in government. At first an ally of Kai-Qobad and his son Kai-Khusrau, he deserted the latter after his defeat by the Mongols and made his way to Karakorum to seek Mongol support. He contributed Armenian troops to the Mongol Syrian campaigns, and the Armenian port of Ayas or Lajazzo on the west shore of the gulf of Alexandretta became a great mart, rivalling Acre in the extent of its trade.

At Lajazzo it was Genoa that had the greatest advantages. Its support of Michael Palaeologus had brought it handsome, if not always continuous, dividends, and it had on the whole the patronage of his successors. Their trading stations in the Troad and at Lesbos and Chios gradually passed into their complete control. At Caffa in the Crimea they formed an important depot, which eventually became a strongly fortified town, and the centre of a flourishing Black Sea trade. It was in a Genoese ship from there that the Black Death is thought to have come to the West.

The fall of the Latin empire had been on the other hand a damaging blow to Venice, though they still retained many of their gains, Crete, Euboea, Modon and Coron on the south-west prong of Greece and, in semi-independence, the duchy of the Aegean Sea. This last was the creation of a remarkable man, Marco Sanudo, nephew through his mother of the doge Enrico Dandolo, and brother-in-law of the Nicaean emperor, Theodore Lascaris. From his capital at Naxos, where much of his building still remains, he extended his control over the southern Aegean, and established a dynasty that was to survive till the Turkish conquest of 1566. The Christian hold on the sea routes was well based, and had it been united would have been hard indeed to displace.

In 1256, a dispute that broke out in the narrow, close quarters of the Acre streets, where at a crossroad the Venetian, Genoese and Pisan quarters met, led to open warfare, in which Philip of Montfort, a nephew of the leader of the Albigensian crusade and on his mother's side an Ibelin, turned the long-established Venetians out of Tyre and backed the Genoese. The Templars supported Venice, the Hospitallers Genoa, and in June 1258 a great naval battle took place off Acre, in which the Venetians sank twenty-four Genoese ships. A papal legate and the queen dowager of Cyprus, Plaisance of Antioch, between them patched up an uneasy peace, but within three years Palaeologan aid restored Genoa's standing, and the suicidal struggle continued with another Venetian victory off Trapani in Sicily in 1264. Never was the intense local rivalry of Italian politics to be more fatally displayed, for while the two great republics heedlessly quarrelled, events elsewhere were moving rapidly.

SEQUEL TO THE FALL OF BAGHDAD

The fall of Baghdad led to a Mongol advance into Syria. Aleppo was occupied, and Hulagu moved on to Harenc, the frontier fortress that had been long in Moslem hands. The Franks were now to have an opportunity of revisiting it. Hayton of Armenia and his son-in-law, Bohemond VI of Antioch, came to Hulagu's camp, and rode beside him when, on 1 March

139 The castle of Harenc, the great strongpoint between Antioch and Aleppo. The slopes of the mound were paved with a stone glacis.

1260, he entered Damascus. It seemed as though a new era had opened. The local Christians, more akin to Mongol Nestorians than they had ever been to the followers of the Latin Church, found themselves for a rare moment in the ascendant. Kitbogha, the Mongol general left in charge when other happenings called Hulagu eastward, was a Christian, and might well look for Christian support. But in the discussion at Acre it was Venetian argument, stressing the economic importance of Egyptian trade, that was allowed to prevail. When Egypt moved against Kitbogha, free passage was given to the Egyptian army through Frankish territory. It encamped for several days outside Acre, and its generals were entertained inside the town. Among them was the Mamluk Rukn-ad-Did Baybars, already distinguished for his leadership at the battle of Gaza, who now noted the weakness of the defences. At Ain Jalut, near Nazareth, the traditional site of David's triumph over Goliath, the Mongol army was completely routed by the Egyptians and Kitbogha was captured and killed. The Mongol advance was checked, Islam triumphed, and within three months Baybars, having murdered the sultan with his own hand, had seized power in Cairo.

Brought up in the Mamluk guard, this tall, blue-eyed Turk was already a proven general. He was to show himself an astute, unscrupulous statesman, a distinguished patron of architecture, and a merciless and convinced foe to Christendom. Aware of his lack of title, he strengthened it by re-establishing the caliphate in Cairo. An uncle of the last caliph had escaped the massacre in Baghdad and Baybars installed him, receiving in return confirmation of his own position. In an elaborate diploma the new caliph gave his patron authority over Egypt, Syria, the Hejaz and Mesopotamia, and urged on him the duties of the Jihad. 'Through you God has preserved the defence of Islam from desecration . . . and your sword has inflicted incurable wounds on the hearts of the unbelievers.' It was shrewd propaganda both against the Mongols, the murderers of Baghdad, and against the Franks; it may well have brought some inner satisfaction to this grim, austere, self-made man. The Mongol allies, Armenia and Antioch, were his first objective, but, at the petition of Hayton, the Mongols sent a force and for the moment the Mamluks were driven back. The years that followed saw a gradual absorption of Frankish territory, Nazareth, Haifa, Arsuf, Caesarea, Safad and Toron. In 1266 it was again the turn of Armenia. Hayton hurried to the Mongol court at Tabriz, but in his absence his country was overrun, and the port of Lajazzo and his capital at Sis put to the sack. He returned to find his country devastated though not occupied, and leaving the kingship to his son, Leon III, he withdrew to the monastery of Trazargh near Sis. More clearly than any of the Franks,

204

140 Beatus initial: from the Riccardiana Psalter.

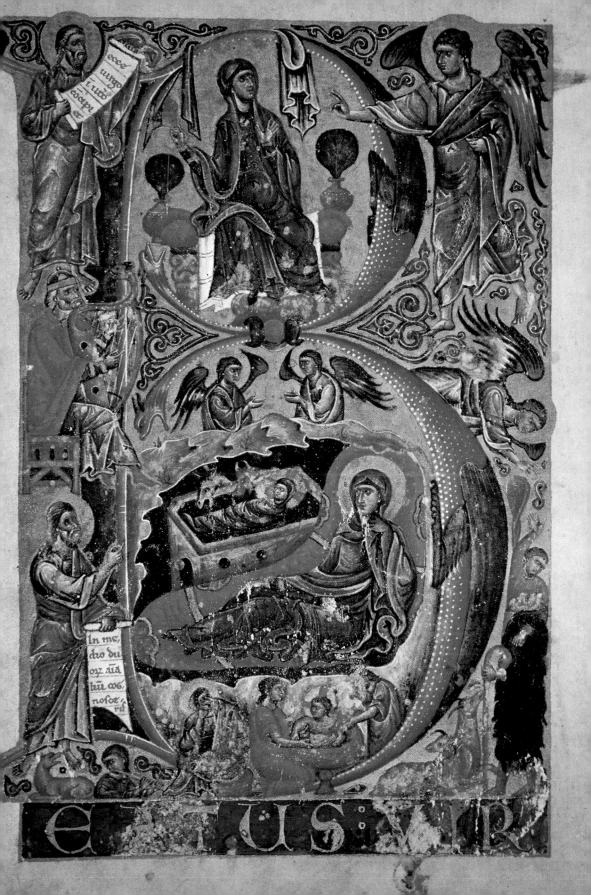

ecce
uirgo
t uo
cocpir
a...

In me
dio du
or aud
bu cog
noscer
....

E T US: VR

he had seen the possibility of the survival of the Christian states under Mongol protection, and even of the gradual conversion of those, already partially Christian, overlords.

In 1268 Jaffa fell. John of Ibelin, who had always enjoyed Moslem esteem, even that of Baybars, had died two years previously. His son Guy was a lesser figure. Disregarding treaties made with the father, Baybars seized the town. From there he marched north to Antioch. Bohemond VI was absent in Tripoli, and the garrison was insufficient to man the vast circumference of the walls. After a siege of only four days the Mamluks broke into the town. The massacre that followed equalled and avenged any that the crusaders had perpetrated. The booty amazed the conquerors. An Armenian scribe working 'in the God protected fortress of Horomkla' added a note to a Gospel book that 'Antioch was captured by the wicked king of Egypt and many were killed . . . the wonderful beauty of the holy and famous temples, houses of God, which were destroyed by fire is beyond the power of words.' It was the close of a long greatness. Now began Antioch's decline into a small township, and the traces of its splendour gradually disappeared as earthquakes shook down rock and earth from the slopes of Mount Silpius.

Hope for a moment arose in Acre. Louis of France had again taken the cross, but this time his ambitious brother, Charles of Anjou and Naples, diverted the campaign against Tunis. There had been a very grudging response to this new crusading propaganda in France. Even the faithful Joinville refused to accompany his master and argued that there was better service to God to be done in his own land. Charles meanwhile urged that a show of force would bring Tunis to Christianity, and Louis was persuaded and went to die of fever on the hillside above Carthage. Charles obtained a favourable treaty with the Tunisian emir. Of the crusaders only Edward of England continued his course to Palestine, and with his small force he could do nothing but urge the baronage to seek Mongol support, seeing more clearly than they the one remaining chance. Baybars feared him enough to send an Assassin to slay him (a similar emissary had recently slain Philip of Montfort in Tyre) but the prince was only wounded, and shortly after the incident returned to England.

With him in Acre had been Tedaldo Visconti, archdeacon of Liège, who had taken the cross when he was on a mission in London. While still in Palestine he received news that on 1 September 1271 he had been elected to the papacy. The efforts of this sincere and determined man, as pope Gregory X, to revive crusading fervour ennoble these last declining years of Outremer. A general Council was summoned to meet in Lyons in 1274, and in preparation for it the pope invited memoranda, not only

207

141 Tartars feasting, representing Gluttony in a late fourteenth-century Genoese work on the Seven Sins.

about the position in the East, on which he himself was well informed, but also on the likely reactions in Europe to crusading propaganda. One of these documents, probably by a Franciscan, Gilbert of Tournai, has received the unpromising title of *Collectio de Scandalis Ecclesiae*. The author had little use for the average crusader, 'soaked in wine, laden with vices . . . returning from the crusades and boasting of their prowess in their cups'. For such as these, whose sins forbid divine help, it is wrong to oppress the poor or despoil the Church. What is required in the Holy Land is a permanent mercenary force. Here he is voicing a view that was more and more generally held, and thoroughly justified by the disputes between crusaders. But how such a force was to be paid for was another matter, and the *Collectio*, in criticizing the use of crusading vows for penance and their redemption by money, attacks what had become a main item of crusading finance. The troubadours, many of whom had links with Provence and remembered the Albigensian crusade, had been more and more outspoken in their satirical verse. Frederick II, too, had had the poets' support. 'You make a truce with the Turks and Persians to kill French and Germans.' This cry against the Church was widely, brutally and sometimes wittily echoed. Even those who had the crusade at heart could find little comfort in papal exhortations. The poet Rutebeuf writing of his hero, Geoffrey of Sergines, St Louis's representative who had stayed on in Acre, exclaims that he can see no sign of succour being sent: 'the horses stumble and the rich men wheeze'.

Other and very different arguments were being used. God had shown his displeasure with the warlike crusades and had deserted even the pious Louis. Ever since St Francis had visited Damietta, the possibility of missions had been growing. 'Teach the Saracens their error and end this carnage.' This idea also figures in the songs, and even more in the minds of those seriously thinking over Eastern affairs and hearing also of the Mongol Christians. When three Tartar envoys appeared at Lyons and professed Christianity these hopes seemed to have some justification, though Gregory must well have known the implacable strength of Islam, and the fanaticism of its present leader, Baybars.

He did what he could. The Council, though only one crowned head, the boastful James of Aragon, was present, made careful plans for financing a crusade, not without some compromise over the sale of exemptions from vows. The old and infirm were encouraged to contribute money; collecting-boxes were placed in all the churches; bequests were encouraged. Only in Spain could other crusading indulgences be allowed and Ottokar of Bohemia's appeal for similar privileges for his border wars was firmly refused. Charles of Anjou was rebuked for his designs

142 Charles I of Anjou, by
Arnolfo di Cambio, *c.* 1277.
Charles succeeded in diverting
the crusade led by his brother
Louis IX of France, against Tunis.

against Byzantium and an embassy was received from Michael Palaeologus.
The whole problem of the crusade received a detailed review. The master
of the Temple urged that even a small force would be useful, and when
questioned about Egypt's sea-power said, probably truly enough, that
when Baybars had attempted to blockade Acre he had had only seventeen
galleys. Worn out by what must have been an intolerable and frustrating
labour, Gregory died at Arezzo on 10 January 1276. His inspiration gone,
his plans were haltingly pursued. Two years later, urged by the master of
the Temple, William of Beaujeu, Acre put itself under the protection of
Charles of Anjou, who was known to have a treaty and friendly relations
with Egypt. To the end the barons of Outremer were legalists, debating
the rival claims to the kingship of Jerusalem of Hugh III of Cyprus,
grandson of Hugh I and Alice of Champagne, and Maria, surprisingly
for those days an elderly spinster, daughter of Melisend of Lusignan, who
was the child of Isabella and Aimery. The marriages of queen Isabella
were still cause for confusion. Should the grandson of an elder sister have
priority over the daughter of a younger? Maria sold her claims to Charles
of Anjou, and his *bailli* was installed at Acre.

143 The Mongol khan Abagha (d. 1282) and his son Arghun (d. 1291). Abagha
married Maria Palaeologina, the daughter of the emperor, Michael Palaeologus.

144 The nun Melane, probably Maria Palaeologina, from a mosaic in the church of St Saviour in Chora (Kariye Cami), Istanbul.

Meanwhile the new Mongol khan, Abagha, was ready for Christian support. The Armenian alliance held good, and Michael Palaeologus had given him one of his daughters, another Maria, in marriage. The Mongols called her Despina Khatun, and showed her great respect. Her gentle, pious presence is a redeeming feature of the intrigues of the time. When her husband died she returned to Constantinople and built there the church still known as St Mary of the Mongols, one of the few churches that has been continuously in Christian use. She can be seen too in a mosaic in Kariye Cami, kneeling before Christ, and thus is a link with this marvellous expression of revived Byzantine art. But her influence on her

211

Mongol husband was never invoked by the Franks, and when in 1281 a Mongol army entered Syria, Acre made no move to join it, and instead made a treaty with Egypt. Baybars had died three years earlier, but Kalavun, his leading general, had displaced his son and ruled in his stead. The Hospitallers, under Nicholas Lorgne, always more aware of the true situation, gave the Mongols their only support with a contingent of knights and a raid from Marqab. Mamluks and Mongols met near Homs in October 1281. It was an indecisive battle, from which in the end both sides withdrew, but the Mongol power was not broken, and still threatened the militant Islam of Egypt. A Hospitaller, Joseph of Chauncey, writing to Edward I of England, could still urge that 'the Holy Land was never so easy of conquest as now', though in Acre they were short of men and hard-pressed for food. It had been a parched summer and much of the land now was untilled; and 'the king of Sicily will suffer no provisions to be sent out of his dominions into Syria because of his war with the Greeks'.

The great design of Charles of Anjou, in which the survival of Acre was a mere detail, was the conquest of Byzantium, the old Norman policy that he had inherited with Naples. But his ceaseless scheming was now brought to an abrupt halt. On 30 March 1282, the Sicilians rose in revolt against their Angevin master; soon Aragon was involved and the western Mediterranean had no time or energy for the East. It was a blow both to Acre and to Egypt, and it loosened any mutual interest between them. In May 1285, still at truce with the Franks, Kalavun besieged and took Marqab, avenging himself on Hospitaller help to the Mongols.

One last opportunity was given to Christendom. The Mongol khan, Arghun (1284–91), though not himself a Christian, sent messages to Rome, France and England with detailed plans for a joint, co-ordinated attack on the Mamluks. It was an offer that might have changed the course of history, but the papacy, without a man of Gregory's integrity to guide it, was more interested in technical details of Nestorian belief, and Philip of France and Edward of England were busy with their own affairs. Venetians and Genoese once more fought in Syrian waters, and in Tripoli, on the death of Bohemond VII, there was a dispute over the succession in which some of those involved appealed to Kalavun. It was a welcome excuse to dis-regard the treaty, and the Egyptian army marched north and took the town, massacring the inhabitants, and laying waste the port. While Baybars rebuilt and maintained the castles and inland towns, a genuine resettlement of the country, the westward-looking ports were to be allowed no chance of revival.

Acre awaited its fate, but not without some spirit. In 1286, with no hope from Naples, it had reverted to Cypriot rule, and the young king Henry

145 The Mongol khan Arghun with his two wives and his son Ghazan, who stands to the left of the throne.

was crowned at Tyre and fêted in Acre. For a fortnight there were tourneys and pageants 'and many other games fine and delectable and pleasant'. The knights dressed as women and enacted the battle of the Amazons, no doubt much as it is represented in the pages of the *Histoire Universelle*. The gaiety and romance was indeed deep-seated. Then in 1290 there was a riot in these narrow, noisy streets. A band of north Italians, an unruly lot, the poor, grotesque product of half-hearted papal preaching, had in their enthusiasm killed some Moslem merchants, surprised no doubt to find how freely these circulated in this Christian town. Kalavun at once prepared to strike, vowing he would not leave a Christian alive in the city. But as he set out from Cairo it was he himself who died. His son al-Ashraf resumed the campaign in the spring of 1291, bringing an army, which, if the figures given are clearly exaggerated, was a very considerable one, a final tribute to Frankish prowess. On 18 May the city fell. The defenders had fought well. William of Beaujeu, whose pro-Egyptian policy was now so bloodily proved false, fell in a last counter-attack. Some escaped, Henry of Cyprus among them; most perished. The crusading kingdom ended as it had begun, in pillage and carnage.

146 The harbour of Alanya, showing the Red Tower and the fortification which rises to the citadel. It was built by Ala-ad-Din-Kai-Qobad between 1226 and 1231.

147 The fort at Alexandria: a sketch made in 1742.

Rhodes and Cyprus 8

Pope Nicholas IV was already busied with crusading propaganda when the news of the fall of Acre reached him. Earlier in the year he had issued a bull forbidding, under pain of excommunication and perpetual loss of civic rights, all trading of any kind with the sultan. It was a policy that had to a lesser degree already been enunciated, and it was hopeless to look for any complete acceptance of it, but never before had the prohibition been so fully stated, and it was to remain a much-quoted document. It had the full support of Charles II of Naples, the pope's vassal and ally, who had succeeded his father in 1285 and now disowned the pro-Egyptian policy that had hitherto characterized Angevin designs. He urged that the maintenance of a fleet in the eastern Mediterranean to enforce the blockade would be far more feasible than any *passagium generale* or full-scale military attack. He also urged that the military orders, whose disputes had been so notorious, should be unified under one rule, a view that found considerable support. The pope as an earnest of his interest sent a fleet of twenty galleys to Cyprus, to which king Henry added fifteen more. Their aim was to aid Armenia, obviously the next Egyptian objective, but the place chosen for attack was the Karamanian stronghold of Alanya, opposite the Cypriot coast, and of little defensive import against Egypt. The great Red Tower of the port was stormed, but the walled hill-town held out, and the Christian fleet, abandoning Alanya, made a hesitant attack on Alexandria. Nothing came of it, but these ventures were to be the basis of later Cypriot policy.

In April 1292, Nicholas IV died, and there were two years of dispute among the cardinals as to his successor, ending in a desperately pious solution in the election of the inexperienced hermit Celestine V. Meanwhile, in the eastern Mediterranean little had been learnt by the Christians.

Armenia was filled with civil disputes; in the harbour at Lajazzo the Genoese defeated a Venetian fleet, capturing twenty-five ships; the Ibelin family at Episcopi in Cyprus were raided by a Genoese landing party who carried some of them away as prisoners. In the case of these Italian ventures, which lacked firm control from their city-states, there was no clear-cut distinction between piracy and warfare. Al-Ashraf Khalil, the Egyptian sultan, was murdered in 1293, but no advantage was taken of a time of turmoil in Cairo. In the West, emotions were roused by detailed accounts from survivors of the atrocities of the sack of Acre. But from the end of 1294, the papacy, under the determined and cynical rule of Boniface VIII, was too busied with its own problems to heed the reproaches against its lack of crusading fervour. Looking back on these years Dante wrote that the papal enemies were Christians, not those who conquered Acre or traded with the sultan's lands. Yet it was a period in which there were still hopes and possibilities. In 1299 a Mongol army, with Armenian and Georgian detachments, had swept down through Syria, and for a brief period held Jerusalem, entrusting it to the Georgians. The Mongols had summoned help from Cyprus, and both the military orders organized expeditions, but nothing came of them save sporadic raids on Egypt and the Syrian coast. Then, in 1304, the Mongol khan, Ghazan, declared for Islam as the official faith of his people. This was the end of the tentative missionary efforts of the West. Too late, men were realizing that conversion by teaching and persuasion, and by strengthening Eastern Christian communities, might play a great part in the relations of East and West. The papacy had formed an outline scheme of Eastern archbishoprics, based on travellers' accounts. In far Cathay a most remarkable Franciscan, Giovanni of Monte Corvino, had created a considerable community and had been appointed by Clement V archbishop and patriarch of the whole East. But by the mid-fourteenth century this branch of the Church had lost its original fervour, its last archbishop was murdered and nothing more was heard of it. Elsewhere there were martyrs. Even during St Francis's lifetime some friars had been tortured to death at Ceuta in Tunisia, and now in 1315 the Catalan, Raymond Lull, who understood better than most the possibilities of work by competently trained missionaries, was, at the age of eighty-two, stoned to death at Bugia, on the North African coast.

In Greece, Catalans of a very different stamp were making their mark. The Morea had declined in power under absentee Angevin overlords; the force and panache of Frankish Greece was represented by the de la Roche family in Athens. Under Guy II a great festival of three weeks' jousting was held there in 1304, with a splendour and gaiety strangely at variance

148 Martyrdom of Franciscan monks at Ceuta in Morocco: fresco by Ambrogio Lorenzetti. With the growth of missionary activity there were many martyrdoms in North Africa and in the Far East. The subject was a topical one in Siena, for a Sienese brother, the blessed Pietro, had been martyred in India in 1322.

with the departed glories of Outremer. Here too it was jousting on the eve of disaster. Guy died without a son in 1308, and was succeeded by Walter of Brienne, grandson of the heroic count of Jaffa, great-grand-nephew of John of Brienne, one time king-consort of Jerusalem, and heir to Athens through his mother; here was another family that found new scope by moving East. In 1311, under this Walter, the Franks of Athens received a crushing defeat at the hands of the Catalan Grand Company, a band of mercenaries that had been employed by the Palaeologi, but had earned their masters' distrust and been driven out to seek for new fields of action. For three-quarters of a century they were to rule in Athens, and their castles at Livadia and Salona still recall their power. Walter was killed in the battle, and twenty years later his son Walter, to become famous as the Florentine Duke of Athens, made an unsuccessful attempt to regain

217

his father's duchy, with the sad consequence that the Catalans as a pre-
cautionary measure pulled down the great castle at Thebes, which under
the family of St Omer had been the chief seat of Graeco-Frankish culture.

In Cyprus, the course of history was little more peaceful. In 1306 king
Henry II's brother, Aimery, organized a *coup* against him and ruled as
governor until, in 1310, he was stabbed to death by one of his own most
trusted supporters. In the opening of these disputes the Templars had
supported Aimery, the Hospitallers the king. It was the last chance of
rivalry between the orders. They both held lands in Cyprus, to which they
had withdrawn with any of their members who had escaped the débâcle on
the mainland. Their central administration was in confusion, but they
retained their great financial network throughout Europe. Both were
aware that they were under criticism and that there were many pressures
for uniting them. In 1306, James of Molay, the new grand master of the
Temple, elected in Cyprus, was summoned to Avignon, where he presented a document on his views as to his order's future. It is an unimpressive
series of arguments against union, and shows little sense of urgency in

formulating new policies. The master of the Hospital, Fulk of Villaret, was also summoned to Avignon, and his report is a more detailed survey of crusading possibilities: he himself, delayed by a new undertaking, did not reach France till 31 August 1307, a week after the pope had announced an inquiry into the order of the Temple.

The four years' agony of the Templars, with trial, torture and execution constantly taken over by the king's officers, is a miserable story. The accusations of blasphemy and sodomy in their initiation rites were almost common form in the procedures of the time. No doubt in this celibate order, leading a camp life, in constant often friendly contacts with Islam, there was much licence of speech, probably also homosexual attachments. In the policies of the Kingdom, they had often played for their own hand. But the accusations on which they were condemned, admitted under torture and then repudiated, were a farrago of nonsense directed to the satisfaction of salacious popular imaginings. The real aim was their wealth, above all its concentration in the Temple at Paris, the great stronghold of the order. Clement V, constantly outplayed by Philip's advisers, sought to save something for the Church by the transfer of the Temple property to the Hospital. Philip agreed subject to the latter order also being investigated. It was a sinister clause, but the Hospital had by then taken action to give new lustre to its name. On 5 August 1307 Clement issued a confirmation of the order's possession of Rhodes, 'that island which, not without great labours, outlay and expense you have taken under your powerful arm, and which today by God's grace you hold, having driven thence the schismatics and completely overthrown the infidel.'

While still a Byzantine possession, Rhodes had already been talked of as a new outpost for crusading endeavour. In 1249 it had been momentarily occupied by the Genoese aided by William of Villehardouin, but had soon been regained by the Nicaean emperor, John Vatatzes. More recently there had been Arab raids on the island and some occupation of it. There were both schismatics and infidels to be attacked. In June 1306, in surreptitious league with a Genoese pirate, the Hospitallers had sent a small force against the island. The knights had shown awareness of the need to develop a fleet, and, under a new officer, the Admiral, had been acquiring ships. Now these were to be put to use. There are uncertainties about the conquest, and Clement's statement in September 1307 that they held the island may have been premature, but by 1309 the town of Rhodes had become the new headquarters of the order.

During the first half of the fourteenth century there was, however, much criticism of the order's comparative inactivity. The assignment of the Templars' lands to the Hospital was a considerable cause of jealousy, and also of considerable obstruction, by the states concerned, to the Hospitallers' new claims. From France in particular little came to the order, except writs for debts due to the crown. Marino Sanudo, writing in 1329, estimated that responsions, the technical name for remissions from their estates, brought into the Hospital an annual income of 180,000 florins, from which much more action could be expected. But the reorganization of their finances after the loss of Palestine; the cost of the capture and fortification of Rhodes; the building up of a navy; the settlement of several of the islands of the Dodecanese; and trading readjustments so as to exclude Rhodian war material going to the Egyptians, particularly wood for shipbuilding in Alexandria, are ample explanations of the comparatively minor raids carried out by the knights. In 1320 they owed 500,000 florins to the Bardi and Peruzzi houses, and it is clear that, as so often, critics of their wealth took little account of their commitments. The debt to the bankers was gradually met, and by the mid-century the knights were in credit with the Italians. Then, in 1343, the Peruzzi failed, followed three years later by the Bardi. These famous bankruptcies which shook the whole financial system of Europe were a serious blow to the knights who lost about 360,000 florins. This was followed by the years of the Black Death, with the consequent impoverishment of many estates and reductions in the responsions from them.

The long mastership of Hélion of Villeneuve (1319–46) could in fact show considerable achievements. Ludolf of Suchem, who visited Rhodes under his mastership, describes the city as built with high walls and impregnable advance works, 'out of huge stones, which it would seem impossible were placed by human hands'. This implies that the curtain and lower outer wall, as they still in places exist, had already been built,

152 The street of the Knights in Rhodes, as restored by the Italians in the 1920s. It is one of the finest medieval streets in existence.

and that much of it was re-used classical material. Hélion's arms can still be found on the walls, but reset, so that they do not date the work where they are now placed. An English traveller in 1345, writes that the master is 'one of the lords of the world, that he has 400 knights with him, and all the artificers necessary to a city or royal castle. In the hospital the sick are cared for, and Christians assemble from every part of the world to fight against the Turks or Saracens.'

There had been one substantial success, the capture of Smyrna, or at least of the castle controlling the port, in 1344. Smyrna in 1261 had been assigned by the Palaeologi as a sphere of influence for the Genoese, who also held Chios. There was, however, a break between the Genoese and Byzantium in 1328, and during this dispute Smyrna was occupied by the emir of Aydin, one of the independent Turkoman emirates that had grown up among the ruins of the Selchukid empire. Umur of Aydin was a young leader of considerable ability. From Smyrna his fleet raided as far as Greece, at one point laying siege to the castle of Bodonitsa; furthermore he was working in alliance with the emperor, Andronicus III. It was a situation highly disruptive to Christian trade in the Aegean and Clement VI's crusading enthusiasm found here an objective. The Hospitallers had been active in the Aegean, defeating Umur's father in a battle off Chios in 1319 in which they had provided twenty-three ships. Clement, notwithstanding, had been rebuking them for their idle and luxurious lives in Rhodes and exhorting them to further effort. They provided six galleys for the Smyrna expedition and eventually were entrusted with the charge of the port. Umur was killed in 1348 in an attempt to retake the port castle and a precarious hold, sufficient to provide an invaluable naval base, was maintained till in 1402 Timur and his Mongols captured Smyrna.

Elsewhere other Turkish powers were taking shape, as the Selchukid empire, whose history had in time so closely corresponded to that of the Kingdom, gradually disintegrated. A Turkoman leader, Mohammed ibn-Karaman, built up an independent domain in the south, and in 1328 the Karamanids occupied Konya. Two years earlier, in the north, Brusa had been captured by another Turkoman leader, Orkhan, whose followers came to be known as Ottomans. Constantinople, or rather one party in the disputes over the empire, regarded them as possible allies, and in 1345 the elderly Orkhan married Theodora, daughter of the emperor John VI Cantacuzenus, a match which did not prevent him in 1356, at the end of his long career, from occupying Gallipoli. His son Murad I extended his conquests in Europe, and also kept in check the Karamanian power on his southern borders. A new and decisive factor had appeared in the eastern waters, but for the time being its full significance was not appreciated.

222

153 Christ leading the crusaders: from a fourteenth-century Apocalypse.

The fourteenth century is the great age of Cyprus. Famagusta, hitherto a small port, became a great emporium for Eastern goods: it was 'the furthest of Christian lands, so that all ships and all wares, be they what they may, and come they from what part of the sea they will, must needs come first to Cyprus, and in no way can they pass it by, and pilgrims from every country journeying to the lands over the seas must touch at Cyprus'. Refugees came from all parts, some of them poverty-stricken and needing succour, such as those rescued by Cypriot ships when the Mamluks captured Lajazzo in Armenia; others took to profitable trades, and with the resilience of these Near-Eastern peoples, prospered in them. The Lakha family in Famagusta entertained king Peter I to a banquet whose lavishness became a legend, and founded a Nestorian church, probably that of St Peter and St Paul still standing, with its triple semicircular apses set in a square base, its vaulted nave and aisles, and its finely carved angels on the consoles of its north doorway.

Opposite this church, across the small central square, stands the cathedral of St Nicholas, with its twin, though unfinished towers, its sharply pitched gables over the porches, and its splendid west window, whose tracery belongs to that phase of French art when the geometric style was used with great freedom, but had not yet passed into the flowing lines of curvilinear. The central doorway has niches for column figures, but these, if ever installed, have not survived Turkish iconoclasm. The chevet

154 Kantara castle, built in the late thirteenth century. It guards the long promontory of the Karpass in north-east Cyprus.

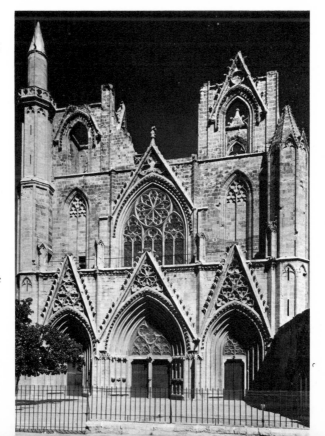

155 West façade of Famagusta cathedral which was built in the fourteenth century.

with its three apses rising the full height of nave and aisles is an impressive architectural concept, completing the great silhouette that commands this ruined city of dead churches. Inside, whitewashed for its use as a mosque, it lacks the colour and variety which it must have held when it was the crowning place of the Lusignan kings. There is little trace of elaborate carving, and probably the decoration was mainly paintings – there was certainly a lively school of painting on the island but now only dim and damaged patches of frescoes survive. The prime mover in building the cathedral was bishop Guy of Ibelin; at his death in 1308, he left 20,000 bezants for the work. By 1311 this sum had been expended, and Guy's successor in the see of Famagusta, Baldwin Lambert, marked the progress of the work by an inscription on a buttress by the south doorway. The date of completion is uncertain, but the consistency of the work suggests a fairly steady and continuous programme. Scattered throughout the now largely empty space enclosed by the Venetian walls are many other churches, some identifiable as Orthodox or Armenian, Franciscan or Carmelite, among them the gaunt but lovely Gothic skeleton of St George of the Latins, whose vaults were destroyed in the bombardment of 1571, but whose masonry and carvings are some of the finest in Cyprus. Whatever the harshness of the Cypriot Latin Church – in 1358 the intransigence of the legate Peter Thomas provoked a riot in Nicosia and a rebuke from the king in Famagusta – the various Christian churches were allowed to build and adorn their places of worship.

While St Nicholas of Famagusta was being built, St Sophia of Nicosia was completed by archbishop John del Conte (1318–32). He added the west porch, and the carving of the doorways probably dates from his time. The foliage is a full, crinkled leaf, a little heavy and coarse, which became the characteristic feature of Cypriot decorative work, a clumsy adaptation of Gothic forms to make a native masonry tradition. On either side of the doorways are flat niches, which must be designed for paintings, and carved above them two hands holding crowns, presumably those of saints and martyrs. In 1948 the crumbling plasterwork of the central tympanum was repaired, and underneath it were found, marvellously intact, three rows of voussoir figures, fifty-eight kings, queens, prophets and bishops. Figure and niche are carved from the same block. The mason who directed the carving knew something of French patterns, and gestures from Rheims are clumsily interpreted by not very skilful workmen. But there is a charming, provincial naïvety about these little figures, so strangely preserved, the largest assembly of Western figure sculpture in the eastern Mediterranean. Unfortunately Moslem susceptibility requires that most of them shall normally be kept boarded over.

226

SAINT SOPHIA, NICOSIA

156–9 Details from the west porch
showing: the porch as fully uncovered in
1948, a censing angel, a queen and a
prophet.

Elsewhere, in Nicosia, there were many churches, and close to the cathedral, a strange triple church, with some figure carving and Gothic vaulting, presents some nice problems as to its use and origin. Our Lady of Tyre, now an Armenian church, has a remarkable collection of the incised tombstones with which the Cypriots commemorated themselves. But of the eighty churches that are recorded there, many perished when, in face of the Turkish menace in 1567, the Venetians decided to withdraw the town within a new and shorter circuit of ramparts, those that exist today, and to flatten to the ground everything beyond them. In particular the great Dominican church was pulled down, the centre of an order very powerful in the island and one of its less conciliatory elements. The royal palace adjoining it, famed for its great rooms, balconies, golden ornaments, tapestries, pictures, organs, clocks, baths, gardens and menageries, was also sacrificed to the desperate need of defence. Only occasional carved doorways and a splendid curvilinear window preserved in the medieval museum recall the domestic magnificence of an over-luxurious régime.

It was in these two main towns that most of Cypriot medieval buildings were carried out. Cathedrals were built at Limassol and Paphos, but little remains of them. In the villages many of the small Byzantine churches continued unaltered. Even the great monastery of Stavrovouni, conspicuous on its hilltop, with its great relic, the cross of the penitent thief, hanging in the air without visible support, was mainly Byzantine in con-

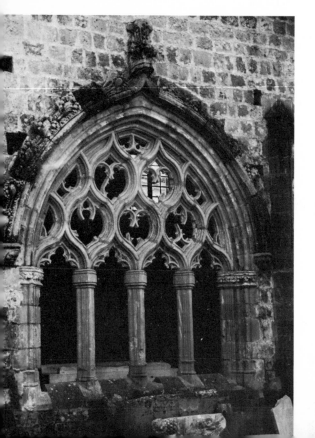

160 A window from the Lusignan palace at Nicosia. The palace was demolished in 1879.

161 The cloisters of the Premonstratensian abbey of Bellapais. Two Roman sarcophagi have been re-used as lavabos.

162 A view over the northern plain from a Gothic window in the castle of St Hilarion.

struction. The notable exception is the Premonstratensian abbey of Bellapais. It was much patronized by Hugh III (1267–84); the main buildings date from his reign, though the great refectory and cloisters were probably added in the following century, when Hugh IV frequently visited it and added 'marvellous apartments'. Its Gothic beauty fits admirably into the sloping hillside with the green of its olive and carob trees; below is the sea and beyond, on a clear day, the Turkish coast.

The surviving castles of Cyprus, with the exception of Kyrenia, show curiously little trace of Frankish work. In the upper part of St Hilarion there was some extension of the living quarters, and a fine Gothic window still provides a wide view of the coastal plain. Inaccessible Buffavento required little increase in defence work. Kantara was enlarged under James I to keep guard against Genoese expansion from Famagusta, and its horse-shoe towers may date from this period. After the sack of Limassol by the Genoese in 1373, a new castle was constructed in the shell of a thirteenth-century church, a striking example of new priorities. Kyrenia, which figures so constantly in Cypriot history, often in its sinister role as a prison, had less natural defence on its sea promontory than the castles of the hills. Throughout the thirteenth century the Franks rebuilt and enlarged, probably intensifying the work after the fall of Acre. In its great siege of 1374 by the Genoese, it resisted attack both by land and sea. When the Venetians added to its defences, they retained much of the earlier work.

The life of the island ranged from the wealthy luxury of the court and great merchants to the poverty of the local peasantry. Slaves were brought from Greece and Turkey and, the chronicler Makhairas (writing some time after 1426) tells us, were so brutally treated that many were driven to suicide. Justice gave way to intrigue; Famagusta was a sink of unnatural vice. Yet Makhairas, while he makes these strictures, admires the bravery and vigour of his heroes, Peter I and James I. He was a lively product of this mixed society; he wrote in the local Greek dialect but used Latin sources and Latin romantic methods of narrative. His story is full of strongly marked characters, great undertakings and sudden changes of fortune.

The reign of Peter I (1359–69) was the climax of Cyprus's power and repute. He came to the throne at the age of thirty, much under the influence of the papal legate, Peter Thomas, who crowned him in Famagusta. This legate was a man of rigid piety, fanatically devoted to crusading ideals, who had risked the dangers of a solitary journey to Jerusalem and then as Latin patriarch of Constantinople travelled over much of the eastern Mediterranean. Questions of the union of the churches made the patriarchate more than a nominal post, but Thomas's fierce intolerance of any schismatics made him little suited to negotiations, and early in his reign Peter had to curb his ruthless treatment of the Cypriot Orthodox Church. Equally under his influence was the king's friend Philip de Mézières, whom he made his chancellor. Both men were eager for exploits against the infidel; Peter, while praying before the Holy Cross in the monastery at Stavrovouni, had a vision urging him to war against the unbeliever. In him the religious intensity of earlier times revived. No psychological interpretations disturbed these men's trust in their emotional experiences bred of conviction, sentiment and sense of guilt. Already, as heir to the throne, he had founded a new order, the Knights of the Sword, half a band of followers, half a pledge to crusading endeavour. An opening came from Armenia. The death of Leon IV in 1342 had brought to an end the Haytonian dynasty. Constant inter-marriages had linked the Cypriot and Armenian royal houses, and Leon was succeeded by Guy, a son of Aimery of Lusignan, the ambitious brother of Henry II, who for a time (1306–10) had usurped the Cypriot throne.

Armenian power was by now reduced to the mountain capital of Sis and a precarious hold of the coast. External dangers, however, could not restrain their civil turbulence, and Guy was assassinated in 1344. In 1361 it was a usurping ruler, Constantine, who offered the port of Gorhigos, with its island castle, to the Cypriot king, being himself unable to defend it. Of the neighbouring Moslem states, Antalya and Alanya no longer had the prestige acquired in the previous century when they were the favourite residence of Ala-ad-Din Kai-Qobad. Now they were minor emirates, dependent on and jealous of the power of the Karamanids who had carved out a Turkoman state on the northern slopes of the Taurus mountains. Gorhigos was an encouragement to further action, and Peter aided by the Hospitallers surprised and captured Antalya and exacted recognition from the emir of Alanya. The nearest ports on the mainland, outlets for the trade of Asia Minor, were now in Cypriot control.

The second undertaking was on a larger and more exacting scale. Between October 1362 and June 1365 Peter toured the courts of Europe: Venice, Milan, Genoa, Avignon, the Rhine towns, Paris, London, Bordeaux, Prague, Cracow, and back to Venice. The legate Peter Thomas and Philip de Mézières both accompanied him. This young and handsome king, 'the athlete of Christ', whose own dominions were the bulwark of Christendom, awoke new crusading enthusiasms, though the cautious monarchs of the West were not ready to commit themselves personally. In the summer of 1365, 165 vessels were assembled at Rhodes. The secret of their destination had been well kept, and it was not known till they were under sail that they were directed against Alexandria. It was a bold move, not without some political sense. Egypt was at the time weakly governed, and if Alexandria could be captured and held, Mediterranean trade would be in Christian hands, and Cairo so weakened that an inland campaign against it might be possible. To Peter and his closest circle Jerusalem certainly remained the ultimate aim. The surprise was effective. The inhabitants even came out to barter with the ships, thinking it was some great merchant flotilla. The landing was effected and the town was stormed. Then followed days of hideous massacre and pillage. The gates had been destroyed in the attack, and Peter had failed to demolish the bridge on the Cairo road before reinforcements had arrived to hold it. He found himself with a council of leaders over whom he had little control and who

163 Carved inscription commemorating the capture of Antalya by Peter I of Cyprus on St Bartholomew's Day, 23 August 1361.

were anxious only to depart with their booty. His plans to restore the defences and hold the city were unheeded, and in the end he had to return, by a storm-tossed passage, to Cyprus.

It was long before Alexandria recovered. Venice and the trading states were indignant at the course of events, and disowned all knowledge of the attack. Revenge on Cyprus became the key of Egyptian policy, and in the West, though some enthusiasm was aroused, many realized it had been but a plundering raid, and abandoned hope of the Holy Land or else looked for other profitable undertakings. The next two crusading expeditions, those of Amadeus of Savoy and Louis of Bourbon, were directed respectively to the aid of Constantinople and to a raid on al-Mahdiya in Tunis.

Meanwhile the Ottoman menace grew. In 1396 a crusading army of approximately 100,000 men set out to conquer the whole of Turkey, and to march into the kingdom of Syria and the Holy Land. In the Danube valley at Nicopolis they met the Turkish army, and were completely routed. Rarely has an army been so totally destroyed. After it there was never again serious hope that a Western army could regain Jerusalem.

The end of Peter was a tragic one. He returned to rumours of his wife's infidelity, while she in her turn had been brutally handling his mistress in the hope of causing a miscarriage. The queen, Eleanor of Aragon, was a fierce, passionate, courageous woman, devoted it seems to her husband,

164 Kyrenia castle, from the harbour. Kyrenia, which has buildings of Byzantine,

however she might at times pay out his many amours with some of her own. Domestic disturbance and endless negotiations as the aftermath of the Alexandrian expedition soured Peter into morose and tyrannical cruelty. In the early morning of 17 January 1369, some of the nobles penetrated to his sleeping apartment and brutally murdered him. His two brothers, John, prince of Antioch, and James, constable of Jerusalem (for they clung to old, meaningless titles), were privy to the conspiracy, though probably not intending murder. Eleanor was determined on vengeance but bided her time. Meanwhile she wrote to the courts of Europe, where the murder made no little stir, and appealed to Genoa for intervention on her behalf. It was a useful pretext. In 1373 the Genoese sent a fleet to Cyprus and overran the island. This was more than Eleanor had bargained for; she escaped from her Genoese allies, and fled to Kyrenia where James the constable was holding out against the invaders. Kyrenia, after a siege of some months, was still untaken, but in the end had to come to terms. Famagusta was handed over to Genoa, with an indemnity of 900,000 ducats. The constable was carried off to prison in Genoa as a hostage for its payment, while Eleanor, luring the prince of Antioch to dine with her, suddenly displayed Peter's bloody shirt and had him dispatched by her guards. Her son, Peter II, now of age and married to Valentina Visconti, wisely sent his mother back to Aragon, where she reached a ripe and apparently peaceful old age.

Lusignan and Venetian construction, has been a place of many sieges.

Amid these fierce doings, another family came to a sorry end. Among those executed by the Genoese as participants in Peter's murder was Philip of Ibelin, seneschal of the kingdom. The story went that he would have been pardoned, but that his wife had become the mistress of the Genoese commander and demanded her husband's death. He was the last of the Ibelins to play any prominent part in the affairs of Cyprus, a kingdom where five women of his family had been queens.

The cession of Famagusta marked the beginning of the decline of Cyprus. The Genoese monopoly reduced its trade, and also ruined the fiscal system of the island. James the Constable, who succeeded his nephew Peter in 1393, was a hardworking, sensible man, who did something to reorganize the island and to contain the power of Genoa. In 1373 Antalya had been surrendered to the Turks as it was impossible to hold it in the Genoese crisis. This was the final blow to the kingdom of Armenia. In 1375 it was overrun from Aleppo and Leon V, a Lusignan by blood, was carried off to captivity in Cairo. Released in 1382, he wandered the courts of Europe, seeking support; he died in 1393, a pensioner of France, leaving his empty title to his cousin, James of Cyprus.

THE LOSS OF RHODES

Another voice still proclaimed the obligations of a crusade towards these waning kingdoms. The implacable Peter Thomas, who had taken part in the raid on Alexandria, died shortly afterwards, and miracles were soon occurring at his tomb, but Philip de Mézières lived on. Absent from Cyprus at the time of Peter's murder, he decided it was wiser not to return. Withdrawing to the convent of the Celestines in Paris, he busied himself with writing till his death in 1405, pouring out a great corpus of crusading theory and propaganda, much of it full of sound, experienced advice. But his was a lone voice. Nicopolis proved his contention for unified command and the need of dedicated religious zeal, but Europe was finally disillusioned as to the Via Sancti Sepulchri. It was well for Philip that he did not live to see the revenge of the Mamluks on Cyprus, when, in 1426, on the battle-field of Khirokitia, Janus, the young king, was captured and taken in chains to Cairo, and Nicosia was occupied and sacked. Makhairas the chronicler was in charge of the wine at the battle, and the horror of the times lives in his pages.

In Latin Greece the Ottoman raids into Thessaly turned the Catalans into a frontier post of Christendom, rather than the often excommunicated dispossessors of the legal heirs to the princes of Achaia. In 1372 pope Gregory XI summoned the Latin rulers of Greece to a conference at Thebes to discuss measures against the Turks. The conference never met,

165 Philip de Mézières presents his plea for a new crusade to Richard II. The Lamb was the emblem of the order of chivalry, the Order of the Passion, that de Mézières hoped would be established to further the crusade.

but the proposal marks a change in policy. In 1377 the Hospitallers acquired the town of Vonitza in Epirus. Greece had always been of some interest to them, and in 1349 they had occupied a fortified position in Negroponte. In 1377 the new master of the order, provided to the post by the authority of Gregory XI, was an Aragonese, Fernández de Heredia, who already in Aragon and at Avignon had shown considerable, if self-seeking, diplomatic skill, and was well aware of the conflicting Spanish interests in the Peloponnese. He had too a learned interest in classical Greek literature and had commissioned the translation of parts of Plutarch and Thucydides into Aragonese. The exact intentions of a small force of Hospitallers led by him from Vonitza remains uncertain. It was directed against the Albanians, who now occupied the northern shore of the gulf of Corinth. Lepanto was taken, but turning northwards, Heredia was ambushed and captured. The order, indignant already at Gregory's appointment of him, now had to find his ransom. When Heredia returned to Rhodes, a dissident

235

brother attempted to stab him during a meeting of the order in its church of St John. Despite these internal disturbances, the knights continued their interest in Greece and, in 1378, in order to strengthen their forces, enlisted some 150 men of the Navarese Company, a mercenary band unemployed in a pause in the Hundred Years War. In 1379, the Navarese, acting in their own interest, seized Thebes from the Catalans. The folly of this sordid, unprincipled strife between so-called Christians repeats the miserable story of the last years of the Kingdom.

The great defeat at Nicopolis, in which Heredia's successor, Philibert of Naillac, led a detachment of Hospitallers, left the Ottoman menace unimpeded. The following year the Hospitallers occupied Corinth and for seven years manned its fortifications. It is arguable that this defence, initiated by an appeal from the Greek despot of Mistra, preserved the Morea for another fifty years of Greek and Latin rule, and allowed the Florentine family of Acciaiuoli to replace the Catalans in Athens for a period of some prosperity and much family dispute, until the Turks entered the city on 4 June 1456. More important than any doings in Athens, it protected also the last flowering of Byzantine civilization in Mistra, where many of the churches, some with traces of Western influence, and their superb frescoes are the product of the early fifteenth century, a time when the despotate reabsorbed much of the Morea. Then, on 16 January 1449, the despot Constantine Palaeologus was crowned emperor in Mistra's cathedral of St Demetrius, with its great painted figure of the Virgin looking down from the apse on this moment of glory for a doomed hero who, on 29 May 1453, was to fall gallantly in the Kerkoporta postern as the Turks entered Constantinople.

Before that great disaster, a dividing mark in history however long foreseen, there had been a time of respite for which the overthrow of the Ottomans by Timur and his Mongol hordes, a conquest that led to no lasting settlement on the shores of the Mediterranean, was largely responsible. In 1402, as the Mongols swept over Asia Minor, Smyrna was taken from the Christians. The loss of any port on these shores was a blow to European commerce, and Philibert of Naillac, master of the Hospital from 1396 to 1421, was anxious to regain some hold on the mainland. He occupied Bodrum, opposite the island of Cos, already held by the order, and thereby controlled one of the main channels used by coasting vessels. The castle he built there has a special interest, for the materials were drawn from the Mausoleum of Halicarnassus, which the knights found a ruin, and which they proceeded to use as a quarry. Fragments of sculpture were built into the walls, but when in 1522, in a last effort to strengthen the castle, the knights, excavating for stone, found the tomb chamber, 'a fine

166 The castle of the Hospitallers at Bodrum (Halicarnassus) on the western coast of Asia Minor.

large square apartment, ornamented all round with columns of marble, with their bases, capitals, architrave, frieze and cornice engraved and sculptured in half relief', they for a time 'entertained their fancy with the singularity of the sculpture and then destroyed it.' Fra Sabba da Castiglione in 1505 was more of an antiquarian and sent off to his patron, Isabella d'Este, a marine monster lasciviously embracing a nymph 'lately found amongst the ruins of Halicarnassus'.

Meanwhile Rhodes was no longer a springboard for attack but on the defensive. In 1426, the Mamluks had taken their revenge on Cyprus for the sack of Alexandria and, in 1444, they laid siege for forty days to Rhodes. The attack was most fiercely concentrated on the north-east, from the bay of Mandraki, and it was here that the master, Raymond Zacosta (1461–67), built the great round tower of St Nicholas, with a polygonal outer wall and gunports in each of its twenty sides. A liberal grant from Philip of Burgundy financed the work, and from now on fortifications and guns were to have the first claim on the order's resources.

237

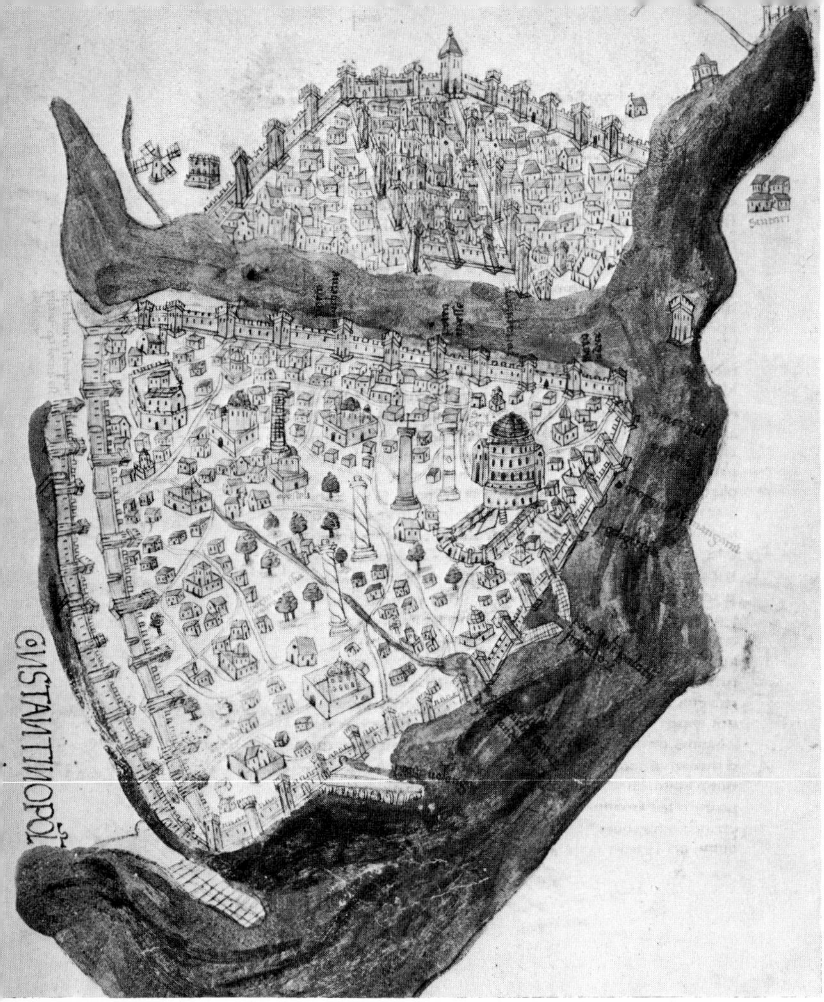

167 A map of Byzantine Constantinople in 1420. St Sophia and the pillars of the Hippodrome are clearly marked as also the lines of the walls.

168 The siege of Rhodes in 1480, showing the attack on the south-east corner of the walls, parts of which have been broken down and repaired with hoardings.

The fall of Constantinople in 1453, when the most famous of city walls were battered down by cannon-fire, had made the new priorities all too clear.

In 1480 came the first great siege by the Turks. The enemy began by attacking the tower of St Nicholas and then switched to the south-west walls. The power of their artillery was such as the knights had not yet experienced. 'The walls were breached, but in the end the Turks were driven off with such loss that they withdrew.' Much had been learnt from the siege. From now on the efforts of the knights were concentrated on adapting the walls for gun emplacements. They were lowered in height and a second ditch was made, leaving a broad bulwark between the two ditches that could be used as a first line of defence, and also widening the distance at which an attack could be launched. At various points polygonal or round bastions (*boulevards*) were built out giving wide fields of fire.

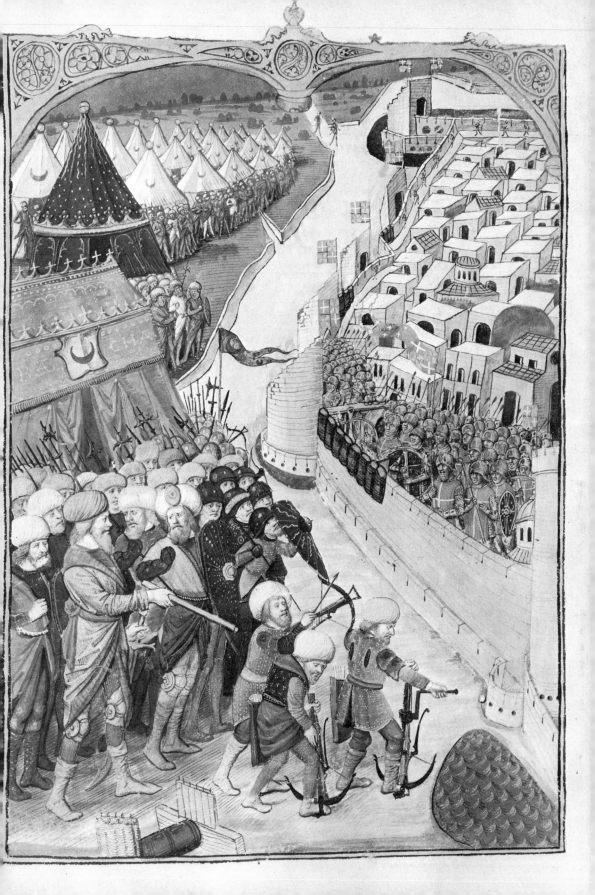

There is much dispute over the claim of originality. Rhodes was certainly one of the earliest and most complete examples of the new type of fortification, particularly associated with the grand master Pierre d'Aubusson (1476–1503). He was the old type of crusader, strict and ascetic, but unusually qualified having a training in mathematics and engineering. In the defence on 27 July 1480, he was five times wounded. In 1489 Innocent VIII created him cardinal-deacon of St Hadrian. The sultan Bajazet presented him with the arm of the Baptist, for he was much admired by his opponents. A severe disciplinarian, he checked all licence within the town, restoring the pristine rigour of the rule, though aware that display in the buildings and state rooms of the master's palace had its uses. When this dour warrior died, they laid him out in the church of St John with on one side his hacked and battered armour, and on the other the elaborate stuffs of his cardinal's robes. His arms can still be seen, carved on the walls, almost everywhere throughout Rhodes.

But walls were not enough. The Turks now controlled Egypt, and Rhodes lay across their lines of communication. In July 1522, Sulaiman I sent a fleet of 300 sail to Rhodes and himself led a force estimated at 100,000 men to the south coast of Asia Minor. The garrison in Rhodes was some 300 knights and about 6000 troops. The siege began on 1 August. On 22 December they capitulated in return for safe-conduct for themselves and any of the inhabitants who wished to leave with them.

The loss of Rhodes may well be taken as closing the age of the crusades. They were still to be talked of and their old propaganda was to be used to stir defence against the Ottomans. But Jerusalem had become impossibly remote. Between 1461 and 1467 the edicule of the Sepulchre was reproduced, with Renaissance variants, in the private chapel of the Rucellai in Florence. Ferdinand I of Florence in 1603 was actually to send in secret to Jerusalem to try and dismantle the tomb and bring it back to Italy. The Sepulchre had become a collector's piece. In drawing and later prints views of Jerusalem remained in strong demand, and artists painting Biblical scenes gave their various versions of the octagon of the Dome of the Rock, such as that which rises in the background of Raphael's *Sposalizio*. Bernard von Breydenbach, whose tense, arresting face still can be seen on his tomb at Mainz, employed an artist, Erhard Reuwich, to engrave the scenes of the pilgrimage that he made in 1483; pilgrimages continued, often under much hardship and danger, and accounts of the journeys continued to be written. In 1335, with the aid of Robert of Naples and his wife Sancia, the Franciscans acquired the site of the Coenaculum, the supposed room of the Last Supper, and some rights in the Church of the Holy Sepulchre. Clement VI assigned to them in 1342

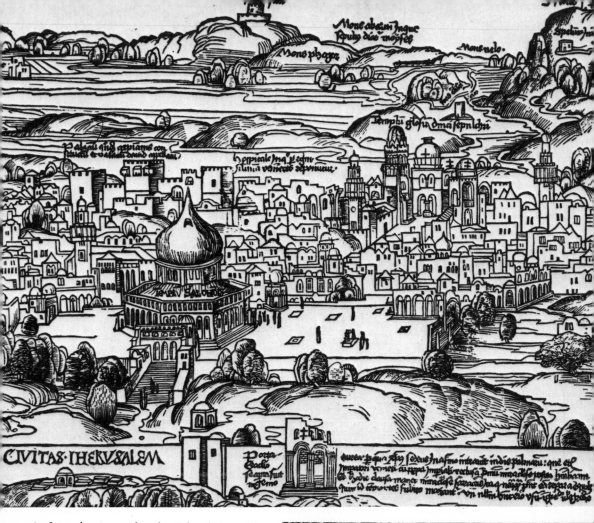

CIVITAS·IHERVSALEM

169 Jerusalem: woodcut by Erhard Reuwich
of Utrecht. Bernard von Breydenbach's
account of his pilgrimage was published in
1486 and contained woodcuts by Erhard
Reuwich which set a new standard in accurate
topography.

170 Bernard von Breydenbach: tomb slab,
Mainz cathedral.

the custodianship of the Holy Land, a task which, with frequent persecution and displacement, they have carried out ever since.

In the eastern Mediterranean only Venice was left. Cyprus had passed under its control in 1473. After the great defeat by the Mamluks in 1426, the Lusignan dynasty had struggled on under Janus's son, John (1432–58), an ungainly, feeble man dominated by his grim wife, Helena Palaeologa. Byzantine tastes and customs reasserted themselves in the island, strengthening its indestructibly Greek quality. They had as heiress a daughter, Carlotta, whose illegitimate half-brother, James, an attractive, unscrupulous man, disputed the succession and called in Moslem help from Cairo, where for a time he resided. There was another long siege of Kyrenia, bravely defended by Carlotta, but it was James who won, and who distinguished his reign by expelling the Genoese from Famagusta. He only did so with Venetian help, and Venice sent him a 'daughter of St Mark', Catherine Cornaro, as his bride. But within a few months of the marriage James died of dysentery and Catherine's posthumous son died as an infant. Venice claimed Cyprus by the terms of a treaty made with James, and in 1473 the queen handed it over to her mother-city. Cyprus became a Venetian outpost, strongly fortified with the walls of Famagusta and the new enceinte of Nicosia. But not strong enough. In 1571 the Turks took Famagusta, and its heroic defender, Marcantonio Bragadino, was flayed alive before the Venetian archway of the palace of the Provveditore.

Genoa, the great rival of Venice, had steadily declined in power. In 1352, in a harsh February gale in the Bosphorus, about sixty-five Genoese ships fought with a combined Venetian, Catalan and Greek navy of some seventy-five vessels. It was a costly but indecisive engagement, one of the largest naval struggles in those waters. The Genoese, however, held their Constantinopolitan station in Pera uneasily as the affairs of the city swung in the internal struggle for power between the Palaeologi and Cantacuzeni families. In 1379 Genoa had her great moment. Her fleet held the northern Adriatic and blockaded Venice from Chioggia. The Venetians brought their great admiral Vettore Pisani from the prison to which they had recently condemned him on his return, defeated by the Genoese at Pola. The success of Pisani's bold and desperate counter-blockade of the Genoese fleet long hung in the balance, but eventually the Genoese were forced to surrender. Genoa, so nearly successful, never recovered from this blow. Her families remained in some of the islands (Chios, Lesbos, Thasos) where castles and carved crests still recall their sojourn, but she was now in the second place. Venetian trade was firmer and more enduring. Petrarch writing from Venice states: 'From my window on the Riva degli Schiavoni I see vessels as large as houses. They sail to all parts of the world, and brave a thousand dangers. They carry wine to England, honey to the Scythians, saffron, oil, linen to Assyria, Armenia, Persia and Arabia, wood to Egypt and Greece; they return laden with merchandise to be distributed all over Europe. Where the sea ends, their sailors quit the ships and travel on to trade with India and China; they cross the Caucasus and the Ganges, and reach the Indian Ocean.' It is an impressive picture, and it stands for high and courageous enterprise, but there was no crusading fervour in it.

In 1517 the Ottoman forces under Selim I defeated the Mamluks outside Cairo and entered the city. From Constantinople to Cairo the seaboard of the eastern Mediterranean was now under one control. Something that for so long the policies of the West had struggled to prevent was now achieved. It meant the end of the Venetian empire. Modon, guarding the western prong of Greece, with its sea-shore walls, had fallen in 1500; Famagusta fell in 1571; Crete held out for nearly a hundred years longer, and then in 1668, after a two years' siege, Candia fell. In 1686, its heroic defender, Francesco Morosini, regained for a brief period some strongholds in the Peloponnese. He has gone down to history as the general whose 'lucky shot' exploded the Turkish powder magazine in the Parthenon, in Our Lady of Athens, that Franks, Catalans and Florentines had all preserved.

Trade proved more lasting in these Eastern questions than religion. Things were done in these wars in the name of Christ that outraged His teaching and deeply impaired the true religious sense of the West. No heroism, no genuine if misconceived devotion, and there was much of both, can redeem the gross misuse of Christian faith. For some 300 years the crusades dominated the mind of Europe, widening horizons, calling new kingdoms into being. European thought was penetrated by their problems, and for better or worse they were a great factor in the making of Western civilization. But they condoned intolerable acts, and Urban II's vision of their purpose proved a fatal heritage.

In the lands they occupied four centuries or more of Turkish domination have obliterated most of their traces. Some linguistic borrowings and folk traditions preserve shadowy memories. Their buildings remain as more positive evidence: Krak des Chevaliers still supreme on its hilltop; the choir of the Holy Sepulchre now restored to something of its original distinction; Famagusta with its graveyard of churches; Rhodes, most complete of all medieval towns, though its walls lowered for artillery have lost something in impressiveness. The order of the Knights of St John has been the most lasting of crusading enterprises. Driven from Rhodes, they had some years of uncertain wanderings until in 1530 the emperor Charles V gave them the island of Malta, a barren, rugged contrast to fertile Rhodes. Here, in 1565, they were to resist as great a siege as any they had faced before and in holding their fortress and harbour against the assault of the Turks saved the western Mediterranean for Christendom. Their heroism and devotion rekindled the old crusading spirit, and inspired by such an example, Europe six years later, forgetting its feuds, destroyed the Turkish fleet at Lepanto. But the great painting of the victory that pope Gregory XIII commissioned Vasari to paint on the walls of the Sala Regia in the Vatican has as its neighbour a fresco of another Catholic triumph, the Massacre of St Bartholomew. The wars of religion now had another context. Yet in Jerusalem, that much-tried town, one finer tradition has survived, and the Hospital of St John, albeit refounded by the English Protestant branch, still cares for the sick in the Holy City where the order had its origin.

171 Alberto Aringhieri, a knight of St John, painted by Pinturicchio in Siena cathedral. He wears the robes of the Order of the Hospital; behind him can be seen the walls of Rhodes.

Philippopolis

Adrianople

Cons

Durazzo

Salonica   THASOS   Br

AEGEAN

Larissa   Adramyttium

CORFU   Pergamon

Artah   LESBOS   Smyrna

EUBOEA

Bodonitsa   SEA

Thebes   CHIOS

Patras   Athens   Nymphaeum   Ephesus

Clermont   Corinth

Andravida   PATMOS

Karytaina   PAROS   LEROS

Mistra   NAXOS

Sparta   COS

Navarino   Rhode

Modon   Coron   RHODES   Lindos

Monemvasia

Canea

Candia

CRETE

M E D I T E R R A N E A

N
↑

0 ————————————— 250 Kms
0 ————————————— 150 Mls

Trebizond

Neocaesarea

Kharput

Melitene

Gargar

Caesarea

Marash

Hromgla

Edessa

Bira

 rylaeum

Iconium

Sis

Turbessel

Tarsus

Lajazzo

Alexandretta

Antalya

Baghras

Artah

Aleppo

Alanya

Silifke

Antioch

Harenc

Anamur

Saone

Apamea

Kantara

Latakia

Shaizar

Hamah

Kyrenia

Masyaf

Montferrand

St Hilarion

Bellapais

Marqab

Rafaniyah

Nicosia

Tortosa

Homs

Famagusta

Safitha

Paphos

CYPRUS

Tripoli

Krak des Chevaliers

Limassol

Gibelet

Arqah

Baalbek

Beirut

Sidon

Damascus

Beaufort

Subeibe

Tyre

Banyas

Montfort

Toron

Acre

Safad

Hattin

Haifa

Tiberias

Athlith

Belvoir

Caesarea

Nazareth

Ajlun

Arsuf

Sebastia

Ramla

Jaffa

Lydda

Nablus

Ibelin

Bait Nuba

Ascalon

JERUSALEM

Gaza

Bethlehem

Damietta

Blanchegarde

Hebron

Kerak

Monréal

Petra

Cairo

Aqaba

S E A

247

The Royal House of Jerusalem

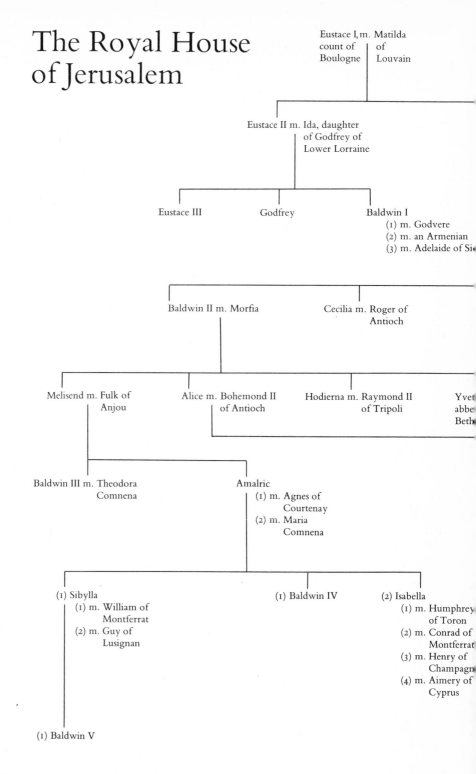

Eustace I, m. Matilda
count of | of
Boulogne | Louvain

Eustace II m. Ida, daughter
of Godfrey of
Lower Lorraine

Eustace III   Godfrey   Baldwin I
(1) m. Godvere
(2) m. an Armenian
(3) m. Adelaide of Si

Baldwin II m. Morfia   Cecilia m. Roger of
Antioch

Melisend m. Fulk of   Alice m. Bohemond II   Hodierna m. Raymond II   Yvet
Anjou   of Antioch   of Tripoli   abbe
Beth

Baldwin III m. Theodora   Amalric
Comnena   (1) m. Agnes of
Courtenay
(2) m. Maria
Comnena

(1) Sibylla   (1) Baldwin IV   (2) Isabella
(1) m. William of   (1) m. Humphrey
Montferrat   of Toron
(2) m. Guy of   (2) m. Conrad of
Lusignan   Montferrat
(3) m. Henry of
Champagn
(4) m. Aimery of
Cyprus

(1) Baldwin V

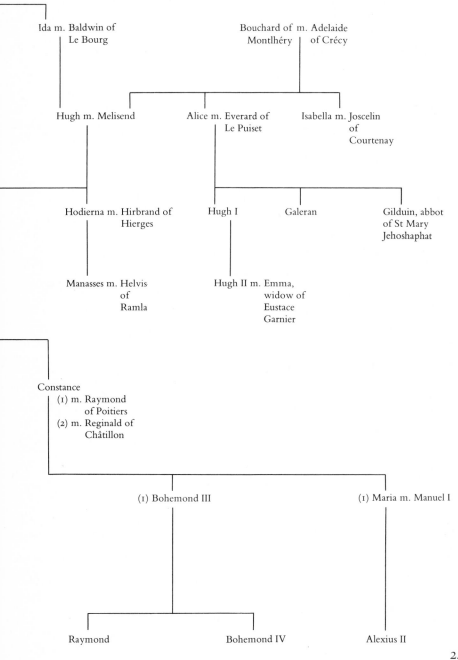

Ida m. Baldwin of
 Le Bourg

Bouchard of m. Adelaide
 Montlhéry | of Crécy

Hugh m. Melisend

Alice m. Everard of
 Le Puiset

Isabella m. Joscelin
  of
  Courtenay

Hodierna m. Hirbrand of
  Hierges

Hugh I

Galeran

Gilduin, abbot
 of St Mary
 Jehoshaphat

Manasses m. Helvis
  of
  Ramla

Hugh II m. Emma,
  widow of
  Eustace
  Garnier

Constance
 (1) m. Raymond
   of Poitiers
 (2) m. Reginald of
   Châtillon

(1) Bohemond III

(1) Maria m. Manuel I

Raymond

Bohemond IV

Alexius II

249

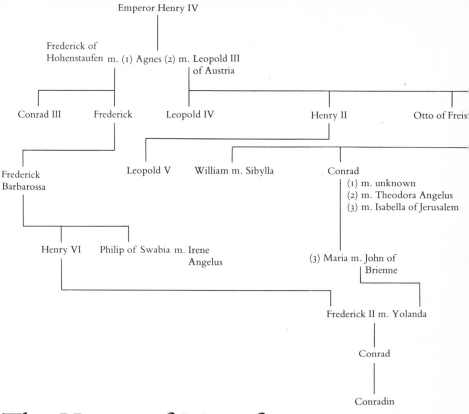

Emperor Henry IV

Frederick of
Hohenstaufen m. (1) Agnes (2) m. Leopold III
of Austria

Conrad III   Frederick   Leopold IV   Henry II   Otto of Freis

Frederick
Barbarossa   Leopold V   William m. Sibylla   Conrad
(1) m. unknown
(2) m. Theodora Angelus
(3) m. Isabella of Jerusalem

Henry VI   Philip of Swabia m. Irene
Angelus   (3) Maria m. John of
Brienne

Frederick II m. Yolanda

Conrad

Conradin

The House of Montferrat

The House of Ibelin

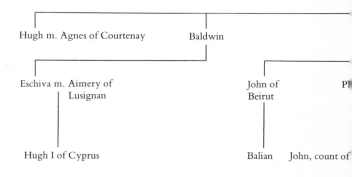

Barisa
(Balian the C

Hugh m. Agnes of Courtenay   Baldwin

Eschiva m. Aimery of
Lusignan   John of
Beirut   P

Hugh I of Cyprus   Balian   John, count of

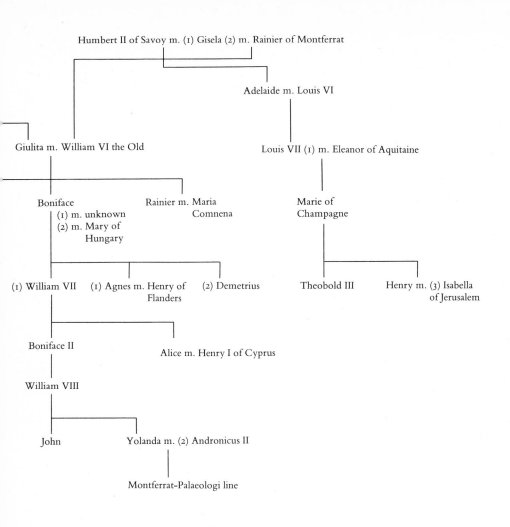

Humbert II of Savoy m. (1) Gisela (2) m. Rainier of Montferrat

Adelaide m. Louis VI

Giulita m. William VI the Old

Louis VII (1) m. Eleanor of Aquitaine

Boniface
  (1) m. unknown
  (2) m. Mary of
     Hungary

Rainier m. Maria
    Comnena

Marie of
Champagne

(1) William VII   (1) Agnes m. Henry of   (2) Demetrius
                  Flanders

Theobold III   Henry m. (3) Isabella
                       of Jerusalem

Boniface II

Alice m. Henry I of Cyprus

William VIII

John

Yolanda m. (2) Andronicus II

Montferrat-Palaeologi line

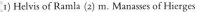

(1) Helvis of Ramla (2) m. Manasses of Hierges

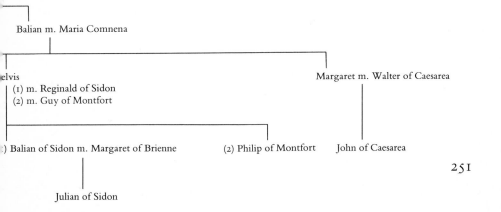

Balian m. Maria Comnena

elvis
  (1) m. Reginald of Sidon
  (2) m. Guy of Montfort

Margaret m. Walter of Caesarea

) Balian of Sidon m. Margaret of Brienne   (2) Philip of Montfort   John of Caesarea

Julian of Sidon

251

Chronology

1071	Battle of Manzikert		Châtillon marries Constance of Antioch
1095	Urban II preaches the crusade at the Council of Clermont	1154	Damascus submits to Nur-ad-Din
1097	First crusade reaches Constantinople: Alexius Comnenus emperor (1081–1118): siege of Antioch (21 October 1097–3 June 1098)	1155	Crusading alliance with Manuel Comnenus (1143 to 1180)
		1157	Great earthquake in northern Syria
1098	Baldwin occupies Edessa (March)	1163	Accession of Amalric (1163–74)
1099	Capture of Jerusalem (15 July): Godfrey of Bouillon elected Advocate of the Sepulchre: Battle of Ascalon (12 August)	1163–9	Campaigns against Egypt
		1169	Saladin occupies Cairo for Nur-ad-Din
1100	Death of Godfrey: Baldwin I (1100–18) succeeds as king	1174	Death of Nur-ad-Din and of Amalric: accession of Baldwin IV, the Leper (1174–85)
1109	Capture of Tripoli	1180	Marriage of Sibylla and Guy of Lusignan: death of Manuel Comnenus
1112	Death of Tancred		
1115	Roger of Antioch defeats Bursuk at Danith	1186	Marqab ceded to the Hospitallers
1118	Accession of Baldwin II (1118–31)	1187	Defeat of crusading army by Saladin at Hattin (4 July): Conrad of Montferrat arrives at Tyre (14 July): Jerusalem surrenders to Saladin (2 October)
1119	*Ager Sanguinis* (28 June): defeat and death of Roger of Antioch		
1124	Capture of Tyre		
1131	Accession of Fulk of Anjou (1131–43), as husband of Melisend, daughter of Baldwin II	1188	Saladin's northern campaign: capture of Saone and of Kerak
1132/3	The Assassins settle in the Ansariyah mountains	1189	Guy of Lusignan begins siege of Acre
1137	John Comnenus campaigns against Armenia and Antioch	1190	Death of Frederick Barbarossa in Cilicia
1142	Krak des Chevaliers ceded to the Hospitallers	1191	Arrival of Philip II of France and Richard Cœur-de-Lion at Acre: recapture of Acre by the crusaders: departure of Philip
1143	Death of Fulk, accession of Baldwin III (1143–63): death of John Comnenus: accession of Manuel		
1144	Zengi captures Edessa	1192	Assassination of Conrad of Montferrat (28 April): Guy of Lusignan buys Cyprus from the Templars, to whom Richard had assigned it after his conquest of the island: departure of Richard: refortification of Kerak by al-Adil
1147/8	Second crusade, led by the emperor Conrad III and Louis VII of France		
1149	15 July, dedication of Church of Holy Sepulchre		
1153	Capture of Ascalon: Reginald of		

1193	Death of Saladin	1261	Michael Palaeologus reconquers Constantinople
1197	Aimery of Lusignan crowned king of Cyprus (1197–1205)	1266	Mamluks under Kalavun devastate Armenia: Baybars captures Safad and overruns Galilee
1198	Leon II crowned king of Armenia (1198–1219)		
1200	al-Adil, Saladin's brother, proclaimed sultan of Egypt and Syria	1268	Baybars captures Jaffa, Beaufort and Antioch
		1270–2	Crusade of Edward of England
1204	Constantinople taken by the crusaders	1271	Baybars takes Krak des Chevaliers
1205	Battle of Koundoura: the Franks conquer the Morea	1277	Death of Baybars: succeeded after two years of dispute by Kalavun
1207	Death of Boniface of Montferrat		
1218	Death of al-Adil: al-Kamil succeeds him in Egypt	1281	Kalavun defeats the Mongols near Homs
1219	Capture of Damietta by crusaders	1285	Kalavun takes Marqab
		1287	Fall of Latakia
1221	Crusaders evacuate Damietta	1289	Kalavun captures Tripoli
1229	Frederick II regains Jerusalem, Nazareth and Toron by treaty with al-Kamil	1290	Death of Kalavun: succeeded by his son, al-Ashraf Khalil
1232–6	John of Ibelin leads the baronage against Frederick's bailie, Richard Filangieri	1291	Khalil captures Acre (18 May): Athlith and Tortosa evacuated
		1307–14	Suppression of the order of the Temple
1239–40	Crusade of Theobald of Champagne: treaties with Damascus and Egypt restore Galilee and Ascalon to the crusaders: Jerusalem occupied by an-Nasir of Kerak	1309	Hospitallers occupy Rhodes
		1311	Catalans defeat Walter of Athens
		1344	Crusaders capture Smyrna
		1361	Peter I of Cyprus (1359–69) occupies Antalya
1244	Jerusalem sacked by Khorezmians: Egyptians and Khorezmians defeat a crusader-Syrian army at Gaza	1365	Sack of Alexandria
		1373	Famagusta ceded to Genoese
		1375	Armenia conquered by Mamluks
		1379	Navarese company capture Thebes from the Catalans
1249	Louis IX lands in Egypt and captures Damietta		
1250	Louis defeated and captured by Egyptians; ransomed by surrender of Damietta	1396	Battle of Nicopolis
		1402	Timur captures Smyrna: Hospitallers fortify Bodrum
		1426	Battle of Khirokitia: Mamluks sack Nicosia
1250–4	Louis in Palestine		
1258	Hulagu and the Mongols capture Baghdad and kill last Abbasid caliph	1453	Fall of Constantinople (29 May)
		1473	Cyprus ceded to Venice
		1480	First siege of Rhodes by Ottomans
1259	Battle of Pelagonia		
1260	Mongols under Kitbogha take Damascus, but are defeated at Ain Jalut by Mamluk army under Baybars: Baybars becomes sultan	1517	Ottomans occupy Cairo
		1523	Loss of Rhodes
		1565	Siege of Malta
		1571	Ottomans capture Famagusta: Battle of Lepanto

Bibliographical Note

An admirable bibliographical guide to the crusades exists in H. Mayer, *Bibliographie zur Geschichte der Kreuzzüge* (Munich, 1960), and his supplement covering publications of the years 1958–67 published as Sonderheft 3 of the *Historische Zeitschrift* (1969). A. S. Atiya, *The Crusade: Historiography and Bibliography* (Indiana University Press, 1962) is a useful guide in English.

A bibliography aiming at any completeness would run to many pages. The notes that follow are highly selective, and indicative of my particular indebtedness, though even in that context there are many omissions of books and articles that I have consulted with profit.

GENERAL   Of general histories, R. Röhricht, *Geschichte der Königreichs Jerusalem 1100–1291* (Innsbruck, 1898), remains the foundation of modern crusading studies. R. Grousset, *Histoire des croisades et du royaume franc de Jérusalem*, 3 vols (Paris, 1934–36), and S. Runciman, *A History of the Crusades*, 3 vols (Cambridge, 1951–54), are both, in very different ways, brilliantly readable narratives. Grousset writes with a certain propaganda sense of French claims in Syria; Runciman has a preference for Byzantium rather than Outremer. A. Waas, *Geschichte der Kreuzzüge*, 2 vols (Freiburg, 1956), ranges over a wide number of topics and is controversial and stimulating. The University of Wisconsin *History of the Crusades*, a corporate work by various scholars, designed by J. L. Lamonte and now in charge of K. M. Setton, has as yet produced two volumes: I. *The First Hundred Years*, ed. by M. W. Baldwin (1955); II. *The Later Crusades 1189–1311*, ed. by R. L. Wolff and M. W. Hazard (1962). Three more volumes are to come, and the work has already set the standard for many problems of crusading historiography, particularly nomenclature and transliteration of Arabic, Persian and Turkish names. J. Prawer, *Histoire du Royaume Latin de Jérusalem* (Hebrew edition 1963) is in course of publication and is particularly valuable for social and constitutional problems, many of which the author has dealt with in an important series of articles. C. Cahen's articles in *Bulletin de la Faculté des Lettres de l'Université de Strasbourg* XXIX (1950/1) are of first importance, and his *La Syrie du Nord à l'Epoque des Croisades et la Principauté franque d'Antioche* (Paris, 1940) is an

254

essential book. J. Riley-Smith, *The Knights of St John in Jerusalem and Cyprus 1050–1310* (London, 1967), has much enlarged our knowledge of the early history of the order.

Of shorter, one-volume accounts D.C. Munro, *The Kingdom of the Crusaders* (New York, 1936), has a particular place as a final summing-up by the founder of the contemporary American school of crusading historians. W.B. Stevenson, *The Crusaders in the East* (Cambridge, 1907), though overtaken in some points by more recent research, remains a model of careful scholarship and good sense. J. Richard, *Le Royaume Latin de Jérusalem* (Paris, 1953), is an outstanding piece of work. J.B. Glubb, *The Course of Empire* (London, 1965) and *The Lost Centuries* (London, 1967), are highly personal and vigorous accounts of events from the Arab side, based on a unique knowledge of the strategic lie of the land. R.C. Smail, *Crusading Warfare 1097–1193* (Cambridge, 1956), is the standard work on military problems.

For the crusading families J.L. La Monte's articles in *Byzantion* XII (1937) FAMILIES and XVII (1944–45), *Revue historique du Sud-Est Européen* (1938), *Speculum* XVII (1942) and XXII (1947), and *Medievalia et Humanistica* VI (1950) are of basic importance: W. Rüdt-Collenberg, 'Les premiers Ibelins', *Le Moyen Âge* LXXI (1966), is an important recent contribution to the subject. There are now many monographs available on the leading figures of the crusades, such as J.C. Andressohn, *Godfrey of Bouillon* (1947); R.L. Nicholson, *Tancred* (1940) and *Joscelyn I of Edessa* (1954); R.B. Yewdale, *Bohemond I* (1924); J.H. Hill and L. Hill, *Raymond IV of St Gilles* (1962); M.W. Baldwin, *Raymond III of Tripoli* (1936); J.P. Donovan, *Pelagius* (1950): L. Usseglio, *I Marchesi di Montferrato in Italia ed in Oriente* (Casale Montferrato, 1926), has a mass of, unfortunately unindexed, information.

For the theory and origins of the crusade P. Alphandéry and A. THEORY Dupront, *La Chrétienté et l'idée de Croisade*, 2 vols (Paris, 1954–59), is a controversial work, with which the author of the present work largely agrees. See also C. Erdmann, *Die Entstehung des Kreuzzugsgedankens* (Stuttgart, 1935), and P. Rousset, *Les origines et les Caractères de la première Croisade* (Neuchâtel, 1945). For later theory A.S. Atiya, *The Crusade in the Later Middle Ages* remains the main guide: see also P.A. Throop, *Criticism of the Crusade* (Amsterdam, 1940). For trade, W. Heyd, *Histoire du Commerce du Levant*, 2 vols (Leipzig, 1923), retains its magisterial authority: see also E.H. Byrne, *Genoese shipping in the twelfth and thirteenth centuries* (Med. Acad. of America, 1930), and R.S. Lopez and I.W. Raymond, *Medieval Trade in the Mediterranean World* (Oxford, 1955).

NEIGHBOURS   For the states neighbouring the crusading settlements, the new *Cambridge Medieval History IV, Pt. 1, Byzantium and its neighbours*, ed. J.M. Hussey, D.M. Nicol, and G. Cowan (1966), summarizes much recent research: see also D.J. Geanokoplas, *Emperor Michael Palaeologus and the West* (Harvard U.P., 1959); C.M. Brand, *Byzantium confronts the West* (Harvard U.P., 1968); W. Rüdt-Collenberg, *The Rupenides, Hethumides and Lusignans* (Lisbon, 1963); P. Lemerle, *L'Émirat d'Aydin* (Paris, 1957); S. Lloyd and D. Storm Rice, *Alanya* (London, 1958); T. Talbot Rice, *The Seljuks in Asia Minor* (London, 1961); B. Lewis, *The Assassins* (London, 1967).

GREEK SETTLEMENT   For the Greek settlement W. Miller, *The Latins in the Levant* (London, 1908) is still the main account, though in places out of date: see also D.M. Nicol, *The Despotate of Epiros* (Oxford, 1957), and K.M. Setton, *Catalan Domination of Athens 1311–1388* (Med. Acad. of America, 1948). For Cyprus G.F. Hill, *A History of Cyprus*, 4 vols (London, 1940–52), has no competitors. The knights of St John in Rhodes still lack a satisfactory history and J. Delaville Le Roulx, *Les Hospitaliers à Rhodes 1310–1421* (1913), is incomplete and requires considerable revision. There is a valuable series of articles by A. Luttrell, particularly those in *Papers of the British School at Rome* XXVI (1958), *Speculum* XLI (1966), *Annales of Order Souvereign Military of Malta* (1962): Dr Luttrell kindly allowed me to read his forthcoming monograph on Fernández de Heredia.

SOURCES   Many of the original sources are printed in the *Recueil des Historiens des Croisades*, 16 vols (Paris, 1841–1906). Additional or alternative texts are listed by Atiya in his *Bibliography*. William of Tyre is translated by E.A. Bablock and A.C. Krey in the *Records of Civilization Series* (New York, 1943), as is also Philip of Novara, *Frederick II and the Ibelins* (trans. J.L. La Monte and M.J. Hubert, 1936); Odo of Deuil, *De profectione Ludovici VII* (text and trans. V.G. Berry, 1948); and the *Chronicle of the Morea* (H.E. Lurier, 1964). See also Raymond of Aguilers, *Historia Francorum qui ceperunt Jerusalem* (trans. J.H. and L.M. Hill, *Memoirs of American Philosophical Society*, No. 71); Usamah ibn-Munqidh, *Memoirs of an Arab-Syrian Gentleman* (trans. P.K. Hitti, Beirut, 1964); *Gesta Francorum* (trans. R. Hill, London, 1962). R.B.C. Huygens, *Lettres de Jacques de Vitry* (Leiden, 1960), is a recent addition to available printed material. See also his important article on William of Tyre in *Latonus* XXI (1962), pp. 811–29.

ARCHITECTURE   For architecture see C. Enlart, *Les Monuments des croisés dans le Royaume de Jérusalem: Architecture réligieuse et civile*, 2 vols and 2 folders of plates

(Paris, 1925–28), and *L'Art gothique et la Renaissance en Chypre*; H. Vincent and F.M. Abel, *Jérusalem. Recherches de topographie, d'archéologie et d'histoire. II. Jérusalem Nouvelle* (Paris, 1914–22); P. Deschamps, *Les Châteaux des croisés en Terre Sainte 1. Le Crac des Chevaliers. 2. La défense du royaume de Jérusalem* (Paris, 1934–39), and *Terre Sainte romane* (Paris, 1964); W. Müller-Wiener, *Castles of the Crusaders* (London, 1966); T.S.R. Boase and R.L.W. Cleave, *Castles and Churches of the Crusading Kingdom* (London, 1967); A. Gabriel, *La Cité de Rhodes, 1310–1522*, 2 vols (Paris, 1921); A. Bon, *La Morée franque: Recherches historiques, topographiques et archéologiques sur la principauté d'Achaie, 1205–1430* (Paris, 1969), and K. Andrews, *Castles of the Morea* (Princeton, 1953).

H. Buchthal, *Miniature Painting in the Latin Kingdom of Jerusalem* (Oxford, 1957), created a new branch of crusading studies, to which K. Weitzmann, 'Icon painting in the Crusading Kingdom', *Dumbarton Oaks Papers* xx (1966), has added yet a further dimension. See also C.L. Striker and Y. Dogan Kuban in *Dumbarton Oaks* xxii (1968). For Armenian illumination see S. der Nersessian and L.A. Dournovo *Armenian Miniatures* (London, 1961). ILLUMINATION

C.N. Johns, *Palestine of the Crusades*, 3rd ed. (Jerusalem, 1946), is the most useful map of the Kingdom, pending an English edition of J. Prawer and M. Benevenisti, *Crusader Palestine*, sheet 12/IX of the *Atlas of Israel* (Jerusalem, 1960). GEOGRAPHY

List of illustrations

258

17 View of Jaffa by W.H. Bartlett, 1834. From John Carne, *Syria, the Holy Land, Asia Minor Illustrated*, 1837. Photo R. B. Fleming.

18 Coronation of Baldwin I of Edessa. From a French translation of William of Tyre's *History*. Thirteenth century. Paris Bibliothèque Nationale, MS. fr. 9081, folio 99v.

19 Interior of the church of the Nativity, Bethlehem (Jordan). Photo A.F. Kersting.

20 Capture of Jerusalem in 1099. From William of Tyre's *History*. French, early fourteenth century. Paris, Bibliothèque Nationale, MS. fr. 352, folio 52v.

21 Map of the world with Jerusalem at the centre. From a Psalter. English, thirteenth century. London, Trustees of the British Museum, MS. Add. 28681, folio 9.

22 Castle of Gibelet (Lebanon), seen from the classical remains. Photo A. F. Kersting.

23 Clerk, Knight and Labourer. From *L'Image du Monde*. Franco-Flemish, late thirteenth century. London, Trustees of the British Museum, MS. Sloane 2435, folio 85.

24 Reconstruction of the eleventh-century church of the Holy Sepulchre, Jerusalem, as found by the crusaders. Courtesy of Père Charles Coüasnon and Mr T. Ball.

25 Interior of the church of the Holy Sepulchre, Jerusalem, showing the sepulchre. From M. Corneille le Bruyn, *A Voyage to the Levant*, 1702. Photo R. B. Fleming.

26 Interior of the church of the Holy Sepulchre, Jerusalem, looking east. From M. Corneille le Bruyn, *A Voyage to the Levant*, 1702. Photo R. B. Fleming.

27 Domes and bell-tower of the church of the Holy Sepulchre, Jerusalem. Photo A. F. Kersting.

28 Windows of the south façade of the church of the Holy Sepulchre, Jerusalem. Photo courtesy of l'École Biblique, Jerusalem.

29 Section of the crusading church at Ramla. From C. Enlart, *Les Monuments des Croisés dans le Royaume de Jérusalem*, 1929. Photo R. B. Fleming.

30 Interior looking east of the crusading church at Ramla. Twelfth century. Photo courtesy of l'École Biblique, Jerusalem.

31 Crusader doing homage. From a Psalter. English, thirteenth century. London, Trustees of the British Museum, MS. Roy. 2.A.XXII, folio 220.

32 Massacre of the Witnesses. From an Apocalypse. Thirteenth century. London, Trustees of the British Museum, MS. Add. 42555, folio 30v.

33 Nebuchadnezzar and his Warriors. From Gloss on the Lamentation of Jeremiah by Gislebert of Auxerre. Mid-twelfth century. Courtesy of the Walters Art Gallery, Baltimore, Maryland.

34 Courage. From the Virtues and Vices, socle reliefs of the centre portal (west façade) of Notre-Dame, Paris. Early thirteenth century. Photo Archives Photographiques.

35 Combat between Roland and Ferragut. Capital from the palace of the dukes of Granada, Estella (Navarra). Second half of the twelfth century. Photo Mas.

36 Tomb of Bohemond at Canosa (Apulia). Twelfth century. Photo Courtauld Institute.

37 Bronze doors by Ruggiero di Amalfi on the tomb of Bohemond at Canosa (Apulia). Twelfth century. Photo Mansell-Anderson.

38 Baldwin I receives a message from Adelaide, countess of Sicily. From a French translation of William of Tyre's

History. Flemish, late fifteenth century. London, Trustees of the British Museum, MS. Roy. 15.E.I., folio 185.

39 Cope of Roger of Sicily. Imperial workshop, Palermo. 1133/34. Vienna, Kunsthistorisches Museum.

40 Medieval plan of Jerusalem. *c.* 1170. The Hague, Koninklijke Bibliotheek, MS. 69.

41 Roman road between Antioch and Aleppo.

42 Enamel grave plate of Geoffrey of Anjou. *c.* 1150. Le Mans cathedral. Photo Giraudon.

43 View of Jerusalem. From the translation of the *Descriptio Terrae Sanctae* by Burchard of Mount Sion (1283), made for Philip of Burgundy in 1455. Paris, Bibliothèque Nationale, MS. fr. 9087, folio 85.

44 Battle between Jews and Philistines. From an Old Testament. French, *c.* 1240. In 1507 the manuscript was presented by Cardinal Maciejowsky of Poland to Shah Abbas I of Persia, who had the miniatures captioned in Persian. New York, Pierpont Morgan Library, MS. 638, folio 23v.

45 Initial from The Wisdom of Solomon. Latin, late fourteenth century. Durham cathedral, MS. A.II.3, folio 225v. By permission of the Dean and Chapter of Durham cathedral.

46 Arab doctors at work. From a Treatise on Surgery by Gerard of Cremona. Second half of the fourteenth century. Vienna, Österreichische Nationalbibliothek.

47 View of Tripoli in the nineteenth century. From John Carne, *Syria, the Holy Land, Asia Minor Illustrated*, 1837. Photo R. B. Fleming.

48 Isaiah sawn asunder. From an English Bible. Twelfth century. Oxford, Bod-leian Library, MS. Laud. Misc. 752, folio 146.

49 Cecilia of Tripoli appeals to Fulk to rescue her husband (above); and attack on Hugh, count of Jaffa, in Jerusalem (below). From a French translation of William of Tyre's *History*. Thirteenth century. Paris, Bibliothèque Nationale, MS. fr. 9081, folio 160v.

50 Castle of Shaizar and the river Orontes (Syria). Photo A. F. Kersting.

51 Castle of Kerak (Syria). Photo former Department of Antiquities, Palestine.

52 Caring for the sick. Detail from a page of the *Cántigas de Santa María*. Thirteenth century. Madrid, Biblioteca del Monasterio del Escorial, MS. T.I.1. Photo Mas.

53 Scenes of the wars of the Maccabees. From the Winchester Bible. *c.* 1160. Winchester cathedral library, Volume II, tolio 135v.

54 Carved angel, probably the symbol of St Matthew. From the chapel of the Hospitaller castle at Belvoir. Photo Micha Pan, Jerusalem, courtesy of Prof. Joshua Prawer.

55 Crusader capital from the al-Aqsa mosque, Jerusalem. Photo Matson Photo Service, Jerusalem.

56 Templar seal, 1259. Paris, Archives Nationales. Photo Brompton Studio.

57 Knights riding out of a fortified town. From a wall-painting of crusaders fighting Saracens in the chapel of the Templars at Cressac (Charente). *c.* 1170–80. Copy. Paris, Musée des Monuments Français.

58 Interior of the Dome of the Rock, Jerusalem, showing the rock seen from above. Photo Middle East Archive.

59 Exterior of the Dome of the Rock, Jerusalem; A D 692. Photo J. E. Dayton.

60 Al-Aqsa mosque, Jerusalem. Photo Middle East Archive.

61 Melisend and Fulk out riding (above) and death of Fulk (below). From a French translation of William of Tyre's *History*. Probably written and illustrated at Acre. *c.* 1280. Paris, Bibliothèque Nationale, MS. fr. 2628, folio 146v.

62 St Bernard of Clairvaux preaching the crusade. From a volume of his sermons. Late thirteenth century. Brussels, Bibliothèque Royale de Belgique, MS. 1787, folio 8.

63 Christ in Majesty, detail from the inner portal, centre tympanum of the church of La Madeleine, Vézelay. *c.* 1140. Photo Archives Photographiques.

64 St Bernard of Clairvaux. Detail from the altarpiece of St Bernard by the Master of Palma. *c.* 1290. Palma de Mallorca, Sociedad Arqueológica Luliana.

65 Manuel Comnenus and his wife, Maria of Antioch. From a Gospel book. Twelfth century. Biblioteca Apostolica Vaticana, MS. Gr. 1176, folio 11.

66 Crusading grille in the Dome of the Rock, Jerusalem (before removal). Photo courtesy of the Israel Department of Antiquities and Museums.

67 Vere Dignum initial. From Sacramentary of the church of the Holy Sepulchre. Jerusalem, 1130–40. Cambridge, Fitzwilliam Museum, MS. McClean 49, folio 4v.

68 Vere Dignum initial. From the Missal of the church of the Holy Sepulchre. 1130–40. Paris, Bibliothèque Nationale, MS. lat. 12056, folio 168v.

69 Initial of the Virgin and Child. From the Missal of the church of the Holy Sepulchre. 1130–40. Paris, Bibliothèque Nationale, MS. lat. 12056, folio 187.

70 Initial D. From the Melisend Psalter. 1131–43. London, Trustees of the British Museum, MS. Egerton 1139, folio 74v.

71 Virgin and Child. From the Melisend Psalter. 1131–43. London, Trustees of the British Museum, MS. Egerton 1139, folio 220v.

72 Scenes of the Acts of Mercy. From the ivory cover of the Melisend Psalter. 1131–43. London, Trustees of the British Museum.

73 The Last Supper. From a Syriac manuscript written by a scribe called Bacchus in the convent of the Virgin at Edessa in 1222. Jerusalem, convent of St Mark, Codex 28, folio 116v. Photo R. B. Fleming.

74 Presentation in the Temple. From the Melisend Psalter. 1131–43. London, Trustees of the British Museum, MS. Egerton 1139, folio 3.

75 Façade of the church of the Holy Sepulchre. From Book of Hours of René of Anjou. *c.* 1436. London, Trustees of the British Museum, MS. Egerton 1070, folio 5.

76 Gadroons and frieze on the façade of the church of the Holy Sepulchre, Jerusalem. Photo Ronald Sheridan.

77 Window in the Martorana tower, Palermo. 1143.

78 Hall in the keep of Saone castle (Syria). Photo A. F. Kersting.

79 The Patriarch of Antioch, Aimery of Limoges, exposed on a tower by Reginald of Châtillon. From William of Tyre's *History*. Mid-thirteenth century. Boulogne-sur-Mer, Bibliothèque Municipale, MS. 142, folio 199. Photo Courtauld Institute, courtesy of Miss Alison Stones.

80 Lake Huleh (north of Galilee) before it was drained.

81 Detail of the outdoor pulpit of Burhan

ad-Din on the Haram (platform of the Dome of the Rock), Jerusalem, showing re-used Templar carving. Photo former Department of Antiquities, Palestine.

82 Dikket (reading platform) in the al-Aqsa mosque, Jerusalem, composed of crusader capitals and friezes. Photo former Department of Antiquities, Palestine.

83 Latrun capitals from the Templars' masons' yard. *c.* 1180. Istanbul, Archaeological Museum.

84 St Bartholomew heals the daughter of king Polyrunius who was poisoned by a devil (right), and raises the king's son from the dead (left). Capital from the church of the Annunciation, Nazareth. *c.* 1170. Photo Courtauld Institute.

85 The Temptation. Capital from the abbey of Plaimpied (Cher). Photo CIM.

86 The Prophet Elijah. From a column painting in the church of the Nativity, Bethlehem. Mid-twelfth century. Photo former Department of Antiquities, Palestine.

87 Saone castle (Syria), showing the great needle which once supported a wooden bridge. Photo A. F. Kersting.

88 Musicians. From a Bible. German, mid-twelfth century. London, Trustees of the British Museum, MS. Harley 2804, folio 3v.

89 Siege of Jerusalem. From a French continuation of William of Tyre's *History*. Probably written and illuminated at Acre, 1260/70. Paris, Bibliothèque Nationale, MS. fr. 2628, folio 62v.

90 Crusaders at Constantinople. From a French continuation of William of Tyre's *History*. Probably written and illuminated at Acre, 1260/70. Paris, Bibliothèque Nationale, MS. fr. 2628, folio 293v.

91 Siege and capture of Antioch in 1097–98.

From a French continuation of William of Tyre's *History. c.* 1280. Paris, Bibliothèque Nationale, MS. fr. 9084, folio 53.

92 Entrance gateway to the citadel at Aleppo (Syria).

93 Battle of Hattin: imaginary scene of Saladin and Guy of Lusignan struggling for the True Cross. From the *Chronica Majora* by Matthew Paris. Mid-thirteenth century. Cambridge, Corpus Christi College, MS. 26, folio 279. Photo Courtauld Institute.

94 Marriage of Sibylla and William of Montferrat. From a French translation of William of Tyre's *History*. Thirteenth century. Boulogne-sur-Mer, Bibliothèque Municipale, MS. 142, folio 264v. Photo Courtauld Institute, courtesy of Miss Alison Stones.

95 Frederick Barbarossa and his sons Henry VI and Frederick of Swabia. From a History of the Welfs of Weingarten. *c.* 1180. Fulda, Hessische Landesbibliothek, MS. D.11, folio 14.

96 View of Tyre in the nineteenth century. From David Roberts, *The Holy Land*, 1855. Photo R. B. Fleming.

97 Christian prisoners released by the Saracens. From the *Chronica Majora* by Matthew Paris. Mid-thirteenth century. Cambridge, Corpus Christi College, MS. 26, folio 148. Photo Courtauld Institute.

98 Masyaf castle (Syria). Photo Kersting.

99 A hall in the keep of the castle of Marqab (Syria). Photo A. F. Kersting.

100 Treaty between Richard and the Saracens. From the *Chronica Minora* by Matthew Paris. Mid-thirteenth century. Cambridge, Corpus Christi College, MS. 16, folio 138v.

101 Fulk of Neuilly preaching. From *Conquest of Constantinople* by Geoffrey de

Villehardouin. Fourteenth century. Oxford, Bodleian Library, MS. Laud. misc. 587, folio 1.

102 Crusaders attacking Constantinople. From *Conquest of Constantinople* by Geoffrey de Villehardouin. Fourteenth century. Oxford, Bodleian Library, MS. Laud. misc. 587, folio 1.

103 St Mark's and the piazzetta. Detail of a view of Venice, from *Li Livres du Graunt Caam* by Marco Polo. *c.* 1400. Oxford, Bodleian Library, MS. Bodley 264, folio 218.

104 Byzantine pillar in front of St Mark's, Venice. Photo G. Brocca, Venice.

105 Bronze colossal figure of an emperor, placed before the church of the Holy Sepulchre Barletta. Seventh century AD. Photo Hirmer.

106 Theodosian walls, Thessalonica. Photo D. J. Wallace.

107 Keep of Clermont castle (Greece). Photo A. F. Kersting.

108 Keep of the castle of Bodonitsa (Greece). Photo A. F. Kersting.

109 View of Karytaina in the nineteenth century. From J. P. Mahaffy, *Greek Pictures*, 1890. Photo R. B. Fleming.

110 Castle of Mistra (Greece). Photo A. F. Kersting.

111 View of the port of Beirut in the nineteenth century, showing the castle of the Ibelins. From John Carne, *Syria, the Holy Land, Asia Minor Illustrated*, 1837. Photo R. B. Fleming.

112 Bridge and castle of Silifke (Turkey). Photo A. F. Kersting.

113 Battle of Damietta. From a fourteenth-century copy of *Histoire de Saint Louis* by Joinville. Paris, Bibliothèque Nationale, MS. fr. 13568, folio 83.

114 Frederick II and his third wife, Isabella of England. From *Historia Anglorum* by Matthew Paris. Before 1259. London, Trustees of the British Museum, MS. Roy. 14.C.vii, folio 123v.

115 Game of chess. From *Juegos de ajedrez, dados y tablas*. 1221–84. El Escorial, Biblioteca del Monasterio. Photo Mas.

116 Map of Acre. From *Historia Anglorum* by Matthew Paris. Before 1259. London, Trustees of the British Museum, MS. Roy. 14.C.vii, folio 14v.

117 Mongols besieging a city, probably Baghdad. From *Jami-et-Tawarik* by Rashid ad-Din. Beginning of the fourteenth century. Stiftung Preussischer Kulturbesitz, Tübinger Depot der Staatsbibliothek, MS. Diez. A, folio 71.

118 Louis IX with the True Cross and the Crown of Thorns. From the *Chronica Minora* by Matthew Paris. Mid-thirteenth century. Cambridge, Corpus Christi College, MS. 16, folio 141v. Photo Courtauld Institute.

119 Joinville offering his *Histoire de Saint Louis* to Louis X. From a fourteenth-century copy of *Histoire de Saint Louis* by Joinville. Originally written in 1309. Paris, Bibliothèque Nationale, MS. fr. 13568, folio 1.

120 Castle at Sidon (Lebanon) from the harbour. Photo A. F. Kersting.

121 Stone head of a helmeted knight. From the crusader castle of Montfort. Thirteenth century. Photo courtesy of the Israel Department of Antiquities and Museums.

122 Upper part of the castle of Montfort (Israel). Photo A. F. Kersting.

123 Nave looking east of the crusader cathedral of Tortosa (Syria). Photo A. F. Kersting.

124 Castle of Athlith, Château Pèlerin (Israel). Photo A. F. Kersting.

263

125 Crypt of the hospital of the Knights of St John at Acre. Photo A. F. Kersting.

126 Krak des Chevaliers. Photo Courtesy of C. Gould Esq.

127 Initial showing the Triumphal Entry into Jerusalem. From the Riccardiana Psalter. 1235–37. Florence, Biblioteca Riccardiana, MS. 323.

128 Joshua and Balaam. From the Arsenal Bible. 1250–54. Paris, Bibliothèque Nationale, MS. Arsenal 5211, folio 54v.

129 Initial showing the Resurrection. From a Missal. Third quarter of the thirteenth century. Perugia, Capitular Library, MS. 6, folio 187.

130 Finding of Oedipus. From *Histoire Universelle*. 1270/80. Brussels, Bibliothèque Royale, MS. 10175, folio 90.

131 Scenes of the Creation. Opening page from *Histoire Universelle*. c. 1286. London, Trustees of the British Museum, MS. Add. 15268, folio 1v.

132 Death of Hector. From *Histoire Universelle*. c. 1286. London, Trustees of the British Museum, MS. Add. 15268, folio 114v.

133 Pyrrhus fighting Penthesilea. From *Histoire Universelle*. c. 1286. London, Trustees of the British Museum, MS. Add. 15268, folio 123.

134 Nativity, detail of an icon from Mount Sinai. 1256–60.

135 Crucifixion. From a Gospel illustrated for archbishop John, brother of Hayton I of Armenia. 1287. Erevan, Matenadaran, MS. 197, folio 101v.

136 Archbishop John ordaining a deacon. From a Gospel illustrated for archbishop John, brother of Hayton I of Armenia. 1287. Erevan, Matenadaran, MS. 197, folio 341v.

137 Death of John the Baptist. From a Gospel

illustrated at Hromgla by Toros Roslin. 1262. Courtesy of the Walters Art Gallery, Baltimore, Maryland, MS. 539, folio 66.

138 Portrait of prince Leo (later Leo III) and his wife, Keran, receiving Christ's benediction. From a Gospel illustrated at Hromgla by Toros Roslin. 1262. Jerusalem, Armenian Patriarchate, MS. 2660, folio 288.

139 Castle of Harenc (Syria). Photo A. F. Kersting.

140 Beatus initial from the Riccardiana Psalter. 1235–37. Florence, Biblioteca Riccardiana, MS. 323, folio 14v.

141 Tartars, symbolizing gluttony. From *De Septem Vitiis*. Genoa, late fourteenth century. London, Trustees of the British Museum, MS. Add. 27695, folio 13.

142 Charles I of Anjou. By Arnolfo di Cambio. Rome, Capitoline Museum.

143 Mogul khan Abagha and his son Arghun. From *History of the Mongols* by Rashid ad-Din. Composed for Ghazan before 1304. Paris, Bibliothèque Nationale, MS. Suppl. Persan. 1113, folio 198v.

144 The nun Melane, probably Maria Palaeologina. Detail of the Deesis mosaic. Istanbul, church of the Kariye Cami. Photo courtesy of the Byzantine Institute Inc., Washington D.C.

145 Mogul khan Arghun seated with two wives and his son Ghazan (who stands to the left of the throne), detail. From *History of the Mongols* by Rashid ad-Din. Composed for Ghazan before 1304. Paris, Bibliothèque Nationale, MS. Suppl. Persan. 1113, folio 203v.

146 Harbour of Alanya (Turkey) with the Red Tower, and the castle on the hill in the background. Photo A. F. Kersting.

147 Turkish fort at Alexandria. By Ludwig Mayer. 1742. Munich, Bayerische Staatsbibliothek, MS. Germ. 2967, folio 45.

148 Martyrdom of Franciscan monks. Fresco by Ambrogio Lorenzetti. 1324–27. Siena, church of S. Francesco. Photo Anderson.

149 Arrest of the Templars. From *Chroniques de France*. Late fourteenth century. London, Trustees of the British Museum, MS. Roy. 20.C.vii, folio 42v.

150 Templars brought before the pope and king Philip IV. From *Chroniques de France*. Late fourteenth century. London, Trustees of the British Museum, MS. Roy. 20.C.vii, folio 100v.

151 Burning of James of Molay, grand master of the Templars, and Geoffrey de Charney. From *Chroniques de France*. Late fourteenth century. London, Trustees of the British Museum, MS. Roy. 20.C.vii, folio 48.

152 Street of the Knights, Rhodes. Photo A. F. Kersting.

153 Christ leading the Crusaders. From an Apocalypse. Early fourteenth century. London, Trustees of the British Museum, MS. Roy. 19.B.xv. folio 37.

154 Kantara castle (Cyprus). Photo A. F. Kersting.

155 West façade of Famagusta cathedral (Cyprus). Photo A. F. Kersting.

156 Voussoirs on the façade of St Sophia, Nicosia (Cyprus). Photo Courtauld Institute, courtesy of the Department of Antiquities, Cyprus.

157 Angel above the west porch of St Sophia, Nicosia (Cyprus). Photo Courtauld Institute, courtesy of the Department of Antiquities, Cyprus.

158 Figure of a queen from the voussoirs on the façade of St Sophia, Nicosia (Cyprus). Photo courtesy of the Department of Antiquities, Cyprus.

159 Figure of a prophet from the voussoirs on the façade of St Sophia, Nicosia (Cyprus). Photo courtesy of the Department of Antiquities, Cyprus.

160 Window from the Lusignan palace, Nicosia. Nicosia, Medieval Museum. Photo courtesy of Prof. Ellis Waterhouse.

161 Part of the north side of the cloisters of Bellapais Abbey (Cyprus). Photo A. F. Kersting.

162 Window in the upper part of St Hilarion castle (Cyprus). Photo A. F. Kersting.

163 Inscription at Antalya commemorating its capture by Peter I of Cyprus in 1361. Antalya Museum. Photo Author.

164 Kyrenia castle (Cyprus) from the harbour. Photo A. F. Kersting.

165 Philip de Mézières presenting his plan for a new crusading order – the Order of the Passion – to Richard II of England. From *Un Epistre au Roy Richard*. 1395. London, Trustees of the British Museum, MS. Roy. 20.B.vi, folio 2.

166 Bodrum castle (Turkey) from the quay. Photo A. F. Kersting.

167 Oldest known map of Constantinople. From *Isolario* by Cristoforo Buondelmonte. 1420. Paris, Bibliothèque Nationale, MS. lat. 4285, folio 37.

168 Siege of Rhodes in 1480. From *Descriptio Obsidionis Rhodiae Urbis* by Guillaume Caoursin. *c.* 1490. Paris, Bibliothèque Nationale, MS. lat. 6067, folio 55v.

169 View of Jerusalem drawn by Erhard Reuwich. From *Peregrinationes* by Bernard von Breydenbach, 1486.

170 Sandstone tomb of Bernard von Breydenbach. *c.* 1497. Mainz cathedral. Photo Bildarchiv Foto Marburg.

171 Alberto Aringhieri, a Knight of St John. Fresco by Pinturicchio. 1504. Siena cathedral, chapel of S. Giovanni. Photo Mansell-Anderson.

Index

This index is selective and does not include many briefly mentioned names.
Page numbers in italics indicate illustrations.

Hromgla 144, 207
Hugh I, count of Jaffa see Puiset, Le, family of
Hugh II, count of Jaffa see Puiset, Le, family of
Hugh I, king of Cyprus see Lusignan, family of
Hugh II see Lusignan, family of
Hugh III see Lusignan, family of
Hugh IV see Lusignan, family of
Hugh see Ibelin, family of
Hugh of Payen see Templars
Hugh Falkenberg see St Omer, family of
Hulagu see Mongols
Huleh, Lake 114, *114*
Humphrey of Toron 134–6, 150
Hungary 156–8, 170

Ibelin (Yabna), castle of 78
Ibelin, family of 49, 150, 174, 179, 203, 216, 234, 250; Balian the Old 108, Hugh 115, Baldwin 135, 136, Balian 137, 143, 144, 146, John of Beirut 167, 168, 174–9, 198, John, count of Jaffa 178, 179, 207, Guy, count of Jaffa 207, Guy, bishop of Famagusta 226
Ibn al-Athir 59, 77, 134
icons 194, *199*
Il-Ghazi, ruler of Mardin (1107–22) 60
illuminations: Armenian MSS. 198, 199, *200*, *201*; Riccardiana Psalter 194, *194*, *205*; school of Acre 191–4, *128*, *129*, *131*, *195*, *196*, *197*; school of Holy Sepulchre 98–103, *99*, *100*, *101*, *102*; *105*
Imad-ad-Din 133
Isaac II Angelus see Byzantium
Isabella, m. Frederick II 173, 194
Isabella see Jerusalem
Islam, western views of 12–13, 68, 108–9, 174, 175, 215
Ismailians (Assassins) 18, 59, 78, 108, 109, 147, 151, 181, 186, 191, 207

Jaffa 27, 40, 49, 115, 150, 151, 183, 187, 207, *28*
James I see Lusignan, family of
James II see Lusignan, family of
James III see Lusignan, family of
James of Molay see Templars
James of Vitry 67, 98, 182
Janus see Lusignan, family of
Jerusalem: capture of 15, 18–20,

33, *128*, *175*; capture by Saladin 144; Church of Holy Sepulchre 15, 36, 42–6, 49, 95, 174, 178, 183, 231, 239, 243, *43*, *44*, *45*, *107*, *240*; churches in 40, 41, 95, 96, 103, 104, 120; hospital, buildings of 89, 95; life in 39, 53, 130, 144; maps *8*, *34*, *62*; Moslem reverence for 59, 144; population of 40–2; temple area 84–9, 96, 118, 136, 144, 175, 190, 240, *86*, *87*, *88*, *97*, *119*; Tower of David 20, 29, 30, 86, 103, 108, *20*, *21*
Jerusalem, kingdom of: assizes of 28, 115, 116, 178, 179; burgesses, courts of 39; ecclesiastical organization of 40–9, 82, 116, 170; elections 20–3, 30, 63, 136; high court of 39, 50, 71, 115, 116, 174, 177, 178; military service in 40, 50; patriarchs of: Daimbert (1099–1102) 29, 30, 35, 42, Arnulf (1099, 1112–18) 29, 42–7, Gormond (1118–28) 47, 98, Stephen (1128–30) 98, William (1130–47) 75, Heraclius (1180–91) 127, 136, Aymar (1194–1202) 170, Albert (1205–13) 170, Gerold (1225–39) 175, William, prior of Holy Sepulchre 100; revenue of 49, 116; royal house of 248: Godfrey of Bouillon (1099–1100) 22–9, 41, 80, 89, 175, *24*, *25*, Baldwin I, count of Edessa (1098–1100) and king of Jerusalem (1100–18) 23, 28, 29–61, 67, 89, *24*, *25*, *30*, *73*, Baldwin II, count of Edessa (1100–18) and king of Jerusalem (1118–31) 56, 58, 63–7, 98, 108, Melisend (1131–51) 65, 66, 75, 76, 79, 89, 95, 98, 101–15, *89*, m. Fulk of Anjou, *q.v.*, Baldwin III (1143–63) 76, 89, 104–15, Baldwin IV (1174–85) 126, 133–5, Baldwin V (1185–6) 134, 141, Sibylla (1186–90) 135, 136, 150, *138*, Isabella (1190–*c*. 1206) 134–6, 150–2, 159, 167, 170, 171, 178, 209; tenants-in-chief 49, 50, 115, 116
Jews 12, 41, 72
Jihad 58, 60, 109, 204
Joan of Sicily 151, 167
John VI Cantacuzenus see Byzantium
John II Comnenus see Byzantium

John II Lusignan see Lusignan, family of
John, prince of Antioch see Lusignan, family of
John of Beirut see Ibelin, family of
John of Brienne, king of Jerusalem (1212–25), m. (1) Maria of Montferrat-Jerusalem 159, 166, 170–5
John del Conte see Nicosia
John, count of Jaffa see Ibelin, family of
Joinville, John of 186, 189, 207, *185*
Joscelin I see Courtenay, family of
Joscelin II see Courtenay, family of
Joscelin III see Courtenay, family of
Julian Garnier see Garnier, family of

Kai-Khusrau I see Roum
Kai-Khusrau II see Roum
Kai-Qobad, Ala-ad-Din see Roum
Kalavun see Mamluks
al-Kamil, sultan of Egypt (1218–38) 174
Karamanids 214, 222, 230, 234
Kerak 39, 49, 79, 134, *79*
Kerbogha, governor of Mosul (d. 1102) 19, 67
Khirokitia, battle of (1426) 234
Khorezmians 182, 183
Kilij Arslan see Roum
Kitbogha see Mongols
Koundoura, battle of (1205) 161
Krak des Chevaliers, Hospitaller castle 80, 120, 147, 190, 191, 243, *193*
Kyrenia 178, 229, 233, 242; castle of *233*

Lajazzo (Ayas) 202, 216, 225
lance, the sacred 128
Lascarids of Nicaea 158, 165, 203
Latakia 73, 74, 148
Latrun, Templar castle 118, *119*
Leon II see Armenians
Leon III see Armenians
Leon IV see Armenians
Leon V see Armenians
Leopold IV of Austria 139
Leopold V of Austria 150–2
Leopold VI of Austria 170
Lisbon 93
Lombards 32, 213